CORPORATION, BE GOOD!

The Story of
Corporate Social Responsibility

William C. Frederick

First published by Dog Ear Publishing
4010 W. 86th Street, Ste H
Indianapolis, IN 46268
www.dogearpublishing.net

ISBN: 1-59858-103-1
Library of Congress Control Number: 2005938362

This book is printed on acid-free paper.

Printed in the United States of America

TABLE OF CONTENTS

Dedicated with gratitude

to my doctoral students

Albert Borelli

Rogene Buchholz

Denis Collins

Robert Hogner

Nancy Kurland

Harry Leonardi

Cliff Montgomery

Lyman Reed

Diane Swanson

William Tiga Tita

Robert Toy

David Wasieleski

James Weber

Richard Wokutch

Donald Wygal

EXECUTIVE OVERVIEW

This book takes you on a journey through time, social tumult, fierce arguments, shameful actions, agonizing tragedies, inspiring acts of courage, deep into the core of corporate culture and the souls of corporate executives, into the frustrating but oh-so-satisfying successful quest for ethical wisdom, and even to the far realms of spirituality and cosmic meaning. All of these things—and more—are found in these pages. It is a story of how the business world discovered, resisted, and then came to embrace the idea of **Corporate Social Responsibility**.

And just what is "corporate social responsibility"? The simplest meaning is "learning to live with, and respect, others." If that sounds like something you first heard in your own family, you've got the basic idea. Now, try picturing any of today's big corporations—Wal-Mart, Exxon, Microsoft, Google, General Motors, MacDonald's—and think of them as your neighbors. After all, you meet them face-to-face nearly every day. Like the family next door, you'd like them to be friendly and to show consideration for you and yours. That's all "corporate social responsibility" is—finding ways to live peacefully and respectfully with one's neighbors.

It is a doctrine with roots deep in business. Business firms have always had to learn to live with their neighbors. Long before the catch phrase "corporate social responsibility" was coined, ancient merchants, peddlers, bankers, and tradesmen of all stripes did their business within the shadow of the temple, synagogue, mosque and under the watchful eye of village elders and the ruling authorities. Caught up inside this network of neighborly relations, profit making is no stranger to social constraints.

Five major lessons about Corporate Social Responsibility are taught in this book.

Lesson One. In the United States, Corporate Social Responsibility (CSR) emerged around 1950, struggled for acceptance during the 1960s and 1970s, turned the corner in the 1980s, was given an unexpected boost by President Ronald Reagan, and became an article of corporate faith by century's end.

Lesson Two. The values and ethics that support CSR are embedded in corporate culture itself but must be discovered and managed with the professional help of management experts, social scientists, and business ethics philosophers. The range and variety of these values and ethical precepts are global in scope but are reducible to sets of universally agreed moral principles.

Lesson Three. The corporation and those who work in it are subject to the laws of nature, which are capable of driving and shaping business decisions in both agreeable and ethically disastrous ways. Hard-wired executive minds are fearful to contemplate and difficult to tame, but nature harbors equally hardy community impulses.

Lesson Four. Business schools that train and condition young minds for business careers have a moral responsibility that matches the social responsibility of corporations. Their task is to alert future practitioners to the perils, possibilities, and opportunities of a business leadership that seeks to be socially and ethically responsible.

Lesson Five. Corporate Social Responsibility propels the corporation, its managers, employees, and neighbors far beyond mere money matters—into the realms of science and spirituality, into the age-old quest for personal and cosmic meaning amid all the awesome challenges of an indeterminate future. CSR is the place where corporate executive, community neighbor, and academic scholar join hands to find ways satisfying for all.

A subtext runs along with the main story. It is about the author's professional search for CSR's broader significance and its impact on business, society, and humankind generally. The two stories are intertwined because they both began at the same time, in mid-20th century America, and the protagonists of both stories grew, struggled, matured, and achieved their respective goals during a half-century's development. In the most literal sense, CSR and the author have defined and elucidated each other's professional *raison d'etre*.

So, come along for the trip. Find yourself, your company, your neighbors here—all a part of that rich tapestry of people we call humanity. It's a marvelous, inspiring adventure. Take it from someone who's been there, done that.

THE AUTHOR

William C. Frederick is one of the founders of the study of Corporate Social Responsibility in the United States. He initiated some of the field's key concepts and analytic categories: successive developmental stages of CSR, core values of corporate culture, the global culture of CSR ethics, social auditing of corporate operations, and the influence of evolutionary biology on managerial decision making. He was one of the organizers of the Social Issues in Management (SIM) division of The Academy of Management and recipient of SIM's Sumner Marcus Award for outstanding contributions to the CSR field. He coauthored five editions (1980–96) of the textbook, *Business and Society,* and one of the first books on social audits, *Social Auditing* (1976). Oxford University Press published his *Values, Nature, and Culture in the American Corporation* in 1995. He is coeditor of two volumes of empirical research on business ethics. In 2002, he was Ruffin Lecturer on the theme Business, Science, and Ethics at the Darden Graduate School of Business at the University of Virginia.

As president of The Society for Business Ethics, he helped found *Business Ethics Quarterly* and serves on its editorial board. Other editorial board service includes 6 years at *Academy of Management Review* and present board membership of *Emergence: Complexity and Organization*. He is past president of The Society for Advancement of Socio-Economics, and past chair of the Social Issues in Management division of The Academy of Management.

Professor Frederick has served as mentor and role model for three or four generations of young scholars nationally. Several of his doctoral students have become leaders and major contributors to the CSR field.

As consultant to the Ford Foundation, he made field studies of management education in Spain, Italy, Egypt, and Yugoslavia. For the Gianni Agnelli Foundation, he developed a 10-year plan for management education in Italy. For the Australian University Commission, he made recommendations that led to the establishment of the Australian Graduate School of Management. For the University of Pittsburgh, he advised business schools in Ecuador and Nigeria. For several U.S. corporations, he has developed and taught programs for top-management executives. He was dean of the business schools at the University of Kansas City and the University of Pittsburgh. His PhD in economics and anthropology was conferred by the University of Texas at Austin.

This book, *Corporation, Be Good! The Story of Corporate Social Responsibility*, draws on the author's half-century of thinking and writing about the social and ethical responsibilities of the modern corporation.

Bill Frederick can be reached at billfred@katz.pitt.edu

INTRODUCTION

PRESENT AT THE CREATION

Strange, isn't it, the way a life can unfold, guided by invisible and unanticipated events that turn out to be the drivers of one's professional life? When I emerged from the protective cocoon of a four-year university education in 1950, the idea that corporations ought to pay heed to social concerns was not on the national radar screen. But it was lurking in the shadows, ready to grow legs and propel me into a race to overtake and understand it that continues to this day, a half-century later. Neither one of us has won, nor have we yet crossed the finish line, so we lurch onward, joined at the hip. The track is now full of many other marathoners, all seeking the same goal, not to outrun the idea but to secure its meaning and assure its place within the American business mind.

This book records my race, my journey, my story. It is an eyewitness, I-was-there account of how corporate social responsibility emerged as a public issue, told in time-freeze frames the way it looked as the action unfolded. A gallery, I guess you could call it, of the best and the worst, the voices of winners and losers, and my own gropings to understand the possibilities, limitations, and future potentials of a corporation's responsibilities to society. Others undoubtedly would tell the CSR story in a different way.

My Travel Companions

The quest to find the CSR Grail has not been a lonely one, for many other pilgrims trod the pathways with me. Some of us are economists, others philosophers, still others management scholars, a handful boasted religious credentials, and toward the end came a hardy band of biologists, environmentalists, and evolutionary psychologists. Discovering CSR's meaning has been a group enterprise and remains so to this day.

In those formative days, CSR ideas emerged from a handful of universities and first-generation CSR scholars who could truly be said to have been "present at the creation."

- At **Harvard Business School:** George Albert Smith, Kenneth Andrews, Edward Bursk, Benjamin Selekman, Raymond Bauer

- At **Columbia University Graduate Business School:** Clarence Walton, Richard Eells, Neil Chamberlain
- At **University of California-Berkeley Business School:** Dow Votaw, Earl Cheit, Edwin Epstein, Prakash Sethi
- At **University of California-Los Angeles Business School:** George Steiner, Neil Jacoby
- At **University of Washington Business School:** Joseph McGuire, Sumner Marcus
- At **Arizona State University Business School:** Keith Davis
- **Other early entrants** included Howard Bowen, Raymond Baumhart, Gerald Cavanagh, William Greenwood, Alvar & Carol Elbing, and Morrell Heald

These pioneers by themselves could not do much more than sketch the broad outlines of what others, coming later, would fill in.

Hailing from a little known, marginal business school at the University of Kansas City (now the University of Missouri-Kansas City), my own early involvement in the late 1950s was entirely serendipitous—and undertaken without any awareness of what others were doing at the time. My business school colleagues had put in place a brand new curriculum that built upon UKC's liberal arts traditions and placed a strong emphasis on the sociocultural functions and responsibilities of business. We were subsequently bowled over when James Howell, an author of the forthcoming 1959 Ford Foundation report on business schools nationwide, told us that we had already accomplished exactly what the Gordon-Howell report was to recommend for all business schools. My course on The Place of Business in Modern Society, first offered in 1958, was at the center of that curriculum. Unknowingly, I had taken a first step on a journey that was to generate an entirely new field of management studies about corporate social responsibility—and, equally unaware, had joined those other seekers who were there at the field's genesis.

How the CSR Story is Told

The story is laid out in chunks of time that correspond to my thinking at those moments but also arranged by themes that reflect my own personal approach to the central issues of corporate social responsibility. In Part I, six points of time illustrate the gradual emergence of CSR as a national public issue. Four other chronological markers in Part II set off the central role played by values in shaping the executive mind. Part III offers more recent vistas from natural science that reveal an executive mind perplexed by hard-wired contradictory impulses both to attain and deny CSR. Part IV, in five time bites, confronts the baffling question whether business schools can instill CSR awareness in their students. The tale ends in Part V by pondering what the new century will bring and whether scholars who study CSR and managers who are urged to practice it are up to the task.

Some readers may rightly feel a sense of *déjà vu* in a few chapters previously published but now greatly condensed from the originals, made more reader friendly by omitting all academic references and notes, and bearing cool new titles. There is another advantage for readers coming to grips with corporate social responsibility for the first time, and perhaps even for some veterans. The combined whole is greater than the sum of its separate parts. There is more revealed in these pages than my personal odyssey.

Corporate social responsibility is a large-scale social and intellectual upheaval spread over a half century of American life. The urgency of its persistent appeal is best understood by watching as it emerged from that tumultuous period of economic, political, and global change. That is what this book attempts to do. In the end, CSR is about more than business. It is about the nourishment of humane values that sustain societies around the globe. In the most literal sense it is about the future of life on this planet. It is what peoples everywhere seek for themselves and for humanity. CSR is "realer" than the business profession knows.

Listen up, business! Corporation, be good!

PART I

EMERGENCE AND STRUGGLE

These chapters recount the appearance and evolution of the core idea of corporate social responsibility. What had begun as the mere wisp of an idea at mid-20th century emerged as a full-blown business philosophy by century's end. Acceptance of CSR unfolded in very uneven ways, generating heated debates in business circles and in academia. The march towards CSR, though unsteady, nevertheless moved ahead to a cadence of distressingly frequent and widely publicized examples of irresponsible and unethical corporate actions. Demands for socially responsible business behavior became both insistent and strident during the socially tumultuous 1950s, 1960s, and 1970s, as business faced a host of social protest movements. Before it was all over, leading corporations had learned, though grudgingly, to adjust to these social expectations, both through public policy and private initiatives.

THE 1950s

[Public approval of big business: 66%]

FIRST LIGHT: CSR'S HERALDS

Corporate social responsibility—the idea that business firms should be held accountable to society for their decisions and actions—did not first see the light in 1950. Human history is too fluid to draw a line across social change and declare, "It began here and then." But what did happen around mid-20th century was a coalescence, a drawing together of scattered ideas and attitudes that, when combined, eventually could be recognized as a coherent, and to some observers an appealing, idea that business owes something to society beyond making profits.

The early 1950s also saw the timorous beginnings of what would become a new field of management study in the nation's business schools: an effort to understand the meaning of corporate social responsibility and teach it to aspiring business practitioners.

Both developments—the idea of CSR and convincing future business leaders of its importance—would involve decades of controversy amid alternating cycles of acceptance and rejection, until by century's end CSR would again be in the ascendant. It is the story of that half-century's exciting and often bitterly contested struggle for and against CSR that is chronicled here. First light dawned around mid-20th century.

CSR's Curious Origins

It is popularly believed that business opposes CSR and must be dragooned into compliance with social directives. In this powerfully mythic scenario, corporations, their managers, and directors are driven by greed to seek "profits before people," generally disregarding the public interest as their decisions and policies run roughshod over employees, environment, and community. Long lists of anti-social corporate misdeeds may testify that business practitioners are, at the very least, indifferent to the harms suffered by society, and at the very worst, seem uncaring and arrogantly unmoved by social protests. CSR seems remote indeed from the corporate mind. Or so goes the popular myth.

For that reason, it is all the more remarkable—and totally surprising to both advocates and critics of CSR—to learn that the core idea of corporate social responsibility first took root within the minds of big business executives. Corporate philanthropy, social give-back philosophies, community service, the executive as public trustee, codes of conduct, religious guidelines—all were alive and well during the 1920s in American business circles. Only the Great Depression of the 1930s and the Second World War of the 1940s stifled and slowed the widespread adoption of CSR by leading corporations.

CSR was not born in opposition to the business order but was encapsulated within the capitalist system and became an integral part of the free-enterprise market economy—and was subordinated to that system's central values. Until one understands the original provenance of CSR, all attempts to "curb" excessive business behavior in the name of social responsibility or ethics can be seen as historically naïve and socially futile. CSR, whatever form it takes, *serves* corporate interests and goals—and has been intended to do so since its inception around the turn of the 20th century. This need not mean, and does not take that turn here, that wily corporate titans, seeing the writing on the wall, conspired to foist an insincere doctrine on a gullible public. Quite the contrary, CSR was a natural outgrowth of the corporate system itself. It had to evolve from executive minds attuned to their own and their companies' interests. Grasping this reality is the key to understanding just why the doctrine of corporate social responsibility emerged in full view during the 1950s.

Frank Abrams

No more blue-blooded corporate titan strode the earth in 1951 than the chairman of the board of directors of Standard Oil of Jersey (now Exxon). Beginning in 1913, Frank Abrams worked his way up the corporate ladder, becoming something of an elder statesman by mid-century. In what became an iconic statement, published in 1951 by that paragon of corporate correctness, *Harvard Business Review*, Abrams urged his fellow executives to think of themselves as professionals in the manner of physicians and lawyers, imbued with responsibilities going beyond the narrow bounds of their daily work. Businessmen (it being a one-gender activity in those days) as professionals have responsibilities to many groups besides themselves and their shareholders. Management's duty is "to conduct the affairs of the enterprise to maintain an equitable and workable balance among the claims of the various directly interested groups, a harmonious balance among stockholders, employees, customers, and the public at large." Since "business firms are man-made instruments of society," management should see itself "as a good citizen" acting in socially responsible ways. "Business managers can more effectively contribute to the solution of the many complex social problems of our time. There is no higher responsibility, there is no higher duty of professional management."

Abrams' opening salvo was seconded by others during the following ten years. The management guru Peter Drucker, writing in *HBR*, declared that "productivity is a social if not a moral principle, and not just a business principle...it is not enough for it to contribute to profits [alone]." The editors of *HBR* had struck a mother lode. For the remainder of the decade, the *Review's* columns echoed with calls from business executives, philosophers, theologians, consultants, professors, and laypersons to argue that business should assume the mantle of social responsibility. The arguments ranged from historian Arnold Toynbee's reminder that great leaders have always minded their publics, to Reinhold Neibuhr's case for using Christianity to produce corporate good, to O. A. Ohmann's iconic "skyhooks" to elevate business minds above grubby materialism (he thought "we need a spiritual rebirth in industrial society"), to professor Harold Johnson's literally affirmative and managerially detailed answer to his question "Can the Businessman Apply Christianity?"

These in-your-face religious and social appeals to corporate executives finally got under the skin of Harvard Business School professor Theodore Levitt who in 1958 produced a blast heard 'round the corporate world. The doctrine of social responsibility "has become a deadly serious occupation, the self conscious, soul-searching preoccupation" of business executives, "a prevailing vogue, a new tyranny of fad and fancy." Levitt was sure that no good, and much harm, could come of it. But he was too late, the genie was out of the bottle. CSR was now official doctrinal belief within the corporate command structure.

The CSR Doctrine

What did CSR mean in the 1950s? Three core ideas stand out: corporate managers as public trustees; balancing competing claims to corporate resources; and philanthropic support of good causes.

The manager as trustee had became popular in the 1920s. A thoroughly paternalistic attitude, it evolved from the sheer economic power that corporate executives wielded plus their influence on local, state, and national governments. The resources they commanded—technology, materials, money, and employees—were transmogrified into a kind of quasi-religious charge or mission and, for some, even a calling. As Abrams had said, business is an instrument of society, so its directors and managers are bound to look beyond the company's gates in promoting public purposes.

Foreshadowing by four decades the concept of corporate stakeholder, the principal managerial task was finding a fair and just balance between the competing claims of all who worked for or whose lives were affected by business operations. General Electric's Richard Eells in 1960 coined a name for such a company: "the well-tempered corporation" whose leaders are mindful of employees' needs and dignity, customers' expectations of quality products at fair prices, suppliers' dependence upon reliable links and fair dealing, the community's desire for good corporate citizenry, and, yes, the shareholders' pursuit of profitable return on investment. The managerial nightmare of trying to balance these often contradictory claims appeared to be less important than setting forth the new ideal. Corporate pride and philosophy swelled equally, while overlooking the nitty-gritty details of how it would all be done. The article of CSR faith outran the managerial reality of it all, at least in those early days.

More doable was philanthropy. The Community Chest, later known as the United Way, was business's first large-scale, organized philanthropic activity, beginning in the 1920s. Support for education, the arts, social welfare agencies such as YMCA, and various charitable causes were additional social obligations assumed by business. In the mid-1930s, business leaders even lobbied Congress for a "five-percent amendment" that gave corporations a tax break for making charitable contributions. That paved the way for philanthropic largesse to flow from corporate treasuries to deserving social causes.

The scholar who gathered all of these social impulses into a single CSR writ was Howard Bowen, 1953 author of *The Social Responsibilities of the Businessman*. A surprising source of radical insights—he was at the time a business school dean—Bowen fashioned a theory that justified, not just a new philosophy for business practitioners but one that anchored in academia what later became an entirely new field of management studies. Even earlier, Bowen had argued in *Toward Social Economy* that a society's social institutions shape economic outcomes, so it took only a small step to embrace CSR fully. No wispy-eyed idealist, he acknowledged that business advocacy of CSR was rooted in a self interest best advanced by promoting the public interest. Support for education, good human relations at work, community philanthropy, harmonious relations with government, improving productivity, achieving economic stability, tempering competitive zeal, and conserving natural resources—these were the heart of the New CSR canon, and they paid in cash and burnished a company's reputation. The executive as social steward and public trustee was the ideal he preached, all to be accomplished voluntarily and with minimal government direction.

Reflecting on his ideas some 20 years later, Bowen reluctantly admitted that he had been overly optimistic. "I have come to the view that voluntary social responsibility cannot be relied upon as a significant form of control over business. The power of business overwhelms the weak reed of voluntary social responsibility. My experience and observation since [1953] have led me to the conclusion that the social responsibility concept is of minimal effectiveness." But like Theodore Levitt's earlier warning about CSR's dangers, Bowen issued his gloomy conclusion too late. A new era of corporate social responsibility had already opened by the end of the 1950s decade.

Back to the Future

None of those pioneering CSR stalwarts actually realized what they were creating, nor did the few hardy business school scholars who dared presume the superiority of society over an All-American Free Enterprise System triumphantly regnant following World War II. Both groups slouched towards social controls over business, largely innocent of its larger meanings and dimensions. Little did they know that their labors would eventually tell more about the nature of business and society and their interlinked moral character than could be discovered in any other way.

The puzzle is this: human society's need for a process that sustains the whole and enables humanity to flourish and achieve its fullest potentials, side-by-side with business's goal of generating that life-giving, life-expanding process with minimal interference from external societal pressures. The newly-minted advocates of CSR focused attention on the first half of this formula, while the Luddite-like CSR opponents computed only the last half.

Underlying and driving the entire interlinked business-and-society system to this historic crisis point was the powerful engine of industrial technology—the Age of Mechanism—that at once boosted the economy's productive powers ever higher even as it threatened, eroded, and sometimes pulverized many cherished human customs and institutions. Little wonder that technology's sponsor, the private enterprise market-based business corporation, was judged to be the heavy, the villain, the very essence of Mammon gone berserk. Neither should it have been considered unusual that a small cadre of corporate executives—the guys with their feet on the accelerator of the technological juggernaut—had paused to consider what they and their companies might be doing to their fellow humans. Even as they perched on the upper rungs of corporate power and privilege, did they dimly sense in themselves an even more ancient and deeply ingrained urge to identify with the human species as a whole? Should not business yield to society, technology to custom, economy to humanity? The answers would remain elusive long into the future.

Successive layers of cultural reaction against an accelerating techno-logical, economizing corporate thrust were already scattered throughout the 1950s: religious rejection and curbs (Ohmann's "skyhooks" and Johnson's workplace Christianity), self-imposed restraint generating corporate phil-anthropy (support for Community Chest), paternalist trusteeship and stew-ardship (Abrams' managerial professionalism), corporate partnering with organized labor (John Kenneth Galbraith's countervailing power), and grudging acceptance of government regulation of imperfect markets (post-war oligopoly pricing and exploitive advertising). Here were the crude raw materials for a newly evolving CSR philosophy. But their thick cultural lay-ers concealed the true nature of the forces drawing business and society into a relationship that was at once necessitous but also vexatious, acidic, and corrosive.

The interplay between business and society in the 1950s looks suspi-ciously and intriguingly like a spontaneously evolving, self-organizing rela-tionship between "business and society" or between "company and community." In later decades, scholars would refer to these linkages as "interpenetrating systems" while others would label them "complex adap-tive systems," drawing upon the language of complexity/chaos theory. Self-organizing relationships of this magnitude emerge spontaneously in response to natural forces at work within large scale ecological systems. The economic gain-seeking activity of a business firm—its central econo-mizing mission—is one such natural force, shaped by diverse cultural tra-ditions. Nature-based also is the human social impulse towards reconciling the typically wide range of diverse human needs and interests found among people living together in communities. The resultant binary partnership tying business to society, which was the seedbed for CSR thinking, would prove in time to be nothing more nor less than a product of nature—a stun-ning insight of natural science still hidden in the mid-1950s.

Outwardly, the popular issue became one of how much and what kind of economizing would business cede to society in order to retain its power and control over the production process. CSR advocates were prepared to voluntarily grant some concessions in the forms and amounts mentioned earlier: for them, economizing would yield, at least minimally, to a com-munity's ecologizing needs. The ensuing cultural debates of the 1960s, 70s, 80s, 90s, and on into the new century would center around the question of the best means (voluntarism, public policy, self regulation, moral principle) to adjust this balance between economy and society.

Generally overlooked in the search for means was the nature of the ends being sought, particularly their rootedness in nature itself. The business-and-society, company-and-community, economizing-ecologizing linkage is more than an invented cultural institution. These pairs are coevolving partners responding to Darwinian-like natural selection pressures, where life itself, along with its quality and meaning, are at stake and the ultimate prize. CSR is not merely the religious or philosophical whim of the well-fed corporate executive, nor can it be explained as a pragmatic tenet of competitive strategy, and certainly not as a character blip on a psychological grid. All notions of responsibility, of fair dealing in the marketplace, of justice and fairness must find meaning within the strictures of natural selection if they are to serve the human species' survival and potentials for flourishing. From that naturological process, the corporation as a complex adaptive system emerged to become a prime economizing vehicle totally dependent upon its ties to others in society. CSR was to be the operational bridge between the two, integral to corporate operations, not for the cultural reasons often given (fairness, give-back, stewardship) but because nature decreed it. In the end, CSR values embedded in nature would be the key to solving the business-and-society conundrum.

YEAR 1960

CORPORATE SOCIAL RESPONSIBILITY COMES OF AGE

Setting the Stage. Television audiences in the late 1950s were shocked to learn that one of the nation's most watched entertainment shows was rigged. The answers to difficult and arcane questions were secretly fed to contestants who put on a good show of struggling mightily to come up with the right answers. Even more scandalous was the revelation that one of the program's stars was none other than the son of one of America's best known authors. The show's commercial sponsor was roundly criticized, and a Congressional committee held hearings. It was one of the first hints that the media giants had acquired a new kind of social responsibility to insure honesty and integrity of programming. A quickening sense of CSR stirred in the business mind. The race was on to find out just how business corporations might become socially responsible.

The television quiz show scandal, aired last autumn in Congressional hearings, has highlighted an issue that has been of increasing concern to many people—the public responsibilities of private businessmen. Concern about business power is not new, but the past decade has seen a growing consciousness of the problems that business power can create in a democratic society.

This heightened interest in business responsibility can be explained in terms of two developments of the twentieth century, one intellectual, the other institutional. Both are related to the collapse of *laissez faire* as a philosophy and as an economic order.

The Relevance of *Laissez Faire*

The disintegration of the world economy, starting early in the present century, signaled the beginning of the end for the *laissez-faire* philosophy and all its supporting institutions. The trend, accelerated by the First World War and the subsequent monetary panics of the 1920's, culminated in the

early 1930's in what Karl Polanyi has characterized as "The Great Transformation." Free economy was transformed into regulated economy in all
of the advanced nations that stood in the capitalist tradition including
Soviet Russia, where the 5-year plans were initiated; Germany, where
National Socialism was in the ascendant; Italy, which was in the throes of
corporate Fascism; and the United States, where the New Deal was the
symbol of institutional transformation on a grand scale. These and other
domestic economies, seeking to protect themselves from the ravages of a
self-regulating market mechanism, were transformed to an economy in
which centralized state planning and regulations were increasingly the rule
rather than the exception.

At the same time, it became more and more obvious that the world of
business itself was the scene of growing economic power. The growth of
the large-scale corporation, with its tendency to divorce legal ownership
from actual control of operations and with its technique of feeding upon
itself for growth capital, freed the giants of business from the checks formerly put upon them by stockholders and capital investors. In addition,
business had combined two forces to dilute what could be considered "consumer sovereignty": a refined and sophisticated advertising program and
what amounted to programming control of one of the nation's mass media
of communication, thereby making possible the massive tailoring of consumer tastes to the standards of mediocrity that have become so common in
our times.

All of this institutional transformation was remarkable enough. Even
more remarkable (though far less spectacular) was the intellectual revolution that accompanied the institutional change of the old order. It was to be
expected that the maxims that had guided economic thinking for over a century would undergo change as the institutions themselves were transformed, and as early as 1933, Joan Robinson and Edward Chamberlin had
written economic treatises discussing the impact of the large-scale corporation on traditional forms of competition.

The philosophy of *laissez faire* had collapsed as thoroughly as had its
supporting institutional framework. All of the major foundation stones were
disintegrating. Gone, or seriously weakened, was the invisible hand of free
competition which was to guide selfish interests into socially-useful channels. Displaced from the center of the stage were the old forms of business
organization—the proprietorship and the partnership—through which
competition was to work. Gone was the theory of behavior which posited a
free and rational individual capable of promoting his own interests if only
allowed to do so by a meddlesome government. Gone was the theory of
social institutions which found at their core a rational desire of man to solve

his problems. Gone was the theory of a harmony of interests which was to be the automatic outcome of the self-seeking interests of a society of rational men checked in their selfishness by the invisible hand of competition. A type of civilization and a way of thinking were truly "gone with the wind."

The collapse of the *laissez-faire* philosophy created a philosophical vacuum. It is this vacuum that businessmen and others interested in the issue of business responsibility have been trying to fill since the end of World War II. Under the *laissez-faire* philosophy private interests were supposed to be channeled into publicly useful pursuits, but now such institutions as had been responsible had fallen into disuse. Under the *laissez-faire* philosophy, there had been a social theory by which private interests could be harmonized with the interests of society at large. This meant that there was no need to be concerned deliberately with the social responsibility of private businessmen; it would be produced automatically. But now there was no such theory. Quite plainly, the older rubrics no longer furnished an adequate intellectual system for explaining the social consequences of business activities. Hence, the collapse of *laissez faire* posed a giant intellectual conundrum for social theorists: How could a society with democratic traditions and democratic aspirations rationalize the growing amount of power accruing to businessmen? And how could that power be channeled into socially-useful functions without driving the populace into some Orwellian nightmare of *1984* proportions?

Several events conspired to cloak the true nature of the crisis until after the Second World War. It is true that a few questioning voices were raised during the 1930's and the 1940's—most notably those of Adolf A. Berle and Gardiner C. Means in their monumental study, *The Modern Corporation and Private Property* and James Burnham in his analysis, *The Managerial Revolution*. But preoccupation with the Great Depression and with the impending World War II served to postpone a consideration of the major problems of business power that had developed out of the broad-scale institutional changes in the 1930's.

However, with the resumption of peace-time production, and after it became evident that the American economy would not be subjected immediately to another large-scale depression, and particularly after studies which revealed the very great concentration of economic power that had occurred during the Second World War, all of the same worrisome questions were asked once again. Since 1950, as a result, five major currents of thought about business responsibility in American society have developed. Each of these currents attempts to grapple with the problems of power in a complex society and with the resultant issue of business responsibility to the society at large.

Management as Trustee

The first of these currents of thought, and one that has gained increasing favor, is the idea that corporate managers should voluntarily act as trustees of the public interest. They should police themselves and their use of the tremendous amounts of power they possess. The keynote of this concept is the deliberate and voluntary assumption of public responsibility by corporate managers, even though at times such a trusteeship might cause a managerial group to forego immediate profits for the sake of the public good. Management, according to this concept, has a multiplicity of obligations—to the stockholders, to the employees, and to the public at large. This viewpoint, therefore, appeals to the conscience of individual managers to wield their power in a publicly responsible manner. One student of the problem has even called for the development of the "conscience of the corporation" to protect the public against possible abuses of corporate power.

The Relevance of Christian Ethics

Easily the most appealing and the most emotional of these five viewpoints is the notion of relating Christian ethical principles of conduct to the problems of business enterprise. The basic idea seems to be that the businessman needs to think of himself as something more than a simple money-grubber. He needs to have a nobility of purpose that overarches his corporate activities and day-to-day duties. He needs "skyhooks" to orient him toward the nobler ideals of Christian ethical conduct so that he might become a practicing Christian businessman on the job. One spokesman for this viewpoint even argues the direct applicability of such Christian doctrines as the idea of original sin, forgiveness, creation, and the general concept of God to the problems of business. Christian ideals and doctrines are said, therefore, to furnish the Christian businessman with a framework of ethics by which he can approach and grapple with problems of finance, personnel, production, and general decision making.

Balance of Power

One of the most intriguing ideas to reappear in the postwar period is the notion that the answer to concentrated business power is more power. The central theme of this argument is that business power is here to stay and that the answer to this problem is to build up countervailing power in the hands of the other major groups. Government, according to this viewpoint, should play a major role in establishing a balance of power between the major functional segments of the economy, even if it means taking the side of one group against all the others while a sufficient amount of countervailing power is being developed. Thus, the balance of power doctrine handles the problem of business responsibility by permitting all parties, including the business interests, to look out for their own economic and social interests. The public welfare is presumed to be the outcome of the balanced sum of interests represented in the power struggle. This relieves businessmen of deliberately and consciously promoting public responsibility, often in contradiction to their own private interests.

The Viewers with Alarm

Perhaps the strongest currents that have attempted to fill the philosophical vacuum left by the collapse of *laissez faire* consists of the ideas of the group that "views with alarm." Often these spokesmen see the problem of business power as only one facet of a larger process, namely, the drift of the total society toward monolithic and totalitarian control of the human mind and spirit. Huxley, Orwell, Riesman, Whyte, and Mills—all basically humanistic in their philosophical predilections—are dismayed by the press of technology and organization upon the traditions of a free society. They express grave doubts about concentrating so much power in the hands of so few bureaucrats, whether of the industrial, the governmental, or the military type. The members of this group have no clear-cut answer to the problem of concentrated power, counseling a resistance of the spirit against the ravages of organization and mass technology. Business responsibility, they seem to say, will be achieved only when there is a general recognition by businessmen and others of the perils to the individual personality that accompany great aggregations of power.

Capitalist Ethic Reformulated

The fifth major current is an attempt to reformulate and restate the capitalist ethic. Perhaps the most notable attempt is *The Capitalist Manifesto* by Louis O. Kelso and Mortimer J. Adler which argues that the capitalist revolution will not be fully realized until some of the basic capitalist principles—ownership, for example—have been extended to embrace ever larger numbers of citizens. As ownership is more widely diffused, so will the citizen's stake in the prevailing system increase. As a result, interest and loyalty to the modified capitalist system will increase. Thus, a higher degree of responsibility on the part of capitalist-owners will be achieved by modifying and extending one of the basic capitalist institutions.

A Critique

There is a surprising shortcoming shared by these five schools of thought: not one of them offers a clear-cut, substantive meaning of the social responsibilities of businessmen. The public trustee theory and the Christian theory have been heavily influenced by the remnants of the *laissez-faire* philosophy in which "the greatest good of the greatest number" seems to have been a major criterion of social responsibility, although we are still left in some doubt as to the precise nature of the "good" to which the formula refers. The balance of power theory generally suffers from the same shortcoming, although in the case of John Kenneth Galbraith's version of countervailing power it is rather obvious that total over-all economic production constitutes the criterion of value, especially as revealed later in *The Affluent Society*. The basic value assumptions of the "viewers with alarm" are those of individualism and humanism; therefore, socially responsible business behavior presumably would protect the integrity of the individual and humanist qualities generally. But it does seem amazing that throughout most of these writings there appears no precise formulation or description of behavior that clearly bears the label of social responsibility.

The real explanation, of course, is to be found in the precise nature of the intellectual vacuum created when the *laissez-faire* system collapsed. For that vacuum, more than anything else, is a vacuum of values. It is our value systems that have been most sorely bruised in the transformation to the world of large-scale organization and technology. Older value systems have been rendered useless by the advance of knowledge and by vast institutional transformation. And new value systems have not yet had time to emerge. We stand too close to the older systems and to the dust that still rises from the ruins of the fallen order. And as the five major schools of thought seem to demonstrate, the temptation to dart back into the murky ruins of the old order and to snatch at the weakened timbers for use in constructing a new philosophical framework is still great.

Moreover, the public trustee theory and the Christian theory are startlingly naive in some respects. They seem to ignore some of the basic and fundamental realities of historical development and of the contemporary institutional setting in which business enterprise operates. To the extent that they are based on a theory of history at all, it is an idealistic or a romantic one that ignores the essentially materialist and self-seeking basis of business enterprise as it emerged in Western culture. Further, both the trustee and the Christian theories seem to ignore the force of historical tradition and custom in determining the basic value elements of contemporary business institutions and the force that these traditions still exert upon the behavior of businessmen caught up within such a historically determined system. Both theories seem to imply, for example, that private gain can be simply pushed to one side by the force of will of public-spirited businessmen or of those who have been inspired by Christian ethics.

In addition, the theory of behavior that underlies both of these positions on business responsibility ignores some of the basic and most significant findings made by social scientists in the past fifty years. A social role defines for an individual a pattern of behavior to which he is expected to conform in order to carry out his socially approved functions within the society. The businessman's role is defined largely, though not exclusively, in terms of private gain and private profit. To ignore this important facet or to assume that the businessman himself can ignore it simply by force of will inspired by Christian ideals or by public spiritedness is preposterously naive.

Therefore, we find that the businessman, by virtue of historical traditions and contemporary institutional forces, is in a sense "locked into" a going system of values and ethics that largely determines the actions he will take. There is no question that the system itself is subject to change over a period of years. Neither is there any doubt that the force of an individual personality can wield a great influence over the manner in which a person acts out his socially defined role. But there also seems to be little question that at any given time individuals who are active within the system of social roles and institutions are subject in large measure to its prevailing characteristics. This means that businessmen *must* be concerned primarily with private gain and profits, for they are a prime value within the presently existing system of business enterprise.

The balance of power theory, on the other hand, is a grown-up version of the automatic institutional forces that allegedly worked for the social good under the *laissez-faire* order. The argument is basically the same: When countervailing power is brought to bear against the holders of original power, such privately wielded power will be deflected into channels that are not so harmful to the interests of society as would otherwise be true in the absence of such a power struggle. Under the *laissez-faire* order, competition between self-seeking business firms was said to have produced the same effects. Countervailing power in the twentieth century substitutes for the free competition of the nineteenth century.

Some of the most powerful statements on business responsibility have been made by the "viewers with alarm," who, like Galbraith, at least are cognizant of some of the realities of the contemporary scene. But since the alarmists are basically individualistic and humanistic in their predilections and since both individualism and humanism are products of an age before the fantastic aggregations of power that we know today, there is very little the alarmists can do except object to what is going on and to what power accumulations are presumably doing to individuals and to human values generally. For them, there is no way out save by some brand of passive resistance to the organizational society and its many bureaucratic institutions. It is characteristic of this group of thinkers that they have little or nothing to offer in the way of an institutional system that will lead us out of our present difficulties with respect to promoting the social responsibilities of private businessmen.

The Basis of an Adequate Theory

An adequate theory of business responsibility must meet several requirements. First, its criterion of value should be drawn from our increasing awareness of the requirements of socially effective economic production and distribution, and particularly the necessities of economic growth and development on a broad social scale. Some such value criterion has been a part of American thinking since the Great Depression of the 1930's, and it was reinforced by the great emphasis that the Second World War placed upon the value of high production and the efficient allocation and distribution of economic resources. In the current race with the Soviet Union to dominate the world economic scene, we see once again that economic production and distribution constitute a major criterion of value.

All of this suggests strongly that when we invoke the phrase "the social responsibilities of the businessman," we mean that businessmen should oversee the operation of an economic system that fulfills the expectations of the public. And this means in turn that the economy's means of production should be employed in such a way that production and distribution should enhance total socio-economic welfare. Social responsibility in the final analysis implies a public posture toward society's economic and human resources and a willingness to see that those resources are utilized for broad social ends and not simply for the narrowly circumscribed interests of private persons and firms. The television quiz show scandal is a case in point.

The second requirement of an adequate theory of business responsibility is that it be based upon the new concepts of management and administration that are now emerging. There is an increasing awareness of the usefulness of scientific methodology in defining and solving problems within the management environment. The "Great Man" theory of management is being replaced with a concept of the manager as coordinator and planner, as a team member whose main play consists of making significant links between relevant pieces of information. This means that managers need to reconstruct their self-images and to de-emphasize the role that status and authority play in the management function. And finally, the study of human relations is convincing managers that careful treatment must be accorded employees if they are to be fully effective in the work situation and if their jobs are to form a part of the "good life." Any theory of business responsibility that ignores these recent developments in management science would be seriously deficient.

Third, an adequate theory of business responsibility will recognize that the present business system is an outgrowth of history and past cultural traditions. It will recognize that what we are today is, to a very large extent, a function of what we were yesterday. In more specific terms, this means that there is not likely to be any escape from the very powerful motive of private gain and profit which is often at variance with social interest. Rather than denying the importance of this force or wishing it away in an idealistic fashion or assuming that businessmen can or will ignore it as they make decisions, the new theory of business responsibility will attempt to find institutional means for hedging about this motive and for directing it into socially useful channels. This, of course, is the hope of Galbraith in his theory of countervailing power and of Berle who speaks of the need to develop "the conscience of the corporation."

The fourth requirement of a theory of business responsibility is that it recognize that the behavior of individual businessmen is a function of the social role they play in business and in society. This means two things: (a) that the individual businessman, however noble may be his intentions, is often unable to influence significantly the total business configuration within which he works; and (b) that many times the individual businessman will be motivated to take action or make decisions that are not at all consistent with the ideals of social responsibility that he may hold in the abstract. Both forms of behavior are understandable when we realize that the businessman does not operate in a cultural vacuum but within a social role whose total pattern is fairly well defined for him by the mores of his society.

Fifth, there should also be a recognition that socially responsible business behavior is not to be produced automatically but is rather to result from deliberate and conscious efforts of those institutional functionaries who have been given this task by society. There are no magic formulas and no automatic mechanisms which by themselves will guarantee the results that the public desires. Conscience alone, whether of public trustee or of Christian businessman, is not enough. A balance of power is likewise insufficient. Nor is courageous action by public servants enough. The task requires a constant tinkering with the institutional mechanisms of society, employing more and more of the fruits of scientific methodology and the scientific attitude. The job, though difficult, should become easier as social scientists increase their knowledge of human behavior and human institutions. It is true that we cannot totally escape the impact of our cultural heritage, but we are slowly accumulating a storehouse of knowledge about ourselves and about businessmen that should enable us to resolve some of the problems and issues of business responsibility.

YEAR 1973

[Public confidence in big business: 26%]

WHEN SOCIAL RUFFIANS KNOCK ON
THE BOARDROOM DOOR

Setting the Scene: A great tsunami of public outrage and hostility pounded business unmercifully beginning in the 1960s through the mid-1970s. Beginning with Ralph Nader's assault on General Motors, the enormous waves of anti-business sentiment swept across the entire business landscape, reaching deep into the executive suites. This was the stuff of revolutionary protest. Though bewildered and not a little put off by what seemed to be unfair criticism from so many sides, some business leaders began to understand what they and their companies were being asked to do. My faculty colleagues, James Wilson and Mildred Myers, joined me in pointing the way for them.

An entirely new social role is emerging for business. Its eventual acceptance by business is unavoidable because the new role is an outgrowth of deep-seated, long-term trends within Western society generally and within United States society specifically. These trends and developing forces cannot or will not—and in our view should not—be reversed in the foreseeable future. Their transforming force provides no feasible alternative for business except greatly to expand its social role.

This new role calls for businessmen to play a larger, more conscious, more continuous, more humane part in defining, approaching, and seeking a resolution to broad-scale societal problems. It is a role to be played out through the market, yet beyond it; in economic terms, yet enriched and informed by non-economic values; within the purview of profits, yet not constrained simply by the quest for profits.

Business and society enjoy a symbiotic relationship. In our times, each is dependent upon the other. A fundamental change in one brings movement in the other. The business institution of contemporary America is now feeling the stresses and strains being imposed by powerful social

---

* Coauthors: James A. Wilson and Mildred S. Myers

forces at work both internally and externally. These social influences, which seem at times to spring full-blown on the corporate scene without herald and often in menacing garb, are more than the agents of corporate changes. They signal the early phases of fundamental change in the entire institution of business.

Business as Social Change Agent

In 20th century United States society, business corporations are and for long have been major agents of social change. They have helped transform a frontier society of small farmers into a complex urban society of immense industrial power and might. As advocate of mass consumption, the corporate collectivity has shaped our standard of living and has goaded the nation of consumers on to ever higher levels of emulative spending and conspicuous consumption. As controllers and directors of vast resources, corporations have literally transformed the face of the land from primeval wilderness to urban sprawl, from quiet glens to roaring factories, from winding roads to steel and concrete superhighways. As technological innovators and initiators, leading companies have undermined older industries and created new ones, shifted key industrial components from one part of the nation and world to another, introduced new technological and electronic devices (radio and television, for example) with little idea of the societal and attitudinal changes implicit in their widespread adoption and usage, and have continued to substitute machines for the work of men and women in a society where creative, productive work has been considered an important social value. Business corporations, taken as a whole, have served as an engine for vast economic expansion and growth, with all of the potential for change of regions, industries, classes, communities, and persons.

Beyond these gargantuan transformations now obvious to all lie others more subtle but nonetheless important. Business has been and continues to be a prime shaper of values held by the great body of citizens. We readily give allegiance to business- oriented and reinforced principles such as private property, free enterprise, individual initiative, the profit motive, economic expansion, and a rising standard of living. When doubt appears, as lately it has, it is usually business and the business press that leap first to the ideological ramparts to show us the error of our ways. Business urges us on to greater affluence, harder toil, the rewards of leisure, and all of the other manifestations of a secure middle-class suburban life. Corporations have become value centers, where important sociocultural values are formulated, nourished, and promulgated.

Through its central involvement in the mass media of communication, reportage, and entertainment, business exerts a powerful influence on public opinion. As the main consumer of the output of our educational system, business provides both directly and indirectly a major input concerning curriculum, programming, desirable types of faculty, and the extent and nature of research. Interested as it must be in stability at home and security abroad, the business sector attends to both domestic and foreign policy of government, now constituting pressure-group lobbies, now favoring this candidate or that, now issuing policy statements regarding one or another matter of public debate, and frequently furloughing one of its number to serve in elective or appointive office wherein governmental power may be exercised directly.

Perhaps as important as any of these ways in which business shapes our values is the position of leadership that is ascribed to it by the society. From a central position of power and public esteem, the business spokesman is uniquely situated to capture our attention, to incline us to the business way of thinking, and to encourage allegiance to the entire network of values and institutions which buttresses business's general status and social privileges.

In all these many ways, businessmen collectively have caused and guided immense social change, just as they have shaped and influenced social values and attitudes. They have done so *just by being businessmen.* In the normal discharge of business interests, social change has occurred and social values have been shaped.

It is not obvious that society would have deliberately and consciously chosen to place such immensely important social functions in the hands of businessmen, had the matter been discussed, debated, and put to the test of a public referendum. Such a referendum may now indeed be in the making, if one is to judge by the rising anti-business clamor. But the undoubted fact that business has in the past possessed, and does now hold, great social leverage raises a fundamental question. In a society in which leadership is largely industrial and executive, and in which government is often conducted using industrial models—in a society in which there remains a massive amount of trust and goodwill for the corporate concept and for specific corporations—can we afford, and will the society tolerate, less than enlightened, creative, humane leadership in the many societal problems that beset us?

The Social Revolutions

One outcome of business-induced social change is the emergence of a group of "social revolutions." These movements are comprised of distinctive but overlapping constituencies. Each one is fueled by frustration, anger, fear, alienation, aspiration, and expectation. All are determined to bring changes about on behalf of their adherents.

If business does not learn to understand these social revolutions and to cope meaningfully and supportively with the social problems they represent, business will forfeit its greatest opportunity to be a force for good and a service to humankind. We do not speculate further here concerning other possible consequences for the business institution if it fails to respond positively and meaningfully to these social revolutions. We prefer instead to emphasize the opportunities for public good that these movements present to businessmen and their corporations.

The social revolutions that exert the most obvious pressure currently are seven in number. Before discussing their direct significance for business, we will identify the core meaning of each movement as we understand it.

The Black Movement. Its central focus is to achieve complete liberation—economic, social, political, cultural, psychological—from the submerged and servile status that Black people have always occupied in America. It is an attempt to define anew the role and status of *all* Black Americans, literally to create a new cultural meaning for this group, and to define Black existence as simply another phase of the human condition, equal in every essential aspect to the core meaning of humanness. It is an attempt to become free enough from past traditions and current social attitudes to be able to create whatever institutions are necessary and desirable so that Black people may express their style of life and seek the fullness of their potential as human beings.

The Ecology Movement. In its most recent form, it all began rather superficially a few years ago, with a criticism of the unsightly and ugly manifestations of commercialism and industrial operations: billboards, auto junkyards, discarded containers, coal mine tailings, and the like. Then it built rather rapidly, with successive concern for industrial smoke and smog (Pittsburgh and Los Angeles became symbols of each); the dumping of industrial and urban wastes in rivers, lakes, and oceans; the rising noise level of cities; the encroachment of an expanding and affluent population on nature areas and recreational facilities; the disappearance of or threat to various wildlife forms (Rachel Carson's *Silent Spring* alarmed and alerted many); and the possible interference with and irreversible disruption of fundamental life cycles and energy exchanges of the entire biosphere in which plants and animals live on earth. Clean air, pure waters, undefiled nature, and a healthful balance between man and his habitat are the watchwords of the ecology movement.

The Women's Liberation Movement. Only now gathering force, it may prove to be even more profound and dramatic than the Black movement. Women, too, are now seeking liberation from a socially and culturally submerged and dependent status position. Most human societies have been patriarchal or male-dominated—politically, economically, religiously, familially. Women have borne a cultural definition of weakness, passivity, submissiveness—as home maker, child tender, sex object. They are now striving to reverse that social reciprocal, to reject a definition of themselves solely or primarily in sexual terms, to be recognized as full equals with men in all respects, and then to go beyond that equality to seek out the meaning that a human culture freed of its sexual prejudices can have for women. "Sexist" is now as strong an epithet as "racist." This movement is potentially more fundamental than the Black movement because the cultural roots of female status are older and deeper, women are a larger bloc of the population, and the sexual status and attitudes of both men and women are at the very core of human personality and identity.

The Youth Movement. The youth rebellion, according to its rhetoric, is a dizzying, exciting blend of negatives and positives. It *rejects* the tottering remains of Victorian morality and authoritarianism; the single-minded drive for middle class materialistic affluence; the hypocrisy and fakery of many institutions (marriage, formal religion, political democracy); the impersonal bureaucracies of an organizational society (multiversities, corporations); and unquestioning obedience to such national goals as economic expansion, military strength and preparedness, and technological innovation. It seems to *favor* greater involvement of youth at all levels of decision making in all major institutions; freedom to experiment with new patterns of life (sex, dress, appearance, music, speech, career goals, education, religion, mystical and emotional experiences through drugs); and a humanistic ideal of community, brotherhood, love, peace, truth, and a simplistic, uncluttered life. As many have pointed out, the youth movement is bolstered and sustained by the underlying affluence of the middle and upper classes, and constantly fed new energies by the rising educational attainments and social awareness of middle class youth generally.

The Consumer Movement. Considerably less fundamental than the others, it is a demand that the consumer be treated as he was supposed to be treated in the operation of a perfectly competitive market system. This means that he should pay fair prices; receive high-quality goods, free from defects and hazards; enjoy honest dealing; obtain full disclosure and possess near perfect buyer knowledge; have legal and economic recourse when bilked; and experience a choice among real options. Because he works "within the system" and because he seeks a mode of buyer behavior and seller behavior that closely matches the ideal operation of a competitive market system, Ralph Nader is one of our most conservative reformers. His work and that of his fellow consumer advocates is rendered especially difficult in a business world populated by mammoth corporations, oligopoly and accompanying price rigidities, the decline of the centrality of price competition, and the greater complexity of markets and commodities. The radicalism of the consumer movement stems less from philosophic principle than from its belief that an old-fashioned rationality and fairness for consumers might be made to prevail in today's marketplace.

The Anti-War, Anti-Militarist Movement. Its outward and most obvious manifestations have been resistance to the military draft; opposition to the Indochina War; criticism of the influence of the military establishment on foreign policy and (residually) on the setting of national priorities; and opposition to an expansionist foreign policy which brings United States support to non-liberal, authoritarian governments. In a larger sense, the movement grows directly out of a revulsion to the mass atrocities of the Second World War; to the total destruction implicit in unlimited nuclear warfare; to the various and sundry horrors potentially available through chemical-biological weaponry, some now outlawed; and to the overarching military control of the world made possible by space weaponry, and control of civilian populations by force, intimidation and surveillance. Additional fuel for the anti-war movement has been provided by the splintering and divisiveness evident in the Communist world, which therefore seems much less a monolithic threat than formerly. This social movement acquires its revolutionary character from its questioning of the entire theory of the conduct of foreign policy first by diplomacy, then by war—and the underlying premise that business interests and national interests are identical.

The Work Ethic Revolt. Lastly there is another movement, still amorphous and unclear, often referred to as "the Lordstown phenomenon," "the retreat from work," and "the decline of the work ethic." What may be occurring is a decline in allegiance to the Protestant or "work ethic," coupled with the growth of a "leisure ethic." Closely related is an increasing orientation to the *quality* of work, which renders workers, technicians, and middle managers less receptive to authoritarian regimentation and less willing to accept non-creative tasks and repetitious drudgery on the job. At the same time, the lust for power, social position, and money in our society has been dealt a very significant blow by some members of the youth generation. Not all of these youths "drop out" but many of them seem to be moved less significantly than their elders by traditional economic and work-oriented values and goals, even if they associate themselves with the Estab-

lishment by taking a nine-to-five job. Upper-level executives are responding to similar urges, as noticeable numbers of them "drop out" to sail boats
to Tahiti, begin second careers in universities or in Vermont shops, or take
up careers in skilled craft work or the arts. These changing attitudes toward
work expressed by a leading edge of the population probably signal fundamental shifts in general public opinion concerning work and how people
value it and feel about it.

The Social Challenges to Business

Consider now the significance for business of these seven business-
induced social revolutions. Each broad social movement stands in direct
opposition to one or more central practices, values, or traditions of business. Submerged Blacks have provided cheap labor for heavy, unpleasant,
menial jobs in the building of middle-class life in America. Women, too,
have been a source of cheap labor for a limited range of jobs, as well as
obedient and mostly uncritical consumers of the products of business. As
for youth, child labor, before it was proscribed by law, was notably cheap
and docile; and presently, ambitious young men, and women to a lesser
extent, comprise a sizeable segment of the "manpower" which corporations
need. Business has borne only the easily calculable economic costs of production, while the social costs of pollution and environmental despoliation
have been borne by others. In the same spirit, business has benefited from
the gullibility and powerlessness of consumers who have often been vic-
timized by the purchase of shoddy, overpriced, unsafe, and quickly obso-
leted goods. Business has directly and handsomely profited both from
government military contracts and from a militarized and militant government ready to use its armed forces to protect foreign markets, sources of
raw materials, and capital investments. And in a fundamental way, the
entire business culture has rested firmly upon the bedrock belief in the
sanctity of work and the single-minded pursuit of material values. So goes
the indictment posed by the social revolutions.

Giving each movement what it wants, while keeping constant the
business institution as it exists now, is impossible socially and logically. For
one example, it is not just that Blacks are now confronting corporations to
"get a piece of the action," but rather that *corporations cannot provide what
Blacks want and not be changed themselves in the process.* This is the ultimate practical significance of our earlier point that business and society are
unavoidably related to one another and that change in one leads to change
in the other. The business-induced social revolutions inevitably draw business itself back into the vortex of accelerating revolutionary change. As we

shall point out later, such change in the business institution need not be detrimental to the fundamental interests of either business or society.

Four Views of Social Responsibility

How can the corporation be made an effective vehicle for coping comprehensively with social problems and pressures? Current thinking about corporate social responsibility falls into four broad categories.

Corporate philanthropy. The most common meaning, and the one with the longest tradition, goes under the heading of corporate philanthropy. A corporation is thought to be socially responsible if it has a policy and an active program of making voluntary contributions, out of corporate profits, to various educational, charitable, religious, cultural, and other such community agencies. There is much evidence to sustain the notion that business corporations in general have accepted this role as philanthropic contributors to the broad welfare of their respective communities.

Once considered a sufficient way for the corporation to acknowledge its obligations to society, the philanthropic approach is no longer adequate to the social challenges facing today's corporation. A program of voluntary giving, however well motivated, is not sufficiently comprehensive to address current social problems. More is now called for than, in one commentator's telling phrase, "tossing a bundle of money over the ghetto wall."

There is strong belief that the voluntaristic principle has been overwhelmed by market pressures, that companies inclined toward generous contributions have been held in check by those more single-mindedly devoted to the quest for profits. The entire notion of corporate philanthropy assumes a slightly archaic character in a time when social security, adequate health care, access to education, availability of recreational facilities, and emotional rehabilitation are increasingly recognized as matters of legally enforced public right, rather than as the doubtful outcome of gifts given by charitably inclined wealthy donors. The days of the Thanksgiving Turkey and the Christmas Basket, condescendingly dispensed by the Scrooges of the world to the Cratchetts of the world, seem definitely numbered, as another paternalistic practice succumbs to newly designed institutions.

The Manager as Public Trustee. A second meaning of corporate social responsibility is that business managers should consider themselves to be trustees of the public interest—in a sense, stewards whose vast economic powers place upon them a moral obligation to use their power wisely to promote the long-run community welfare rather than selfishly to maximize short-run profits for the few. This view causes the corporation executive to act as mediator among the various groups that have claims on the corporation, seeking to strike an equitable balance among them. *Shareholders* are to receive a fair return on their investment. *Workers* are to be provided decent wages and working conditions, and treated with dignity and respect. *Customers* are to be offered high quality goods and services, improved each year through scientific and technological advances, at prices that reflect costs of production rather than monopoly power. *Suppliers and dealers* are not to be exploited by the mammoth corporation that holds the power of economic life and death over them by favoring them with contracts or refusing to do so on acceptable terms. *Local communities* that host the corporation's various factories and offices have a stake in decisions about plant location and relocation, or expansion and contraction of payrolls, and the socially responsible manager will give careful consideration to the impact decisions might have on that community's general economic welfare.

The essence of this second, very popular, meaning of social responsibility is that executives should be unselfish mediators among the sometimes conflicting claimants on the corporation, with the aim of promoting social harmony and tempering the use of concentrated economic power.

The appealing image of business statesmanship conjured up in this formulation is offset to a considerable extent when one views it in today's social context. In the first place, the approach evokes the Great Man Theory of Management at the very moment when developments in the fields of organization theory and systems analysis appear to signal the end of this particular manifestation of anthropomorphism. There is moreover the troublesome likelihood that the notion of business trusteeship rests upon the unspoken principle of corporate supremacy in a pluralist social setting. Few would question the overriding position of prominence and influence enjoyed by business corporations in contemporary American culture. This is not a society led by philosophers, artists, intellectuals, professors, or aesthetes. It would therefore appear normal to expect the leaders of the central business institutions to reflect a concern for social matters and to act upon them in judicious ways, as the business trusteeship doctrine would have them do. But note the inherent contradiction of pluralist theory implied by such institutional dominance. In a free and open pluralist society, various interest groups are said to seek their own respective interests in competition with others. One might therefore question whether anything approaching social justice could be expected as an outcome of pluralist competition between groups holding such unequal amounts of power, or where the dominant power group, acting in a "statesmanlike" manner, is granted the right to make or at least mediate the final allocation of rights and privileges.

But that is what the business trusteeship doctrine ultimately advocates.

A final weakness of this particular conception of corporate social responsibility is that it encourages talk at the top but inaction at lower levels of the corporate hierarchy. Skeptics have suggested that corporate social responsibility is little more than rhetoric, issued for public relations motives. We believe this to be an unnecessarily harsh indictment. There appears little doubt, however, that a genuine problem exists in matching lower-level actions to top management commitment in the realm of social policy, and that management spokesmen with sensitivity for social matters have themselves not been notably successful in closing the gap between social rhetoric and meaningful social action. The persistence of this gap is a damaging commentary on the workability and sufficiency of the business trusteeship approach to corporate responsibility.

Direct Social Action. Still another meaning of socially responsible business behavior has emerged in recent years. Some corporations now enter directly into confrontation with social problems and seek a solution to them by utilizing the skills, the resources, and the general influence of the corporation itself. Here we have, not a cash contribution to some *other* agency to do the job but direct involvement of the corporation. Examples are programs to train and hire the long-term unemployed residents of Black ghettoes, the sponsorship and financing of new factories to be managed and/or owned by Blacks, the provision of large loan funds to encourage Black enterprise, and taking the initiative, as some companies have done, in pollution control programs.

It is too early to know with certainty whether this direct-action meaning of corporate responsibility will enjoy a long life or suffer a short one. But daily the idea seems to gain greater legitimacy in business circles, as social pressures continue to build and as traditional corporate philanthropy and managerial stewardship appear to provide inadequate responses to Black unrest, charges of business complicity in warfare, ecological imbalance and environmental pollution, and so on.

Direct social involvement by the corporation is an encouraging move but one that has been poorly carried forward. Loan programs to establish new Black enterprises have often proceeded on questionable economic premises, have failed to provide adequate amounts of technical and managerial support, have not sufficiently anticipated continuing capital needs of the newly created firms and have at times seemed to have been as related to the needs of the sponsoring corporations for social goodwill as to the needs of the Black community for more viable economic services and jobs. Ghetto plants, after initial enthusiasm have often failed or stagnated, with insufficient market outlets or as captive satellites of the corporate sponsor with little genuine prospect of an independent and healthy economic future. New jobs and opportunities for gaining managerial expertise have been limited in both the ghetto plants and among the new "Black capitalism" firms. Programs to train and hire the "hardcore unemployed" have not yet been subject to independent audit by outside agencies to verify the claims of success.

However well meaning the supporters of such activities, there is within the corporation simply insufficient understanding of the social and human complexities usually involved. One also often observes the hope for a cheap and simple solution to vexing social problems whose history is long and where resolution may involve steps which will have to be taken beyond the corporation's present knowledge base and value system. In other cases, perhaps the majority, there is an obvious lack of organizational commitment and social resolve to carry through an action program commensurate with stated company policy.

On the positive side, direct social action by the corporation will begin building needed organizational social expertise, will help the corporation to define doable projects, will help inculcate socially innovative traditions within the corporation, and will perhaps open up a company to further social explorations. Even more important and lasting benefits may follow a vigorous program of direct social action. Providing good jobs for Blacks and other oppressed minorities is a tangible way to overcome some of the culturally ingrained racial prejudice of our society. More importantly, it is a powerful way to express the conviction that *all* human beings, regardless of racial or cultural background, have inherent value and that nothing in our society should stand in the way of their achieving such potential. When prejudicial barriers in the job market are removed, broad scale social benefits accrue to all, not just to the newly employed minorities. The corporation is thus in position to initiate social chain reactions of the widest possible benefit to society at large. Having earlier touched off a wave of social effects with many negative consequences, the corporation now holds within its power an opportunity to act in socially constructive ways.

Government-and-Business Partnership. Recently it has been suggested by the Committee for Economic Development (CED) that the proper way for private business to discharge its social responsibilities is to form a partnership with government. The task of government would be "to determine the nation's goals, set the priorities, develop the strategies and create the conditions for carrying out the work most effectively to the satisfaction of the public." Business's role would be "in the actual execution of social programs" carried out under the policy umbrella of government.

This fourth approach to corporate social responsibility casts private

business firms in a distinctly different role from that provided by the previ-
ous three approaches. A business-and-government partnership moves
sharply away from dependence upon self-initiated corporate action in the
field of social problem solving. It implicitly acknowledges the inadequacy
of simple corporate philanthropy, of well-meaning business trusteeship,
and of voluntary direct social action programs as means to resolve pressing
social problems. It counsels a marshaling of national resources and an
assessment of how they should be used within the context of national goals.
Above all, it asserts that current social tensions cannot be successfully
reduced by business alone.

In this emerging partnership, the business record to date is essentially
one of defensive reaction from within a persisting market mentality. Even
the CED statement, with all of its openness, makes obeisance to the traditional virtues of the market as organizer, profit as motivator, and free enterprise as beneficent overseer of economic and social life as if blithely
ignoring the disorganization, dehumanization, and social chaos that have
also accompanied the growth and spread of material comfort. Business allegiance to this outmoded market mentality and its economic benefits is no
doubt partially responsible for widespread business opposition to proposed
laws curbing sexual discrimination. Because businessmen are still thinking
primarily in market and profit terms, they have attempted to weaken the
administration of equal employment opportunity laws, to water down proposed consumer protection laws, and to fight long legal battles over administration of pollution control laws.

So the "partnership" is far from perfect. It functions shakily. Neither
business nor government completely trust one another. The public tends to
be wary and mistrustful, too. But CED advocacy of an active government-
and-business cooperative approach to social problems may represent a
needed breakthrough in business thinking that presages effective social
action on a large scale.

As business moves forward to accept its greatly expanded social role,
it can discover a kernel of value in each of these four major pathways to
corporate social responsibility, although collectively they fall short of the
massive corporate response and transformation needed. *Corporate philanthropy*, at its truest and best sense, holds that the love of profits is an insufficient guide for corporate decision making and should be enriched by a
deeper concern for human welfare. *Corporate statesmanship* advocates the
marshaling of corporation resources to serve the many diverse interests
touched by the company, including social interests. *Direct social action*
implies the need for innovative ways to release creative energies contained
within the corporate system for an attack on social problems. *Government-*

and-business cooperation can possibly provide the legal, political, and economic means for a massive breakaway from traditional market restraints and for a massive breakthrough toward effective and humane social action.

Corporate Power and the Social Revolutions

If one inquires of this society, who holds the power to influence corporate, governmental, and societal decisions; who sets and responds to social values in significant ways; who exerts leadership across institutional demarcations in the society; and who has the power to deny or to respond to community demands, needs, and pressures, then quite clearly the business community and its corporate leaders are a large part of the answer. They occupy this privileged and powerful position by virtue of their control and ownership of the large aggregations of economic wealth and resources represented in our most prominent corporations. Corporations' socially strategic position has made the extent of their "social responsibility" a uniquely important problem of our time.

The call today, echoing throughout all of the social revolutions, is not so much for a redistribution of wealth and income from the "haves" to the "have nots," although one sometimes hears that literal demand and although that would undoubtedly have important social effects sought by some of the social movements. More fundamentally, the insistent concern now is for the quality of community life, for personal autonomy, for the fulfillment of human needs, for the nourishment of humane values, for improved social relationships between diverse segments of the human community, and for a change in the social design of economic and business institutions that now inhibit and repress the full expression and realization of such desired conditions. *That is the meaning of the social revolutions for business and businessmen.* Not redistribution, but re-humanization. Not confiscation of wealth, but shared lives amidst social justice. Not denial of material values, but placing them in the service of human and humane ends.

When businessmen and their corporations see, accept, and act upon this broader formulation, then not only will business have embraced its new social role, but it will simultaneously have crossed the great divide that otherwise separates economy from society, humanity from its habitat, and human persons from one another.

YEAR 1978

WALKING THE TALK:
FROM SOCIAL RESPONSIBILITY
TO SOCIAL RESPONSIVENESS

Setting the Stage. The violent anti-business sentiment of the 1960s and 1970s convinced many business leaders that something must be done—more than philanthropy, more than mere good will. A practical answer was supplied by two Harvard Business School scholars, Raymond Bauer and Robert Ackerman: be socially responsible (CSR₁) by being socially responsive (CSR₂). Others wondered, though, if responsibility and responsiveness were equivalent.

Beginning around 1970, business-and-society thought began an important transition. The origins and scope of this change have yet to be fully clarified, but there is already enough evidence at hand to suggest the major outlines of the transition and to foreshadow its significance for business-and-society inquiry. The change promises to lift business-and-society studies to a new and more realistic plane, thereby bringing them more firmly into the orbit of practicing business and management professionals.

CSR₁ = Corporate Social Responsibility

The idea of "corporate social responsibility," as we now understand the term, began to take recognizable shape in the third decade of this century. By the mid-1920s, business representatives and executives were beginning to speak of the need for corporate directors to act as trustees for the interests, not just of stockholders, but other social claimants as well. Others had spoken of this possibility as early as 1913. Corporate philanthropy, whose history stretched back into the 19th century, was accompanied by a growing belief that business and society were linked together in organic, if not yet well understood, ways. An obligation to provide "service" beyond profits, yet without denying profits, was advocated by some.

These several timorous beginnings of social responsibility thinking suffered ups and downs during the Depression decade of the 1930s and then were largely subordinated to the more urgent demands of World War II. By the 1950s, these long-smouldering ideas about business's obligations to society burst forth with a renewed vigor that has carried them forward uninterruptedly to the present.

The fundamental idea embedded in "corporate social responsibility" is that business corporations have an obligation to work for social betterment. This obligation is incurred and acts as a constant function throughout all phases—mainstream and peripheral—of the company's operations. It may affect those operations and the company's profits either positively or negatively. The obligation may be recognized and discharged voluntarily by preemptive actions of the company, or it may be imposed coercively by actions of government. Regardless of its origin or the particular portion of company operations it affects or its impact on profits, the obligation to work for social betterment is the essence of the notion of "corporate social responsibility."

Over the years, this obligation is said to have arisen from a wide variety of sources, including the economic, social, and political power of the corporation; a fear of government encroachment on private decision making; the possession of technical skills and resources needed for the solution of social problems; the exercise of an enlightened self-interest by corporate executives; the desire of corporations to be good citizens of their respective communities; the decline of traditional checks and balances, primarily price competition, in the marketplace, along with the rise of professional managers as a dominant force of the corporation; the need for some powerful and influential institutions to reconcile the competing claims of pluralistic interest groups; the sometime gap between the profit goals of private companies and an array of changing social values; the simple need of the company to comply with social legislation in order to be a law-abiding citizen; the pressure of humanistic, religious, and democratic values and attitudes; the fear of violence and social disruption; the desire to retain broad public acceptance; and the social contract implications of the corporate charter.

That such an obligation exists or, if so, that it can be made to work has been the subject of intense and sometimes acrimonious debate. Some have inveighed against the very idea as being fundamentally subversive of the capitalist system. Some have scoffed at the voluntarism of the notion as being public relations puffery. Some have been dubious about the efficacy and detachment of government-imposed social regulations. Many believe the obligation is severely— and perhaps fatally—limited by economic, financial, and profit considerations. The radical leftists dismiss the idea as so much liberal apologetics for a corrupt capitalism.

In spite of these and other attacks, though, the idea persists among business executives, scholars, and the public that corporations have an obligation to be socially responsible. A veritable flood of literature attests to the breadth and depth, if not always the logic, of this notion.

Whatever the outcome of the debate might have been had it been allowed to continue unabated, both proponents and opponents of "corporate social responsibility" seem to have agreed that certain key issues loom larger than others. First, the content or substance—the operational meaning—of corporate social responsibility is supremely vague. Does social responsibility refer to company actions taken only in conformity with prevailing legal regulations, or only to those voluntary acts that go beyond the law? Does it refer to those that conform to current public expectations, whether encoded as law or not, or those that anticipate possible future social needs? Are mainstream company operations to be included among socially responsible acts, or only those that are peripheral to the firm's major mission? How far must a company go in cleaning up pollution, reducing discrimination, making the workplace safer, or providing consumer protection to be considered socially responsible? Or what if a firm excels in one of these areas of social concern but fails rather badly in the other three? Is it then socially responsible or irresponsible? The difficulties in finding precise answers to these and similar questions concerning the actual meaning of "corporate social responsibility" have dogged the debate from the beginning.

A second question that has been difficult to answer concerns the institutional mechanisms through which the idea of "corporate social responsibility" could be made to work, assuming that its essential meaning could be clarified. The possible mechanisms include business response to traditional market forces; voluntary business response that goes beyond immediate economic considerations; government-assisted business response through subsidies, contracts, tax relief, etc.; government-imposed social standards of corporate performance; and a much larger role for government planning, nationalized corporations, and federal chartering of corporations. Just which one—or which combination—of these might produce the desired degree of corporate social responsibility remains an elusive matter.

A third unresolved issue in the corporate social responsibility debate is that the tradeoff between economic goals and costs, on the one hand, and social goals and costs, on the other hand, cannot be stated with any acceptable degree of precision. While it may be true that one person's or one company's economic betterment is another group's social deprivation, it is also true that one group's social betterment is another's lower profits, fewer jobs, or higher taxes. The air may be cleaned and the workplace made safer and freer from discrimination, but at the probable price of job losses, decapitalization of the industry, closing of plants, and other types of economic costs. Given the present underdeveloped state of the art of cost-benefit analysis, as well as the highly mercurial political climate created when it becomes necessary to weigh social costs and benefits against economic costs and benefits, the entire question of tradeoffs remains murky indeed.

The fourth and perhaps most difficult issue concerning "corporate social responsibility" is that the moral underpinnings of the idea are neither clear nor agreed upon. One searches in vain for any clear and generally accepted moral principle that would impose on business an obligation to work for social betterment. But one finds only a melange of imponderable generalities concerning public purpose, enlightened self-interest, the social good, equality, human dignity, good citizenship, the responsible use of power, and similar moralistic catchwords. Nor does one fare better in probing for a moral principle that would *deny* the notion of business's social responsibility, for from this side of the aisle come such ponderous and equally elusive phrases as freedom of the individual, protecting economic freedoms, government encroachment on private decision making, preserving individual initiative, etc.

The intractability of these central issues has, until recent times, posed the dreadful possibilities that the debate over "corporate social responsibility" would either continue indefinitely with little prospect of final resolution or that it would simply exhaust itself and collapse as a viable, legitimate question.

But now, since about 1970, one sees the emergence of a new approach to the question of business's role in society. A fundamental theoretical and conceptual reorientation is taking place among those who study business-and-society relationships. This transition represents an attempt to escape the several dilemmas embedded in the debate over "corporate social responsibility."

In order to differentiate the older ideas from the newer and emergent theoretical formulations, it will be convenient to refer to "corporate social responsibility" as CSR_1.

CSR_2 = Corporate Social Responsiveness

Beginning around 1970, a new strain of thought crept into the deliberations about business's role in society. Ever more frequently, one began to hear the phrase "corporate social *responsiveness*" rather than the older rubric of "corporate social *responsibility*." Soon it became evident that the promulgators of the "responsiveness" notion did indeed intend it to be a genuine replacement for the idea of "responsibility" and that it was not simply one of those fashionable changes in phraseology that occasionally takes the scholarly community by storm.

"Corporate social responsiveness" refers to the capacity of a corporation to respond to social pressure. The literal act of responding, or of achieving a generally responsive posture, to society is the focus of "corporate social responsiveness." The key questions are: Can the company respond? Will it? Does it? How does it? To what extent? And with what effect? One searches the organization for mechanisms, procedures, arrangements, and behavioral patterns that, taken collectively, would mark the organization as more or less capable of responding to social pressures. It then becomes evident that organizational design and managerial competence play important roles in how extensively and how well a company responds to social demands and needs. Hence the idea of "corporate social responsiveness" is managerial in tone and approach and its advocates place great emphasis upon the *management* of a company's relations with society.

In order to distinguish this group of ideas from the earlier notion of corporate social responsibility (CSR_1), it will be convenient to refer to "corporate social responsiveness" as CSR_2.

The reorientation of thought implied in this shift from "social responsibility" to "social responsiveness" is profound. While the debate over the merits of CSR_1 has always carried heavy philosophic overtones, CSR_2 shuns philosophy in favor of a managerial approach. The abstract and often highly elusive principles governing CSR_1 are replaced by CSR_2's focus on the practical aspects of making organizations more socially responsive to tangible forces in the surrounding environment. The often speculative generalities that becloud the debate about CSR_1 yield to the analytic posture and methods of CSR_2 scholars and business practitioners who seek to understand the problems and prospects of making specific organizations socially responsive. The moralistic tone of both the advocates and the opponents of CSR_1 is muted by the pragmatic outlook of hardnosed managers who may work either with enthusiasm or only grudgingly toward the ends of CSR_2. The often reluctant and reactive attitude found among business firms concerning CSR_1 (due in large part to the vagueness of the concept, the lack of operational meaning, and shifting performance guidelines) is transposed into a more open, proactive stance as the organization moves closer to a CSR_2 state. During the period when CSR_1 thinking was dominant, companies often exhibited a tendency to treat social problems serially as unrelated phenomena, sometimes in the "knee-jerk" fashion typical of a crisis atmosphere. By contrast, the advocates of a CSR_2 approach stress a process of systems orientation to social pressures, along with an anticipatory scanning procedure to detect emerging problems. Finally, whereas the extent of CSR_1 is often dependent largely upon the individual social conscience of the company's chief executive officer and of the managerial cadre generally, CSR_2 looks to an institutionalized company policy for its successful implementation.

The many philosophic imponderables of the CSR_1 debate—why? whether? for whose benefit? according to which moral principles?—are replaced by the more answerable considerations of CSR_2—how? by what means? with what effect? according to which operational guidelines? *Perhaps most importantly, CSR_2 assumes that CSR_1's central question of **whether** companies should respond to social pressures has already been answered affirmatively by general public opinion and a host of government social regulations and that the important task for business now is to learn how to **respond** in fruitful, humane, and practical ways.*

Close examination of this new theoretical thrust in the business-and-society field reveals that CSR_2 thought has two dimensions or it deals with social responsiveness in two different but interrelated senses. The first is what might be called a *micro organizational dimension.* Here the focus is on a single company and its ability to achieve significant levels of social responsiveness. Raymond A. Bauer and Robert W. Ackerman, both then at the Harvard Business School, were among the first to place major emphasis upon the responsiveness, as opposed to the responsibility, of single firms. Ackerman's now well-known three-stage sequence, through which large corporations move in attaining large measures of social responsiveness, stands as the major conceptual innovation in clarifying the several characteristic traits of a socially responsive firm. The foremost concern is for a single organization to be positively and pragmatically responsive to the pressures emanating from the social-political-governmental environment. Social responsiveness means the ability to *manage* the company's relations with various social groups.

Neil Chamberlain, in what could easily be labeled he culminating theoretical work of the CSR_1 era, argued convincingly that single companies are severely limited in the degree of social responsiveness they can attain. Even the firm that might have successfully combined CSR_1 and CSR_2 would inevitably face not only the limits imposed by economic factors but the unwillingness of the general public to sacrifice its addiction to high levels of consumption for the achievement of less tangible social goals.

But while Chamberlain was thus conclusively demonstrating both the impracticability of CSR_1 and the limits of the micro dimension of CSR_2, others were erecting a conceptual structure that would go a long way toward overcoming these limitations. This second dimension of CSR_2 theory is what might be called the *macro institutional dimension*. It refers to all of the large-scale institutional arrangements and procedures that appear to be essential if each of the individual socially responsive companies (operating in the micro dimension) is to have a significant impact on social problems.

In 1971, the Research and Policy Committee of the Committee for Economic Development (CED) issued its now famous statement entitled *Social Responsibilities of Business Corporations*. Straddling the worlds of CSR_1 and CSR_2, its major contribution was to advocate the formation of a "government-business partnership for social progress." Arguing that the principle had been long established that government could modify market arrangements to achieve a variety of public purposes, the Committee urged the extension of that idea to the arena of social problems plaguing the nation. The CED proposal provided a workable mechanism for overcoming economic obstacles at the firm and industry levels, but it left open the question of how public purposes were to be defined.

Lee E. Preston and James E. Post neatly filled in the answer in their 1975 treatise entitled *Private Management and Public Policy*. The really significant impact that society exerts on business is through the realm of public policy. The central criterion used by society and corporate management to assess a single company's social impacts—a criterion they labeled the "principle of public responsibility"—is derived from a stable yet ever-changing public policy process. CSR_2 companies could take their social cues from public policies, as indeed many of them are doing presently.

Simultaneously, George Cabot Lodge of the Harvard Business School pointed to the decline and slow demise of the older Lockean ideological principles and offered a newer and more socially appropriate set of ideological guidelines that provided a philosophic rationale for the social responsiveness of business.

Hence, as a rounded theoretical construct, CSR_2 stands as more tangible, achievable, intellectually sound, theoretically valid, and philosophically justified approach to the question of business's role in society than can be said of the older and now somewhat passe CSR_1. It is quite likely that the emergence of CSR_2 will have felicitous consequences for both scholars and practitioners in the business-and-society world. Most certainly, the idea of CSR_1 could not long have withstood the onslaughts of all those who argued so effectively that it was either undesirable, unworkable, unlikely, or impossible.

The Implications of a CSR_2 Approach

The transition from CSR_1 thinking to CSR_2 thinking has several important implications.

First, it takes the "moral heat" off business and thereby may tend to make companies less defensive about business-and-society issues. For many years, business firms, including those that have vigorously resisted the blandishments of the "social responsibility crowd," have borne the burden of a guilty social conscience by seeming to fall short of public expectations. With the appearance of the CSR_2 viewpoint, one can now reasonably hope that less attention will be paid to the "moral standing" of a company and more to its tangible activities as a socially responsive entity.

A second implication is that CSR_2 theory puts a strong emphasis on the need for tools, techniques, organizational structures, and behavioral systems most appropriate for a truly responsive company. CSR_2 scholars and practitioners search for tangible ways to respond to social pressures.

Third, a CSR_2 approach encourages the initiation of empirical research into business-and-society issues. Business managers need help in responding to government agencies, social interest groups, and public opinion pressures. They face a genuine problem of knowing how to respond, when and to what extent, and with what specific goals in mind. What is needed is guidance, specific procedures, and an empirical search for tangible answers.

A fourth important implication of the CSR_2 approach is that it draws attention to the internal and external constraints on organizational responsiveness. Internally, CSR_2 theory stresses the importance of the large corporation's divisional structure as a potential obstacle to flexible responses; the lack or underdevelopment of social measurement capabilities; the absence of social factors in the performance appraisal of individual managers; the middle management sabotage of upper management social policies; and the simple bureaucratic inertia typically encountered by any exotic development, whether social or otherwise. The external constraints on CSR_2 include the capital-market monitoring process with its focus on return on investment and similar measures of business success; the heavy and often indeterminate costs of CSR_2; the inherent complexity and stubborn persistence of our major social problems; and the difficulties of evaluating social benefits and costs in precise ways. Having sloughed off the abstract speculations of CSR_1, the CSR_2 viewpoint can concentrate on these constraints as problems to be solved rather than as philosophic principles to be debated.

The Shortcomings of a CSR$_2$ Approach

Fruitful as this new theoretical development is, its advocates have yet to solve some knotty problems about the relation of business to society.

CSR$_2$ does not, in the first place, clarify the meaning of CSR$_1$. We are still left with the puzzle of defining "social betterment." Different companies may be socially responsive in different ways and in varying degrees. We remain without a clear notion of whether or to what extent social responsiveness will produce a general condition of social responsibility, or whether greater amounts of social responsiveness will lead automatically to social betterment, or whether social responsiveness is logically to be equated with social betterment.

The CSR$_2$ approach simply sidesteps the issue of defining "social betterment." It offers little or no help in developing consensual criteria of social performance or a system of social priorities. Preston and Post's "principle of public responsibility" suggests that the content (or meaning) of public policy toward business is open to continual change, thus implying that the search for a single meaning of social betterment is unnecessary. This position is not likely to satisfy either the public or business who want and deserve to know whether specific social actions taken by business are adequate and acceptable.

Closely related to this shortcoming is another. CSR$_2$ doesn't clarify the *nature* of business-and-society relationships—what they are, what they should be, which ones should receive attention. For example, does business *reflect* social values or does it *impose* them? Is business really distinct from society as implied by such terms as "business *and* society" and "environmental influences *on* business" or is this distinction wrongly imposed on a single though complex phenomenon?

A third shortcoming of the CSR$_2$ formulation is that it is essentially a static theory, telling little or nothing about social change, about how new social movements arise and become important to business, about how to anticipate change and adapt an organization so that it may cope with these changes. Business practitioners, as well as management scholars, have provided some insights into these matters, but much remains to be done.

Fourth and last, CSR$_2$ contains no explicit value theory and advocates no specific set of values for business to follow in making social responses. Perhaps the major failing of CSR$_1$ was its inability to enunciate a clear moral principle that would justify in the minds of all an obligation by business to work for social betterment. CSR$_2$ does no better. The result is an implicit reliance on established organizational values and prevailing, if changeable, societal values.

One can sympathize with those who maintain that CSR_2's escape from the hopeless bogs of CSR_1's moralistic debate is gain enough. But it is likely that time will reveal that *social values stand at the core of all business-and-society concerns*. One cannot leave such vitally important considerations unexamined. Business-and-society scholars and practitioners might want to follow the lead of theorists who have begun to fathom the deeps of value analysis and to direct those inquiries toward a resolution of business's role in society. Doing so, they may in time evolve CSR_3, which will clarify and incorporate both the moral dimensions implied by CSR_1 and the management dimensions of CSR_2.

YEAR 1981

[Public confidence in business executives: 20%]

FREE MARKET HAWKS VS. CSR DOVES

*Setting the Scene. The social turmoil of the 1950s, 1960s, and 1970s (see **Year 1973** chapter), which carried a strong anti-business bias, created doubt and division among business leaders who as a group had enjoyed a generally favored place in public opinion in post-World War II years. Now challenged as to motive and their companies' impacts on society, those same business leaders debated what should be done to rescue business's image and social standing. It was during the 1970s that business attitudes shifted significantly toward a reinvigorated defense of free markets and a rejection of government involvement—a kind of symbolic circling of the wagons to fend off renegade social critics. The beginning of that shift, which was to gather greater strength well into the following century, is told here.*

"The modern manager sees the corporation as a social
as well as an economic organization, functioning in
the whole of society rather than just in the marketplace."
Committee for Economic Development, **1971**

"We stress primary reliance on the market system."
Committee for Economic Development, **1979**

Where does business stand on the question of social responsibility after two decades of social ferment? The posture of business toward society can be a crucial determinant of how well a society resolves its major problems. Do we know today the extent to which business is willing and able to commit itself to broad societal tasks?

One benchmark of business commitment is found in business philosophy, those occasional expressions of preference for one form of social action over another. The Committee for Economic Development (CED) is, in a sense, in the business of issuing such statements. It has, in its own words "a special mission that no other business-related organization performs: ...to identify the emerging issues that will confront business and society, analyze them, deduce sound public policies for dealing with them, and communicate those good solutions to thought leaders throughout the country."

Founded in 1942, the Committee for Economic Development is composed mainly of two hundred top-level corporation executives, with a sprinkling of university presidents and an occasional government official with close connections to business. These two hundred members constitute the board of trustees, while another one hundred formerly active members are listed as "honorary trustees." Supported financially by voluntary contributions from business, foundations, and individuals, the committee strives to maintain an "independent, nonprofit, and [politically] nonpartisan" status.

Since its founding, the committee has authored around 119 declarations of preferred policy on a wide range of national issues. Scarcely any major facet of public concern has escaped CED's attention. Economic growth, recession, inflation, government operations, crime and justice, aid to low-income countries, public and private education, housing, agricultural programs, transportation, energy problems, and many other such matters have been the focus of reports intended to shape public opinion. Taken as a whole, these policy statements are a remarkable sample of the thinking of selected top business leaders.

Obviously, CED does not speak for business as a whole. Such organizations as the Business Roundtable, the U. S. Chamber of Commerce, the National Association of Manufacturers, the Conference Board, the American Enterprise Institute, and others all have their distinctive (and sometimes conflicting) views on vital issues confronting business. For now, though, we shall accept the CED's reports as one—but not the only—important indicator of business preferences and business philosophy.

Two of CED's policy statements stand out from all the others as symbolic of the organization's views on corporate social responsibility. In 1971 it issued *Social Responsibilities of Business Corporations*. Coming as it did after a tumultuous decade of rising social protest and disorder, the statement was greeted with high interest by both the supporters and critics of business. In it, CED urged business to adopt a broader and more humane view of its function in society. Eight years later *Redefining Government's Role in the Market System* appeared. It told of the need to reduce government involvement in economic affairs and outlined a program for disciplining those government initiatives that appeared to be unavoidable. This report placed renewed emphasis upon market performance as a way to achieve both economic and social progress.

Perhaps these two keynote declarations—one a capstone of the 1960s and the other a culmination of the 1970s—can provide clues to what business thinks about social responsibility and whether business leaders are broadening or narrowing their social vision.

Social Responsibilities of Business Corporations: The Doves Speak

CED's 1971 declaration invites business to expand its social horizon by thinking of itself as a socioeconomic institution. It states that:

- Business's **social contract** is changing because society now expects more from business than in the past.

- A larger number of better organized and informed **constituency groups**—employees, stockholders, customers and consumers, suppliers, and community neighbors—are making greater demands on business.

- A posture of **"enlightened self-interest"** by business acknowledges that corporate well-being is promoted by social well-being, that social goodwill is essential, and that only deliberate and positive social actions by business can assure the resources and goodwill necessary for survival.

- **Social voluntarism** in ten major fields—economic growth and efficiency; education; employment and training; civil rights and equal opportunity; urban renewal and development; pollution abatement; conservation and recreation; culture and the arts; medical care; and government operations—should be "expanded and intensified."

- Since voluntarism is insufficient, **a government-business partnership** should be forged to achieve social progress. Government should determine goals, priorities, and strategies, and create favorable market conditions. Business should then carry out various social programs at a profit.

- A combination of **government controls, incentives, and disincentives**—contracts, cash loans and loan guarantees, tax benefits, public-private corporations—should be used to encourage positive social performance by business.

- Should social actions by business be blocked by cost factors or failure of corporations to cooperate, **business "logically and ethically**

should propose and support rational government regulation which will remove the short-run impediments from [social] actions that are wise in the long run."

This message was pretty heady stuff for a business community that traditionally had thought of itself as primarily economic and had long harbored a deep suspicion of government intrusion into the private sector. But taking note that "a clear majority of the public thinks corporations have not been sufficiently concerned about the problems facing our society" and noting the even more alarming "pervasive feeling in the country that the social order somehow has gotten out of balance," CED felt compelled to speak out in these bold new directions.

Redefining Government's Role in the Market System: The Hawks React

By 1979 the nation's attention was shifting toward economic rather than social concerns as energy problems, recession, and rampant inflation came to the fore. A tide of public discontent with government operations, regulations, taxation, bureaucracy, and corruption was running strong. CED's 1979 statement reflects these concerns, claiming that:

- The political and governmental system has **reduced the effectiveness of markets and the market system** to the detriment of society.

- Government's role in the economy should be redefined to **moderate government's negative economic impacts.**

- **The pursuit of social goals through government actions** that reduce market efficiency **is self-defeating.**

- **Preference should be given to the use of markets and market incentives** in working toward the nation's social and economic goals.

- To minimize costs and other negative economic effects of government actions, **all existing and proposed government programs should be evaluated** by three criteria: What type of "market limitation" is government attempting to correct and is government action necessary to do it? What social and political goals is government seeking? Is the existing or proposed government solution both feasible and cost-effective? By "disciplining" the policy process in these ways, CED's 1979 statement offers **the hope that expensive social demands will not overwhelm the economy** by reducing efficiency or by further expanding a sluggish and unresponsive government bureaucracy.

CED 1971 versus CED 1979

The contrast between the two documents could hardly be greater. A spirit of social concern and an emphasis upon social equity suffuses CED's 1971 statement while CED's 1979 statement speaks mainly of the importance of the economic efficiency of markets. Private voluntarism and a government-business coalition are proposed as the means of grappling with social issues in the 1971 statement, but a largely unassisted free market is preferred by the later one as the engine of social and economic progress. In the earlier report, government is pictured as a legitimate and indispensable aid to business and society, while the later statement sees government as an adversary of business and a hindrance to society. In 1971 CED favored an expansion of both government's and business's responsibilities in the social arena, but by 1979 contraction and restraint were preferred. Some of CED's 1971 prime policy instruments, such as loan guarantees, became problems for the authors of the 1979 report. Whereas CED in 1971 understood business and social progress to be a function of social well-being, in 1979 it reversed the relationship by claiming that social and economic progress are a function of overall market efficiency.

Basically, CED seems, whether by design or not, to have set up for itself the choice between the pursuit of economic goals through an unregulated market structure and the cultivation of social goals through private voluntarism and private-public cooperation. The 1971 declaration clearly favors the latter course, while the 1979 statement embraces the free market and its associated economic goals. So different are the two views that the more recent statement appears not to acknowledge the existence of the earlier one. It is almost as if an air of slight embarrassment prevailed within the ranks of CED over the excessive attachment to nonmarket orientations that one finds in the 1971 report.

While these differences are striking they should not be allowed to obscure some important similarities. Profits are seen as essential to business and a necessary condition for both economic and social progress in both reports. Market solutions are preferred to government solutions even where the need is acknowledged for some government supplementation of the market. Similarly, both reports maintain that the public sector, even when engaged in its legitimate tasks of setting national goals and priorities, should be subordinate to the private sector, and the authors of both statements agree that government involvement, once underway, can easily expand to a level that hampers the efficiency of markets.

What has happened to CED's 1971 commitment to social responsibility? Was it a brief and expedient response to a turbulent social environment rather than a deep and ongoing commitment to genuine social reform? How can we account for the apparent turnaround in social outlook from 1971 to 1979?

CED's 1971 House of Cards

There were three concepts around which CED's 1971 theory of social responsibility was constructed: social voluntarism, enlightened self-interest, and a government-business partnership. To what extent does CED 1979 draw upon, or ignore, these ideas? A careful reading of the more recent statement suggests that social voluntarism has been retained, enlightened self-interest has been abandoned, and the government-business coalition has been partially retained for economic purposes but largely abandoned as a way to solve social problems.

However inadequate social voluntarism may have proved to be as a social palliative during the 1970s, CED's 1979 statement does not so much reject as ignore the idea. It does not even merit honorable mention.

The boldest philosophic departure contained in the 1971 report is the doctrine of enlightened self-interest. But this doctrine's justification of non-market approaches to social problem solving is an anathema to the 1979 statement, which hails the market as the *deus ex machina* of economic, and thence social, progress.

What about the 1971 government-business partnership of "great promise" that would, by tapping the profit incentive, be responsible for "unleashing the power and dynamism of private enterprise on a scale that will be effective in generating social progress"? The idea of public-private cooperation is a persistent theme in nine of the twenty-eight major policy statements issued by CED between 1971 and 1979. Even in these cases, it tends to be viewed as a necessary evil, definitely not preferred over market solutions.

It seems safe to generalize that since 1971 the concept of a government-business coalition has become an adjunct to a market-centered preference for coping with major national problems. It is seen as an auxiliary method to be used mainly to overcome financial obstacles that inhibit business participation in achieving national goals and policies, not as a broad-purpose tool of social reform or a principal way of breaking through to a resolution of the nation's social problems.

Social Equity, but...

By 1979, CED was rather obviously attempting to establish itself on firmer, more familiar, and altogether more comfortable conceptual terrain. Its leading concept, and the fountainhead of economic and social progress, was the private market system. Nothing that interfered with its operation was to find approbation. While it was acknowledged that controlling pollution, promoting equal opportunity, providing certain public goods, and trying to attain social equity are legitimate functions of government, these well-intended activities can nevertheless produce market distortions, disincentives, and inefficiencies. It is apparent that CED in 1979, while accepting the need for tackling the nation's social problems, believed it could be carried off only through a market system that brooked little government interference with private initiative.

CED's Ideological Aberration

In retrospect, it appears that CED's 1971 call for more attention to corporate social responsibility was inconsistent with the ideology expressed or embedded in CED policy statements before and after 1971. CED's 1971 statement seems to be a somewhat carelessly constructed response to a period of great social turbulence, naïve in the faith it placed in social voluntarism and enlightened self-interest and innocent of the pitfalls of a government-business coalition. Its authors veered away, if ever so slightly, from a market-centered approach to social problem solving.

The environmental pressures of the late 1960s—civil rights disturbances, anti-war protests, consumer activism, ecological fears—were most likely a prime source of this transgression. Business stood accused of favoring a market system that historically had permitted social abuses. Individual companies—some of them well known blue-chip corporations—were said to be indifferent about their impact on pollution, discrimination, job safety, and the quality of consumer products. The beleaguered authors of CED's 1971 report warned their fellow trustees that failure by private business, acting in its own enlightened self-interest, to deal promptly and realistically with social pressures would risk direct government intervention. Better to grasp the nettle of a government-business coalition than to face the more alarming prospect of a growth in the government bureaucracy with its cumbersome restrictions on private decision making. In this way, CED in 1971 offered government, working in tandem with an aroused business community, as an institutional buffer against social criticism.

Environmental pressures eased somewhat by the late 1970s, with street demonstrations replaced by legal and political skirmishing, and business more skillful in advocating its social views. CED's ideological pendulum swung back toward its accustomed position, lamenting the burdens that government places on the market system.

Had the Committee for Economic Development been simply expedient regarding needed social reform and social problem solving, favoring only enough incremental progress to stave off social revolution but not enough to carry business significantly beyond established market rules? But perhaps the 1971 commitment to social responsibility represented a genuine shift in business thinking, even though it occurred in the face of considerable opposition within the ranks of business. If so, *the 1979 statement* would be a discordant ideological note in a pragmatic effort by reform-minded trustees to gain public acceptance and approval of business. Pragmatic reforms, however distasteful, might be preferred to more far-reaching changes in the social order.

If the 1979 statement is "mainstream" business philosophy and the 1971 statement is an aberration, then CED would seem to be signaling an end to any fundamental move toward social problem solving outside of, or involving a modification of, the market system. Even the most innovative social efforts of private companies, including those that may be expedited by cooperative efforts of government, would be limited to localized actions that can reach no farther than the boundaries of the encompassing market system.

Change of Players or Change of Heart?

Before drawing so stark and unpleasant a conclusion about the drift of business philosophy, let us examine a simpler and still more intriguing possibility. Inasmuch as the membership of the CED working groups responsible for developing policy statements changes from time to time and from topic to topic, perhaps the contrasts between CED's 1971 statement and the CED's 1979 statement are due to personnel shifts rather than philosophic reorientation. Could the hawks have replaced the doves?

New Members and Holdovers. Retirements, resignations, and leaves for government service caused a considerable change in membership of the Research and Policy Committee and the various working groups from 1971 to 1979. In the working groups that produced the respective statements, the change of personnel is obvious. In the two research and drafting subcommittees, a membership overlap of only 5.9 percent occurs. An entirely different group of (non-CED) subcommittee advisors was in place for the 1979 research and drafting work, and there was only a 10 percent carryover of 1971 Research Advisory Board membership to 1979. The new majority of 56.7 to 63.3 percent in the Research and Policy Committee and the 90 to 100 percent new majority in the key working groups makes it possible to argue that the change in official viewpoint from 1971 to 1979 was attributable to personnel changes—if one assumes that the new majorities opposed CED's 1971 posture or simply preferred CED's 1979 views.

Assent or Dissent? Another sign that personnel changes, rather than an official change of heart, were responsible for the shift would be if a large number or majority of those serving on the Research and Policy Committee in 1971 and in 1979 (the overlap members) rejected the more conventional stance of CED's 1979 report. But only five overlap members (19.2 percent) recorded memoranda of comment, reservation, or dissent in 1979, and only one member flatly disapproved the 1979 statement. The 96.2 percent who approved the 1971 statement also approved the more conventional 1979 policy, and 81.8 percent approved the latter statement unqualifiedly. The large measure of approval of CED 1979 by those who had earlier been responsible for endorsing the notion of corporate social responsibility would suggest that the shift in viewpoint represents more than just a change of members.

Internal Strains. One other measure of the comparative acceptability of the two statements can be found by noting the number or percentage of memoranda of comment, reservation, or dissent and the number of outright disapprovals recorded for each statement. The social responsibility statement encountered a larger degree of opposition within CED itself than did the policy guidelines for redefining government's role in the market system. Further, of the fifteen dissenting memoranda found in the 1979 report, only four represent disagreements with basic principles.

CED's tradition and the extent of opposition to the statement on social responsibility reveal that it was never entirely comfortable with the prickly subject. Reinforcing its ideological homecoming in 1979 were the ever more intrusive regulatory agencies (OSHA, EPA, FTC, CPSC) with their burdensome and costly bureaucratic trappings. The enduring themes of CED's business philosophy appear to be that profits must prevail over social responsibility, that market solutions are preferred to government-assisted efforts, that government actions must be curbed or "disciplined" to protect the market system, and that social progress is a function of a market-centered economic process.

Business Vision and Social Reality

What has happened to that broader social vision of CED in 1971, the one that spoke of a changing social contract, wider corporate constituencies, a socio-economic corporation, and even a need for government initiatives and regulations to achieve social goals? The only trace is found in CED's other policy statements dealing with the urban poor and urban development generally. On the other issues that constituted the core of social responsibility debates in the 1970s—nuclear power safety, operations in South Africa, affirmative action for women and minorities, job safety, consumer protection, corporate governance, corporate political contributions and questionable payments, multinational corporation excesses and policies, plant closings and dislocations, environmental protection—CED is now silent. It stresses the importance of safeguarding the market and reducing government presence in the economy. In CED's plans to address "the emerging issues of the 1980s," as outlined in the organization's 1979 annual report, the "fundamental forces" and "key problems" seem to be predominantly economic in nature, not social.

Are we not justified in asking the Committee for Economic Development, "What about social responsibility?" Does CED, which claims that it "reflect[s] the best thinking of the business world," now believe that the broad range of social (and economic) problems emerging in the United States can be confronted and successfully resolved through the market system alone? Was Professor Milton Friedman right about social responsibility being little more than well-performed economic activity?

The position is a daring one for business to take and defend. Environmental pressures and tensions remain, though muted, and may well increase in severity as the global struggle for resources goes on apace. A market system "unleashed" from the social controls imposed by government may only exacerbate social problems and abuses. Public policy is not sufficiently or monolithically controlled by business to escape a social veto of private business actions. Rather than turning away from an exercise of political skills and relying upon a negative "disciplining" process, as implied in the ideologically pure position of CED in 1979, business needs to become even more active an expert in politics and public policy formulation if it wishes to maintain its premier status in society.

CED's trustees share with many others in and out of business an understandable ambivalence about how best to move forward against the challenge of mind-boggling domestic and global problems. Perhaps no single ideology will be appropriate as a guide, but the two views of business's role in society set forth by CED in 1971 and CED in 1979 cannot live peacefully in the same house. A business vision that acknowledges social problems and assigns high priority to their solution is worthy of this premier group of business executives. This broader view can lead both business and society toward greater harmony, improved economic performance, and social justice.

YEAR 1983

[Public confidence in big business: 28%]

CORPORATE SOCIAL RESPONSIBILITY:
THE REAGAN LEGACY

Setting the Stage. With the 1980 election of Ronald Reagan as U. S. President, business hopes rose that some of the extreme pressures from social critics would be eased. The thicket of new social regulations and their costs had eaten into profits and complicated corporate decision making. It was a watershed year, signaling a turn away from government regulation and favoring private enterprise. CSR advocates—and some business leaders—wondered, Would this produce more, or less, CSR? Unwittingly, President Reagan had given a boost to CSR.

What are the prospects for corporate social responsibility in the Reagan era? Can, or should, we expect business to become more—or less—active in the social arena? If the federal government is to do less in the way of social problem solving, should or will the private sector do more?

If we are to gain a proper insight into the issues of corporate social responsibility during the 1980s, it will be necessary to view them as an extension of the social issues and problems of the 1950s, 1960s, and 1970s. "Corporate social responsibility"—the idea that business firms have an obligation to act for the social good, even if in so doing they may pursue activities not normally in the business domain, possibly lowering their economic profits in the process—is an idea that has been vigorously debated in the United States since the early 1950s. The philosophical belief that those in power should be called to account for their power by those subject to it extends far back into human history. The application of this principle to the contemporary business corporation was first observed in the early years of the twentieth century. Allowing for the vicissitudes of depressions and warfare, the idea has gathered strength as the corporation became America's primary vehicle for organizing business operations.

A Social Responsibility Agenda

The debate on the role of business in society has generated an agenda of social issues and problems that many accept as a proper focus for socially responsible business actions.

- *Environmental pollution* arising directly or indirectly from industrial operations and from the use and disposal of items produced.

- *Discrimination in employment and other business opportunities* on account of race, sex, ethnic group or national origin, physical or mental handicap, age, religion, and other characteristics.

- *Consumer abuses in the marketplace,* including price gouging; misleading advertising claims; sale of ineffective, unreliable, and unsafe products; difficulty in obtaining satisfaction after purchase of faulty items; sponsorship of advertising and sale of products offensive to good taste, risky to human health, and projective of negative cultural stereotypes.

- *Threats to the safety and health of employees* while at work or due to work processes and materials. Some business firms have exhibited reckless and negligent attitudes toward the physical and mental welfare of their employees, as well as taking a defensive posture when risks are revealed through independent studies.

- *Minimal concern for the quality of work life,* particularly for those employees performing repetitive, low-skill tasks over long periods of time. Authoritarian, non-participative, hierarchical organizational procedures modeled along military lines are typical of most business firms, which excludes significant involvement of employees in determining the conditions under which work is performed.

- *Economic, social, familial, and psychological dislocations* attendant upon business decisions to terminate or relocate industrial and commercial operations.

- *Massive deterioration in the quality of urban life* and in physical characteristics of urban communities, especially in the central core of major metropolitan areas. Business has contributed directly in some cases and indirectly in others—by neglect or disavowal of responsibility—for the decline of the city.

- *Questionable or abusive practices by multinational corporations,* including the payment of bribes and other questionable outlays for securing contracts not otherwise obtainable; explicit and tacit cooperation with and toleration of governments that are repressive of basic human rights; foreign exchange speculation in contravention of the needs of parent and host nations; disregard of the basic economic needs and national policies of parent and host nations; observance of lower standards of public welfare in foreign sales of risky goods, in the safety of foreign industrial workers, and in pollutants generated by industrial production and mineral extraction in foreign nations; and shifting or threatening to shift production to the lowest-cost, and especially the lowest-wage, areas as a means of maximizing profits to the firm.

- *Uncritical support of and direct gain from national defense policies* that advocate high levels of military preparedness, perpetuate a global arms race, support repressive political regimes through sales of weapons, and lead to general preparation for nuclear confrontation among major powers.

Still other items could be added to the agenda: issues of corporate governance; unfair treatment of corporation stockholders by management; business advocacy of favorable tax treatment by local, state, and federal authorities; business acceptance of government subsidies and other forms of support denied to non-business groups; illegal corporate contributions to political candidates; and many of the commonplace, day-to-day ethical excesses encountered in business, such as embezzlement, contract rigging, use of insider information for the purchase or sale of stock, delivering products and services that do not meet contract specifications, and bribery and kickbacks associated with the purchase of supplies and raw materials used in production.

Business Values and Social Control

Two evaluative comments about the agenda are in order. First, the disruptions of the social, ethical, and legal fabric are a function of the business system itself, rather than non-business phenomena imposed on the business order from the outside. Left to its own devices and inclinations, business operating in an unregulated market system produces these effects in the communities in which it operates. The issues and problems that have been at the heart of the social responsibility debate are a natural consequence of the institutionalized quest for profits normally sought through the free market. *They represent the raw edge of business values rubbing against the social values of human communities and the ecosystems that sustain those communities.*

At first, this charge might seem a shockingly harsh judgment, unjustified by the common sense and humanitarian inclinations that all recognize to be a part of business character. Would the typical businessperson consciously and deliberately be so callous, so intent on the Almighty Dollar or the greater glory of The Company, as to create for society this list of grievances? While most would prefer to answer this question negatively, a realistic response reveals that individual actions are often a function of organizational imperatives.

The core values of the business system—economic and organizational growth, the preservation of power, the quest for profits, the rational calculation of gain, the expedient and pragmatic perspective, and loyalty to the ideological spirit that pervades the system—drive all business firms to a social end that is perhaps no part of the intention of the individual businessperson caught in the system's toils. Unless we are willing to acknowledge that the problem of corporate social responsibility lies deep within the business order itself—*within the central values that activate and sustain the whole*—there is little prospect of finding a way out of present difficulties.

The issues agenda also reveals how woefully inadequate the "free" market is as a mechanism for approaching and resolving such problems. That mechanism gives full rein to the very values and inclinations that have contributed to the problems in the first place. How can the patient be made well by administering large doses of the toxin itself?

Society has long recognized the dangers inherent in an unfettered business and commercial system. From ancient times the money changer, the peddler, and the merchant have been on society's list of prime suspects. A recent Gallup poll revealed that only 19 percent of the U. S. public believe business executives rank high in honesty and ethical standards. No society in human history has been willing to entrust its fate to the uncontrolled values of business and commerce for the simple reason that business values, when taken out of social context, will soon eliminate or denigrate those features of community life whose worth cannot be calculated in monetary terms. Humanity's response to this challenge has long been an imposition of social controls: religious, political, governmental, ethical, or ethnic. The market has never been free of social controls.

Corporate Social Responsibility: The State of the Art

What can be said about the current status of corporate social responsibility after nearly three decades of scholarly debate and trial-and-error experimentation by business? A first observation is that many business leaders have accepted the idea of corporate social responsibility. A relatively small, elite group of business executives has been in the forefront of the social responsibility movement from its beginnings in the early twentieth century, speaking of the need to curb corporate power and turn it to broader ends than mere profit taking. Today, the two-hundred-member Committee for Economic Development, the two-hundred-member Business Roundtable, and chief executive officers of many of the larger corporations are on record favoring the broad principles of social responsibility.

Secondly, a small wedge of corporations have put theory into practice by adopting some of the tools of corporate social responsiveness—which differs from corporate social *responsibility*. A responsive corporation responds pragmatically and defensively to social pressures. If a minority group complains about lack of job opportunities in the inner city the corporation responds by constructing a ghetto plant which is staffed by minorities. When abnormal mortality rates are recorded by employees working with an exotic chemical compound, the company adopts safeguards to reduce exposure to the chemical agent. A socially responsive company does not pause long to consider whether these pragmatic actions are ideologically proper; it acts as if they are. It accepts a responsibility for acts that create negative social consequences. In its more advanced form, corporate social responsiveness may be anticipatory. A company may employ environmental scanning, value trend analysis, socio-political forecasting, social auditing, social responsibility committees composed of board members of top-level managers, comprehensive public affairs programs, and various other social innovations intended to enhance the organization's ability to respond to present, and to anticipate future, social pressures.

Thirdly, corporate philanthropy has flourished over the years. Corporate contributions for charitable and similar purposes were $2.7 billion in 1980. Without these funds, many fragile and humanitarian institutions would die: health care for the poor and needy, basic medical research on rare diseases, artistic activities in many fields, educational opportunities for youth, recreational programs for the elderly, family support programs, and many other such undertakings benefit from corporate largesse.

More important than all the foregoing insights into the present status of the corporate social responsibility movement are the basic limits that constrain corporate enterprise as it moves into the social domain. Corporations excel in organizing and directing resources—capital, natural, and human—for the purpose of producing and distributing goods and services, in the hope of making a profit and remaining in business. Their managers and employees are trained for this basic purpose. Performance measures, while imprecise, are well understood and accepted by all. A legal system embodies the principles necessary to sustain and protect the contractual requirements of those engaged in trade. An overarching ideology of free enterprise rationalizes and justifies the pursuit of profit as being not just essential to society but wholly beneficent in its long-run consequences for material welfare, human freedom, and (in some versions) spiritual expression.

Beyond this most formidable system of thought and action, no individual firm or executive can venture without suffering penalties more severe than most are willing to accept. Neil Chamberlain of Columbia University has argued persuasively that corporations are captives of values and motives that drive them to seek profits above all else and are hostage to society's consumption ethic. It is not just business but also society that places limits on corporate and regulatory social initiatives through fear that costly social reforms will threaten jobs, increase prices and taxes, and ultimately reduce the economic effectiveness of the corporate cornucopia from which flow all material blessings. David Vogel of the University of California, Berkeley, came to the same general conclusion in his study of the social protest movements of the 1960s and 1970s. These movements demanded little of business, and they accomplished few of their aims. Corporate authority, though challenged, was not directly diminished. The ability to change corporate behavior directly and substantively proved marginal.

This much we can conclude about the corporate social responsibility movement in the United States: both external and internal advocates of corporate social actions have been, and remain, highly constrained in what can be accomplished through the corporate structure. Corporate philanthropy, while part of a life support system for many important community activities, cannot begin to serve many of the community's most urgent social needs. Corporate social responsiveness appears mainly as a defensive tactic utilized by an elite group of socially aware companies; it is not generally perceived or treated as a broad-scale societal strategy capable of leading humanity to a resolution of its most severe problems.

Social Responsiveness and Reagan

What then are the prospects for corporate social responsibility in the Reagan era? Generally speaking, it appears to be a mixed bag, with some setbacks but not total backsliding.

Voluntary Social Initiatives. In the voluntary sphere, what reason is there to expect business to be either more or less responsible than previously? The basic business values, goals, and practices that presently constrain social reforms in and by business are still in place. The same basic strains of decency and social conscience that motivate some business leaders to be alert to social needs are not likely to disappear overnight, or at all, for that matter. The greed that some observers have remarked upon may be countered, at least in spirit, by a greater generosity on the part of others.

One should not be misled by politically inspired talk about business and the private sector "filling the void" left in social programming as government devotes fewer resources to these tasks. First of all, the dollar gap is very large when compared with current business outlays for social purposes. Figures are slippery but most sources have estimated that the combination of tax changes and budget reductions will deprive individuals and nonprofit organizations of perhaps forty to forty-five billion dollars of federal support through 1984. By contrast, corporations and private foundations in recent years have contributed a total of about five billion dollars annually for charitable and educational purposes.

The Conference Board reported in a survey of 427 companies that 60 percent were planning to increase charitable contributions in 1982 but nine out of ten of these were not doing so in response to federal budget cuts. Nor did the companies have plans to shift contributions to the social programs most affected by budget restrictions, such as job training. Only one-fifth of the corporations headquartered in major cities were planning increases in financial aid to urban programs. Moreover, corporate contributions historically are closely correlated with corporate profits, and the prolonged recession of 1981–82 threatens voluntary contributions. Tax cuts also discouraged greater giving by removing one of the incentives for these tax deductible contributions.

Business leaders have repeatedly said that business cannot and should not be expected to fill the gap. The comment of David Roderick, chief executive officer of the United States Steel Corporation, is typical: "There is a feeling in this country—wrongly so—that corporations are to step up and fill the void...but it should be obvious that we can't do it all." Another executive remarked, "Our company supported the president because we believed in the elimination of a number of these programs. Naturally, we're not enthused about continuing the programs and shifting the burden to the corporate sector."

Mandated Social Requirements. What about business's other social responsibilities—those mandated by government and enforced by regulatory agencies? Will a clean environment, safe workplaces, consumer protections, and equal employment opportunities be pursued in the 1980s with the same degree of success as during the 1960s and 1970s? Here, there is good news and bad news.

First, the bad news. President Reagan came into office having promised to "get government off our backs," a code phrase meaning less government regulation and fewer social initiatives. "Getting government off our backs" has led to a partial dismantling and overall weakening of the federal regulatory structure. Budgets of the agencies have been reduced. Staff cuts have been deep, hampering enforcement efforts in some agencies. Selective appointments—a normal part of the political spoils system—have been made to various agencies, with the apparent aim of shifting regulatory administration to a softer phase regarding environment, consumer protection, affirmative action, and labor union organizing.

All of these changes are usually defended as being cost effective, or as putting regulation in the hands of those who understand business requirements better than their predecessors, or as freeing business decision makers from burdensome bureaucratic routines. These defenses may be justifiable; but the problem is that the changes also may lessen adherence to mandated social responsibility goals.

Business often has charged that government regulations have pushed them "too far." One might reasonably ask: Are workers "too safe" from job hazards? Are women and blacks "too highly paid" relative to men and whites? Are consumers "too well protected" from marketplace fraud and deception? Are the air and water "too clean" for public health? There are many persons, in business and outside of it, who believe that government regulation is essential to the successful pursuit of these and other social goals. If they are even partly correct, then we can expect a lower level of mandated socially responsible actions to be taken by business during the Reagan era.

Reagan's Social Legacy. Although it may be seriously weakened, social responsibility will not fade away, for two reasons. First of all, business has learned during the 1960s and 1970s that social responsibility benefits business. It projects a good and caring image of an otherwise monolithic organization. It dampens down the fires of social upheaval and revolution. It produces a more satisfied and perhaps a more politically stable environment in which to conduct business. It may offset further inroads into business decision making by government or dissident social groups. It may be consistent with long-run profit goals. These are gains worth preserving, and many business leaders are well aware of the positive impact of social responsibility on business.

In the second place, the habits of social responsibility are increasingly embedded in the practices and policies of large corporations. These habits are not likely to fade away, even with less government pressure being exerted. Many social functions have become institutionalized in the corporation: whites and blacks have learned to accept and work with each other; men, with perhaps more difficulty, are learning that women can manage a business or use a jackhammer; marketing professionals realize that placid consumers can turn into raging consumer activists if treated unfairly; production engineers know that social grievances can be avoided by designing low-polluting, safe industrial equipment; and even Detroit seems finally to have caught on that U. S. car buyers prefer small, safe, fuel efficient non-polluting automobiles. Abandoning these socially congenial practices would not be in the interest of business, whose executives might well shudder at the prospect of reactivating the social tensions of the 1960s.

Putting the good news and the bad news together gives this result: voluntary social responsibilities, which by themselves have never significantly addressed society's major social problems, may be expected to remain at present levels; mandated social responsibilities, which have produced the greatest social gains, will be weakened as government relaxes its regulatory purview. If the business community finds itself the target once again of a disaffected and aroused public claiming that business is irresponsible and should be curbed or penalized for social transgressions, business will have brought these charges upon itself. The corporate community favored the election of Reagan and congressional conservatives; supported White House deregulatory initiatives; and, in April 1982, almost two-thirds of them believed Reaganomics was working just fine. To put the matter plainly, the business community seems to favor a government policy whose effect is to exacerbate—rather than ameliorate—social problems and pressures. Under these conditions, there is every prospect that social tensions will increase, public criticism of business will mount, and the agenda of unresolved social issues will grow longer.

A Cooperative Framework for Social Responsibility

What would it take to move beyond this bleak prospect and to make a genuine advance in the art of social responsibility? It would take a development that we are not likely to witness in today's political climate. Those basic business values that have contributed so centrally to the present agenda of social problems and issues would have to be deflected from their natural course and either be replaced (an unlikely occurrence) or supplemented by non-business values that would drive society in more fruitful directions. Enough is known about the dynamics of social change for us to conclude that fundamental value shifts of this order simply do not occur, even when a society undergoes radical revolution. *Plus ca change, plus c'est la meme chose.*

But alternative values do exist and they continue to find expression. What is lacking is *a comprehensive institutional structure* to which these values can be attached and through which they can find full expression in the business arena. By contrast, the modern business corporation is a powerful institutional vehicle giving life vigorously and enthusiastically to the values of business and commerce. *A deeply embedded business value system finds itself unable to respond fully and adequately to the social challenges of our times, while non-business values more compatible with the needs of the populace simmer beneath the surface without institutional structure.*

The institutional structure needed to revivify corporate social responsibility cannot be based exclusively within the business order, for it would then become a captive of the very values from which relief is sought. Nor can it be formed from those external groups whose values would be likely to smother the business system under a blanket of punitive social controls.

The essence of the new institutional system will have to be cooperation, collaboration, and coordination among organizations whose goals, purposes, and values may differ greatly. For want of a better term, it will be useful to call these associations *social partnerships* or *social coalitions.* Neither capitalist nor socialist, such partnerships would be more than pluralism but less than social cartels. Government, business, labor, church groups, the university, social activist groups, trade associations, neighborhood community groups, ethnic groups, professional organizations, and other organizational units constitute the raw material for these social coalitions.

Many, perhaps most, of the successes scored thus far on the social responsibility front are the work of social partnerships—coalitions established among groups whose values are sharply different but who found ways to achieve sufficient harmony among themselves to address serious problems without abandoning their central values in the process. Business has yielded autonomy over pollution control, employment discrimination, job safety, and other matters to coalitions of government agencies, environmentalists, labor unions, and civil rights groups. In doing so, it has not lessened and perhaps has strengthened its status as our society's central institution. Nor have the competing members of these coalitions gained all they desired. The nation's air and water remain considerably contaminated with industrial by-products, women and minorities continue to suffer discrimination, preventable industrial accidents still occur. What *has* happened is tangible movement toward resolving some of the society's major problems. In all these cases, *business values have yielded to social values, but social values have not been allowed to overwhelm the essential economic mission of business.* Surely, the future of corporate social responsibility lies in these directions. Social partnerships are the institutional device to which vital social values can be linked, modifying but not destroying business values, and permitting business to participate fully as one member of a coalition serving broader goals and purposes than those of business alone.

Over a decade ago, one group of business leaders, the Committee for Economic Development, rather courageously advocated the formation of a "government-business partnership for social progress." They understood well that society's problems were too complex and too large to be tackled by business alone. They also feared increased government initiatives in the social arena if business did not act promptly and voluntarily to address society's problems, and these fears were subsequently realized. They believed that the answer to the problem of corporate social responsibility was to be found through a coalition of interests in which both government and business would play central, complementary roles. With the passage of time, that social vision and belief in a social partnership has faded among those executives and has been replaced with a renewed faith in the "free" market (see **Year 1981** chapter, above).

But the notion of social partnerships for resolving social problems is a powerful idea. Its time may not yet have arrived. But like one of those comets that sweeps by the earth at periodic intervals, look for its reappearance when both business and society tire of the current fascination with free market approaches to social problems. Sooner or later, if corporate social responsibility is to have genuine and enduring meaning in society, *a new way must be found to link social values with business purposes.* The social partnership offers that prospect.

PART II

VALUES AND CORPORATE CULTURE

Values—the core beliefs that guide business decisions and shape corporate policies—are the ultimate arbiters of corporate social responsibility. Understanding their behavioral power, their central organizational function, and their origins within nature and culture is an essential lesson to be learned. Core values are the basic foundation on which ethical concepts and rules are constructed, thereby providing the behavioral and philosophical rationale for socially responsible corporate practices. Empirical evidence of the value clashes that often separate corporations and their critics has been scant, though growing in volume since the 1980s. Globalization thrust corporations into the lives of people everywhere, upsetting and overriding long-held personal and societal value systems, and literally demanded a new kind of social responsibility from business.

YEAR 1985

[Public confidence in big business: 31%]

MAKING SENSE OF BUSINESS VALUES

Setting the Scene. During a 1980–81 visiting appointment as professor of business ethics at Santa Clara University, I first became well acquainted with business ethics philosophers. Here was a group as fully committed to morally responsible corporate behavior as the management scholars who had pioneered CSR teaching and research in the nation's business schools. To my amazement and consternation, neither group seemed to know the other, nor did they speak exactly the same scholarly language or even pursue like methods of inquiry. With the help of a few close colleagues in both camps, ways were found to bring the two groups together in common cause. My message to business ethics philosophers, from the beginning of our relationship—and the one found in this chapter—is that values are the key to understanding and promoting moral business behavior. Theirs to me has greatly enriched my own understanding of what philosophy can contribute to an understanding of CSR. One additional thing I did discover: that getting philosophers to acknowledge the research findings of social science was the most difficult thing I had ever undertaken—until later on when I tried to get social science-trained management scholars to pay attention to natural science!

What does science, especially social science, tell us about the ways in which values are formed within the life history of individuals, of organizations, and of culture generally? Without an answer to this question, as well as a willingness to employ it in ethical analysis, all attempts will fall short of touching the vital core of understanding needed for clarifying right and wrong, moral and immoral behavior.

An ethicist is strongly tempted to assess ethics issues in terms of the respective rights of the participants, with a nod towards the utilitarian consequences that flow from the struggle, and to find a "solution" that incorporates a notion of social justice.

A social scientist, on the other hand, would be inclined to view ethical disputes as a manifestation of differential value commitments by people and/or organizations involved, where the values of one party are pitted against the values of another. What the social scientist sees is a clash of *values* and an ensuing contest for the dominance of one set of values over another. More basic than the question of rights is the indisputable fact that each person manifests identifiable values and value commitments that are at odds with equally identifiable value sets of others.

To the question, Are not "rights" and "values" only different ways of referring to the same phenomena? the answer is, "Not quite." *Rights* are typically made to appear as non-contextual (i.e., abstract) assertions of privilege. *Values*, by contrast, are treated as behavioral traits, beliefs, and intellectual orientations that are thoroughly and completely contextual in their origin and subsequent development. *Rights* tend to be imposed on a context of human action, with the language itself being suggestive of a coercive or insistent privilege not to be gainsaid. *Values* grow out of a given context and its history, and the (moral) reasoning that employs values likewise has a life history that can be, and has been in fact, observed and documented. *Values* may and usually do become firmly embedded in individuals and organizations, and in that sense they resemble the coercive, insistent, imperative character ascribed to *rights*; but *values* are not usually assigned, and do not deserve, a superior claim in the overall range of human behavior traits that one often finds to be the case with "human *rights*." *Values* are a fact of human existence and they play a key role in human behavior. It is possible to maintain that *rights* are derivative from *values* and therefore need to be seen in this functional sense rather than from a perspective that assigns a hierarchically superior meaning to them.

Our interest, then, in grasping the fundamentals of value formation in individual persons, human organizations, and the culture process generally turns us away from the byways of philosophic discourse and towards explanations provided by the social sciences. From such a perspective, human behavior, including those features we call values and valuation, appears to be a blend of culturological and ethological phenomena, activated and made dynamic through social interaction, and focused in each one of us by a distinctive patterning of traits that we call "personality."

Values and Culture

The role played by culture in the formation of the human person has long been acknowledged. The version that appears to be closest to the mark is the view that we, as humans, owe our humanity to an ability to engage in symbolic behavior. Symboling is made possible by the comprehensively developed and elaborated neurological system, particularly the structure and functioning of the brain, possessed by the human species alone. By virtue of this unique advantage, humans have been able in the course of a long evolution to learn more quickly, to store information in memory more successfully, to imagine and foresee more comprehensively, to extend the use of tools further, and to accumulate and transmit the species' fund of experience in a more enduring fashion than has been possible for other species. While this fund of human culture has thus been amassed over the years, individual members of the species unavoidably take their behavioral cues from it. Entering the human community as a behavioral, motivational, emotional, and intellectual cipher (according to this view), the infant is encapsulated within the cocoon of human culture and tradition. We thus become what our culture defines for us as falling within the scope of accepted belief and behavior. To the extent that human culture contains within itself dicta of right and wrong behavior and belief, to that extent will the individuals who are nurtured within its folds gain some understanding (not always perfectly grasped or developed) of the meaning of right and wrong. Due to the vastness of time during which human evolution has taken place, as well as to the diversity of circumstances under which humans have lived, an enormously elaborated pattern of human culture and an equally configured design of rights and wrongs present themselves to the observer of the human scene. Human behavior and human values are thus said to be relative to time, circumstance, and culture pattern.

Values and Genetics

Less clear but not to be dismissed is the probable role played by genetic factors in the determination of human behavior. Cultural determinists are inclined to denigrate genetics on two grounds. Methodologically, it becomes difficult, perhaps impossible, to design and carry out experiments that clearly separate and distinguish between genetic and cultural influences; but even if that might be accomplished in such a manner to establish a role for genetics as an influencing factor, culture's influence is said to be so pervasive and all-powerful that it overrides and renders relatively unimportant the underlying structure of genetically determined behavior. Some ethologists are quick to acknowledge both the methodological difficulties and the dominance of culture over genetic inclinations. Yet the tantalizing, if (for some observers) disturbing, possibility lingers that the human organic creature has not by any means been entirely cut off and insulated from the phylogenetic traits that brought the species to the threshold of culture. In a logical sense, such a leap beyond one's selectively adaptive phylogenetic origins would seem not only to violate the experiences of all other organisms and species but is not required as a condition of accepting a culturological explanation of human behavior.

Anthropologists, though lacking a firm conceptual and experimental basis for incorporating biological elements into their cultural analyses, have not been entirely hostile to the idea and as noted, ethologists have freely admitted that genetic dispositions necessarily mingle with learned cultural orientations. Child psychologists, particularly those concerned with the evolution of cognitive, emotional, and judgmental skills, also have acknowledged that biological maturation (a process heavily influenced by genetic factors) is unavoidably involved in an explanation of the developmental and normative behavior of children. Again, in a logical sense, it seems unrealistic to assume that children, once having ceased "growing" in a biological sense, somehow or other turn off the genetic switches and thenceforth guide their behavior during adulthood by a strictly cultural compass. This kind of discontinuity is not generally observable in nature.

The basic ethical implication of ethology is that phylogenetically determined behaviors are selectively adaptive for the human species, thereby creating a fundament—an underlying structure—of ethical predispositions that contribute to the species' survival and continued growth. In this formulation, ethologists maintain that culturally-derived ethical systems that separate the species into contending societal groups may impel humans to engage in behavior that is contrary to their inherent, genetically determined (adaptive) predispositions. Hence, some learned cultural value systems may proved to be selectively maladaptive for the species considered as a whole.

Values and Socialization

Value formation and socialization to moral reasoning that occur in the life cycle of individual persons have been elucidated by child psychologists, sociologists, social psychologists, and anthropologists.

Jean Piaget and Lawrence Kohlberg tell us that individuals develop their moral reasoning capacity by progressing through a series of "stages" or stair steps beginning in infancy and continuing on into early (and perhaps middle) adulthood. These stages are distinguished from one another by the principal justifications given for, or used by, an individual in assessing a situation that involves ethical choices. According to this view, we move continuously and invariantly from an ego-centered to a group-centered ethic, from a specific to a generalized concept of morality, from an externally imposed authoritarian source of moral reasoning to one based on internalized, self-principled notions of justice, and (in the "ideal" case?) from societally-bound moral systems of reasoning to moral concepts embracing humankind at large within a broad cosmos. This sequence has been observed in all cultures and is in some sense independent of the specific content and meaning assigned to right and wrong behavior by a particular society's cultural traditions. To reach the higher stages of moral reasoning is to have escaped the strictures imposed on one in childhood and adolescence and early adulthood by specific portions of the social structure, thus becoming in some cases an admired (as well as perhaps a vilified) moral leader capable of seeing the human moral predicament writ large within the totality of human experience. Few persons, according to Kohlberg, advance this far; in fact, he finds that most remain at the fourth, law-and-order, stage of moral reasoning, with stages five, six, and seven populations becoming increasingly sparse.

The important sociological finding is that adult, as contrasted with childhood, socialization concerns itself less with values and motives than with behavior. In a sense, society seems to "give up" on changing a person's values once he/she has passed through a society's basic socialization process and attained the status of adulthood. For grownups the problem becomes one of finding a niche (or perhaps a whole series of niches) within the social structure where one's values are compatible with those that are part of the roles, role behaviors, organizations, and institutions comprising the social structure. Within varying degrees of flexibility and tolerance, most societies manage to attain at least a "rough fit" or a "match" between the values inculcated through childhood socialization and the values embedded in that society's social structure. Those for whom this socialization process failed may be relegated to special institutions—prisons and mental hospitals are two types—where re-socialization may or may not be attempted. By and large, though, values-socialization—including the learning of proper behavior and of how to reason in right-and-wrong terms—tapers off remarkably once adulthood has been achieved.

Milton Rokeach and his followers have produced another body of knowledge that gives useful insights into value formation as manifested in individual persons. From their work it is apparent that the total number of values held by all people everywhere is relatively small, that they rank them differentially within varying societal contexts, that value change is initiated when a person perceives an inconsistency between one's self-conception and an ordered array of socially-approved values, and that value change in the sense of a reordering of one's value set may occur from time to time but that the amount of value change that occurs over the life cycle tends to be modest and occurs to a greater extent in younger than older persons.

We are brought, then, to the following set of conclusions about values and value phenomena generally:

- Values and valuing behavior are sociocultural phenomena, conditioned by genetic predispositions that are selectively adaptive for the human species.

- A society's social structure is a repository of right-wrong phenomena, providing ethical behavior guidelines for individuals who are socialized into it. Penalties are imposed on those who fail to heed these ethical orientations.

- Value commitments are formed primarily in childhood, adolescence, and early adulthood, with relatively little change occurring in later life. Some kind of "value formation ceiling" is observable, whether one speaks of value rankings or the manner of moral reasoning employed. Few appear to go beyond this ceiling, once adulthood is achieved.

- Value change *for an individual person* may be initiated when a sense of self-dissatisfaction emerges from observing an inconsistency between expected (socially approved) behavior-and-belief and one's own value preferences.

- Value preferences and modes of moral reasoning evolve toward, but do not usually attain, progressively universal, abstract, generalized, humanistic, and cosmic status. A strong implication is that societal systems impose limits on the ability and willingness of individual persons to exceed the value orientations and ethical principles embedded in the social structure.

Values and Business Managers

If we seek knowledge of how these general processes of value formation manifest themselves within the business and management sphere, the work of two scholars is particularly useful.

George England has described the value characteristics of managerial behavior, demonstrating that distinctive types and directions of behavior are a function of a given manager's value preferences, that different societal and cultural traditions produce differential patterns of values in managers, and that it is possible to distinguish between managers and groups of managers on the basis of their orientation towards pragmatic, moralistic, or affective types of evaluation (including a mixture of the three). These studies also tell us that only some, not all, of a manager's total value set is brought to bear as organizational decisions are made: some values are directly "operative"; some are "intended" values that may be subordinated to other contextually determined operative values; others are "adopted" values somewhat removed from personal preference but capable of being activated by situational (organizational) factors; and still others are "weak" values falling within the manager's overall philosophic outlook but not often actually employed.

American managers' values, it turns out (probably to no one's surprise), are operatively oriented toward pragmatic considerations, acceptance of organizational goals, competence, realization of the importance of other reference groups (e.g., labor unions), and achievement; with humanistic orientations being intended, not operative, values; and an outright rejection of organizational egalitarianism. One can conclude from England's studies that managers, like other societal actors around them, have been subjected to a socialization process that has driven or channeled them in the direction of these kinds of value preferences rather than some others.

The process by which these managers and their values have found their way into business organizations has been described by a number of scholars, but the work of Neil Chamberlain is especially worthwhile as a model of how a value consistency is established and enforced between individual and organization. The story is reasonably familiar. Each firm exhibits a "strategy-set" (others have referred to such sets as "corporate culture") which is to some extent a function of the personal value preferences of its primary managers. Organizational norms and values are derived from this strategy-set. Both strategic (planning) decisions and routine (operating) decisions flow from and are consistent with the organization's norms and values. Organizational behavior and performance appraisals also are carried out with reference to the firm's accepted norms and values. Neither behavior nor policy can wander far from the directions embedded in the company's strategy-set or culture.

Chamberlain also tells us, as have many others before him, that business firms pursue a generalized objective of profit and that this quest conditions the nature and character of a company's culture. It is a matter over which the firm exercises little or no discretion. Being in business *means* pursuit of profit. It is the chief goal, the highest good, the primary value, firmly and deeply embedded in the company's culture.

But unlike others who have been willing to leave the matter there,

Chamberlain takes the analysis out into the broader realms of society and culture—out to the locus of value formation that runs through the culture process generally. Thus, we are able to link up what we know of values-socialization that operates within the life cycle of individual persons with the perceived value preferences of their organizations. The conclusion is not surprising: *both firm and individual manager are constrained by the society's dominant value sets. The quest for profit or any other organizational goal is heavily conditioned by prevailing societal and cultural values. Not only are managers within the firm limited in what they can or wish to do by their own embedded personal value systems and the equally embedded value systems of the organization itself, but the entire firm is constrained by the society's long ingrained and widely accepted value systems that have brought it to this point in its evolution. One might refer to this situation as a triple value bind: human action in the value sphere is thrice bound, each time by the outcome of distinct though interrelated values socialization processes: one occurs within the individual person, one within organizations, and one within the culture.*

The Neglect of Values in Philosophic Ethics

Having now laid down the foundations of social science knowledge about values, value formation, and the patterning of values within organizational and societal structures, let us consider the more traditional, philosophic approach to business ethics. One notable fact stands out from the beginning: standard philosophic ethicists pay little or no attention to the insights and perspectives that have been developed by social scientists. A widely used text on business ethics has no mention of Piaget, Kohlberg, Rokeach, or England, although there is brief acknowledgment that ethical notions first appear in our lives during childhood and that they come to us from the society. Three reports on the teaching of business ethics have been circulated nationally in recent years; none of the model curricula, the recommended bibliographies, or the discussion of various ways to approach the teaching of business ethics makes any reference to the major research on value formation, moral development or managerial values.

There is a decided tendency for standard ethics theory to impose abstract and logically consistent categories of philosophic discourse upon the field of business and management action without considering the societal, cultural, and ethological factors involved. As such, it is a good example of culture-binding, for its analytic categories, even though derived from a long tradition of philosophic thought, reflect the value orientations of a selective (narrow) band of cultural experience. Because it does not incorporate the goals, purposes, functions, and ends of value formation or of moral reasoning understood as culturological and ethological phenomena, standard ethics theory can make only limited contact with or contributions to the genuine ethical/value issues and dilemmas that confront managers, business professionals, and their organizations. A danger is that, being culture bound, standard ethics theory may simply serve either (1) to reinforce the dominant value systems embedded in the prevailing culture or (2) to avoid a true confrontation and analysis of a society's values that do not serve a positive (i.e., selectively adaptive) human purpose or experience.

Embedded values *will drive* organizations and individuals along certain pathways. Neither drive is likely to be deflected by an appeal to philosophic reason or wisdom, however attractive the alternatives may appear to be. Here we find the real difference between a philosophic and a social science approach to ethical analysis. The latter deals with the reality—the observed fact—of value conditioning within a sociocultural context, not with the wishfulness that humans committed to one set of values would yield to another, more attractive, set or to the moral reasoning or principles inhering in philosophic categories. *For social science, the locus of the ethical problem is in the value systems that drive individuals, organizations, and societies along certain pathways and towards certain destinations and to reason ethically in certain ways and according to certain culturally and genetically induced principles.* For this reason, most ethical problems, issues, and situations have an *a priori*, not an *a posteriori*, character.

Unifying Philosophy and Social Science

Given these differences, then, how might we direct our thinking if we are to marry the best of both philosophy and social science in the service of greater ethical understanding of business? My answer would run along the following lines.

From social science we need to accept and further develop an understanding of the major value orientations embedded by accumulated experience and genetic predisposition in the human culture process—the value channels that have directed human culture to this point in its long evolution. We need to focus upon and highlight those value orientations that have proved to be the most adaptive and the most liberating of human potentialities. We shall have a truer picture of the ethical dilemmas, as well as the ethical possibilities, faced by organizational actors if we grasp the grim truth that a largely unyielding socialization process leads the actor and the organization to perpetuate value orientations beyond their control which are maladaptive in their cultural function and purpose, while simultaneously nourishing other value principles capable of carrying both parties towards selectively adaptive goals.

What can philosophy, particularly applied ethics theory, contribute? Rather than imposing upon this confrontation of competing and clashing value systems a set of abstract culture-bound analytic categories—utility, rights, duties, obligations, justice—and asking culture (and managers) to yield to reason, philosophy can perform a more important function. It can refurbish its analytic categories by relating them to those cultural and genetic processes that lead to value formation in individuals, social groups, and human culture generally. Utility, rights, and justice contain hints of value orientations and moral principles that have proved, in the course of cultural evolution, to be more selectively adaptive than their opposites. If ethicists could, and would, help to identify and highlight the somewhat shadowy value orientations that lurk behind their principal categories of discourse, a more operational—if perhaps more painful and controversial—ethics/values paradigm could emerge.

Organizational actors—managers and whistle blowers alike, along with all others between these extremes—might then have in full view, thanks to social science, the panoply of possibilities and limitations created and sustained by culture. They might also have, thanks to philosophy, a reasoned way, not *out* of the grip of cultural reality, but rather a way to understand how actors and their organizations might achieve those adaptive value orientations embedded (but still partially concealed) within the principal analytic categories of utility, rights, and social justice.

The views presented here leave many questions unanswered. My choice of language sometimes implies a rigid and unyielding outcome to the values socialization process, but clearly values change over a person's life cycle and within organizations. What stimulates, governs, and nourishes these changes? Are there ways to break through the values socialization ceiling which seems to be imposed on individual and organization alike? Must whistle blowers alone bear the brunt of social value change? Can the decisions of pragmatic managers be deflected into more humane organizational purposes without jeopardizing the adaptive gains made possible by large-scale undertakings?

No enduring answer to these questions is possible without an understanding of the values and valuation processes embedded in persons, organizations, and culture. From that base, and that base only, can ethical analysis proceed on its difficult quest for moral clarity.

YEAR 1986

[Public confidence in business: 28%]

CSR AND THE CULTURE OF ETHICS

Setting the Scene. Can CSR advocates, scholars included, be objective in demanding that business should be socially responsible? Or must their views—and the counterarguments of their business opponents—be tinged with personal bias and narrow vested interests? Is there some objective standard that defines CSR, one that embraces business everywhere? In raising these questions, I managed to create quite a ruckus in the community of CSR scholars. Some questioned the wisdom of "taking sides" on social issues for fear of alienating their corporate consultancy clients. Another declared that CSR theory was nothing but a slightly disguised form of liberal (Democratic Party) political viewpoint. Others charged that speaking of corporate "rectitude" was dangerously flirting with religious zealotry, in addition to being an arrogant assertion of moral superiority. Public policy advocates believed that I had strayed too far away from politically realistic goals and values. Oddly enough, most of the clamor soon died down, as most of the critics themselves turned increasingly to moral analysis of business behavior, now called "business ethics," which proved to be a more congenial and acceptable way of speaking about social responsibility.

Item: General Electric and some units of General Dynamics are barred temporarily as government contractors due to irregularities. **Item:** E. F. Hutton pleads guilty to charges of improperly managing its banking deposits. **Item:** Three top officers of a film recovery laboratory are convicted of on-the-job homicide after an employee died wile working with toxic materials. **Item:** Ford Motor Company, Pan American Airways, and Pepsico pull back from operations in South Africa. **Item:** A global boycott of Nestle Corporation ends when new marketing practices are adopted for its infant formula product.

These events—some regrettable, others admirable—testify that normative (that is, ethical) issues are alive and well in corporate America. To be understood, these episodes and others like them call for careful, balanced study, rather than anguished hand wringing by those hostile to business.

Many scholars who investigate the relationships between business and other institutions in society realize that they must ultimately deal with normative or ethical matters. As a result of this inherently normative character of their work, they incur a threefold responsibility. Part of that responsibility is to make clear the values that are at stake as business and society interact with one another. Another part of the scholar's responsibility is to identify where one stands with respect to those values. The third responsibility is to use one's scholarly knowledge to point out to business practitioners the moral consequences of pursuing the values they and their companies hold. In short, those who study social and ethical issues in management are compelled to form and to declare moral judgments concerning those issues. This moral imperative arises from the inherently normative nature of the topics being studied.

The Inevitability of Normative Issues

"Normative" here refers to what happens when business comes into contact with other parts of society. Each party exerts an influence on the other so that the fortunes of both, and perhaps the directions in which they move, are altered. As these alterations occur, the norms or standards that usually govern relationships between the two may undergo stress and consequently may be subject to questioning and change. These normative alterations may be viewed with alarm or they may be praised, as in the examples given above. Seldom are they thought to be without importance. Often, the changes are believed to be profoundly significant.

An example can be seen in current concern about toxic substances. There is now widespread societal agreement—in the form of social norms—that toxic materials used in production, and those discarded as wastes, should be handled with great care in order to protect workers, consumers, neighborhoods, and future generations. When companies do not do so, they have violated social norms or standards. Such violators, for one reason or another, have allowed their corporate interests to override observance of social norms that seek to protect the public against these poisons. A tension point has been created as business interests impinge upon public health.

Or consider an employee who is faced with repetitive routines that dull one's interest in the work performed, rob one of opportunities to influence the quality or pace of the work done, and tend to reduce workers to something resembling human automata. Most observers would agree that this kind of interplay between business and society is best avoided altogether if possible or should be ameliorated at the very least. In this example, social norms have invaded the workplace, in opposition to business practices that contravene widely accepted views of desirable working conditions. Once again, a tension point has appeared where business intersects a body of social norms intended to protect and preserve important, even vital, human qualities.

Ethical problems arise precisely at these normative junctures, where alterations of interests occur and norms come under stress. At these points of stress, one often finds human rights being defended, demands for social justice being made, cost-benefit calculations being computed—all in an effort to find an appropriate ethical course of action. Additional problems of obligations owed, duties to be performed, virtues to be displayed, and values to be pursued make their appearance at these normative fault lines that erupt in the midst of human life.

The normative alterations generally accepted as being the most far-reaching are the ones in which business operations affect human consciousness or have some visible impact upon human community or upon long-run human continuity. The norms or standards defining and controlling human consciousness, human community, and human continuity are among the most central concerns of all humankind.

However, it is important to remember that business-and-society relations are reciprocal in character. Social norms may constrain business in serious ways. Business decision makers may point out that the burden on themselves and on society is high when social controls that seek to protect human consciousness and human community override the economizing process. Economizing, they rightly argue, is essential to the entire human enterprise. If they are to carry out their expected societal function of supervising the economizing process, then a balance must be found between the demands of humanizing and the demands of economizing.

It is because both parties—business *and* society—have the power to affect each other profoundly that the relationship between the two is unavoidably normative and laden with value issues. When a single firm can, through a plant closure decision, cause widespread distress for an entire human community and many individual lives within it, an act of profound normative significance has occurred. One is bound to question the norms that allow such far-reaching decisions to be made. Or when a punitively high tax or a hasty cleanup schedule forces a business firm to close its doors, society may well have unwittingly deprived itself of an otherwise effective and needed economizing unit, while simultaneously penalizing the firm's employees, suppliers, customers, and stockholders. Here, too, one wishes to raise a question about social norms that lead to such negative outcomes for business and others.

The normative significance of these episodes *emerges from the interplay and interactions* between business and other parties. Evaluative significance is not simply imposed on or imputed to the parties by others. It is the actual clash of interests, the competition of values held by each party, the threat posed by the one to the other, and the reciprocal counter threat that gives these situations evaluative meaning.

Normative Events and the Scholar

Is it possible for scholars who specialize in the study of business-and-society relations to look at these normative interplays and not be drawn into them as advocates for one or another of the parties involved? Can they stand back from the fray, coolly detached, merely observing and not caring about the outcome? *Should* they do so, or should they at least *try* to strike a disinterested stance? What is their function and responsibility in these matters?

There is a sense in which the answers to these questions are foreordained. It matters not that a scholar-observer may *wish* to avoid normative entanglement or may consciously declare an intention to remain clear of advocacy, if the studies undertaken in fact clarify a problem in such a way as to strengthen the position of one party over another. If, for example, research demonstrates a statistically significant correlation between habitual cigarette smoking and various health hazards, this information makes its own normative statement, not only about the dangers of habitual smoking but about the norms that permit unrestricted marketing of cigarettes. In fact, a series of normative positions is created by such research, some permitting doubts to be raised about continued smoking, others allowing arguments in defense of tobacco use. The researcher may have wished for or intended another outcome or may have declared at the outset complete disinterest in the eventual findings or in what use might be made of them by others. Never mind. The work he or she has produced tells its own story, teaches its own lessons, makes plain that an evaluative significance exists between smoking and health.

More than this, the researcher's very choice of this area of inquiry is laden with normative baggage. Such choices are not made in an evaluative vacuum. As one government researcher once said of her own work on poverty, "There is no particular reason to count the poor unless you plan to do something about them." In general, scholars choose an area for research and are justified in doing so because they have a strong (sometimes a vested or even a subconscious) interest in the outcome.

Some who have written on these matters have emphasized the personal, subjective factors that may enter into a researcher's choice of topic. It is true that all scholars manifest political bias, religious commitment, social class standing, ethnic prejudice, gender outlook, and regional viewpoint. Every researcher leaves these telltale autobiographical fingerprints on his or her work, for they constitute the essence of the person, and together they reveal the researcher's most personal, most individualized values.

However, important as these personal factors may be in bringing values to bear upon research, an even more compelling force is at work, far more basic because it goes to the heart of this field's subject matter. The *primary* reason why a business-and-society scholar has no power to escape the normative implications of her or his teaching and research—even though the individual scholar's *style* may suggest or prefer detachment—lies within the contextual nature of the research. The *general* subject of research is a complex web of interactions where vital interests are affected—business's and/or society's. *Any* information or insight about these interactions that is developed through systematic study or exposition affects the fortunes of one or the other, or both. When you explicate the health effects of using infant formula under unsanitary conditions of Third World poverty, you are making a normative statement, whether intended or not. You unavoidably raise a question about the norms regulating the promotion and sale of such products in those circumstances. Although an individual researcher may prefer not to act out the normative implications embedded in the research findings, others will. It is the combination of interacting interests and competing values—the normative context—that makes the researcher a captive of normative analysis from which there is no escape.

Even the most seemingly remote specialized studies—those that employ the most advanced quantitative research methods in rigorous ways—gain their meaning from some center of normative disturbance. These studies are like the tremors and aftershocks that radiate outward from the epicenter of some great normative earthquake. They are the outermost vibrations and resonances recorded on our Richter-like scale of normative sensitivities. One reads these empirical scribbles in an effort to trace the course of normative disturbances that have occurred deep within human consciousness and human community.

CSR₁ as Normative Inquiry: Reluctance and Hesitancy

Two great waves of literature about a corporation's interactions with society have been created. The first wave—called here CSR_1—began in the early 1950s and carried forward into the mid-1970s. Its main focus was corporate social *responsibility*. The second wave—called CSR_2—overlapped the first, running from around 1970 to the present [mid-1980s]. It concentrated mainly on corporate social *responsiveness*. (See **Year 1978** chapter.)

As a group, those who have studied business-and-society relations have not grasped or accepted their role as normative analysts. The pioneering works dealing with corporate social responsibility (CSR_1) never successfully came to grips with the value questions that caused these writings to be created. They groped through a normative fog, seeking but not finding the moral principles that surely were there. Guided by hunches that the business-and-society interface was in need of adjustment—hence, the emphasis on responsibility and accountability—their work was normative in tone but quite unspecific regarding the values that were in conflict. They struck a general moral stance whose foundations were never revealed, thus exposing the field to the familiar and largely justified charge of vagueness and subjectivity.

In spite of this shortcoming, these pioneers did in fact establish the normative nature of business-and-society studies. They sensed that something was wrong with the norms governing business conduct. Business was somehow out of tune with changing social trends, its economic power overbalancing its social responsibilities. It stood, as the title of one conference volume expressed it, on "unstable ground." The pioneers' social criticism may have been bland and timid, may have lacked the theoretical spine that is required when value inquiry is undertaken, but it was a fruitful beginning of the task of unraveling the normative complexities that characterize business-and-society interactions.

CSR₂ as Non-normative Inquiry: Shunning the Obvious

Considerably less credit for normative clarity can be given to the wave of corporate social responsiveness (CSR_2) literature that followed the pioneers' work. By the early 1970s, it had become clear that corporations should learn how to respond to the many social demands being pressed upon them. The focus of scholarly interest shifted to the firm, as ways were sought to enhance the skill and effectiveness with which corporations could cope with social pressures. These learned social responses could be self-induced or could be encouraged through public policies. These were contributions of an undoubted significance, for they operationalized the meaning of corporate social responsibility, thus moving inquiry beyond the sterile philosophic debates spawned by Milton Friedman and others of his persuasion. At least, managers and scholars alike could see what might be involved in adjusting the margins between business and society.

But this body of literature, too, left unanswered the central questions of value guidance, partly because some scholars preferred to adopt a neutral, positivist posture. They have shunned normative questions by trying to erect "value-free" shields that would shut out such matters entirely.

So while corporate Rome was burning, many scholars were fiddling, pretending their indifference to the outcome of great events occurring around them. In the worst instances, it was as if they had become mere scribes, recording corporate tragedies as they occurred without injecting any of their acquired knowledge or their emotions into the unfolding events. Even without these explicit and somewhat crudely wrought attempts to dodge the normative issues found at the business-and-society interface, the entire CSR_2 period has represented a decided drift away from the normative roots of business-and-society studies.

In general, CSR_2 advocates have urged corporations to eschew philosophic questions of social responsibility and to concentrate on the more pragmatic matter of responding effectively to environmental pressures. One way to do this, they say, is to develop the various tools of social response—social forecasting, social auditing, issues management—and to integrate social factors into corporate strategic planning. Another way is to increase the corporation's involvement in public policy matters. Political action committees can help ensure legitimate corporate input into the elective process, while grassroots lobbying campaigns, computerized letter-writing blitzes, and other media-assisted techniques can help influence legislation, as well as the administration of regulations directed against corporate interests. If all these things are accomplished, then any given corporation can be expected to be a more effective responder to external social pressures.

This focus on the effectiveness of social response has pushed CSR_2 thinking in directions it perhaps never intended to go. When large companies deploy this dazzling array of new social gadgets to the full, they are indeed "effective" in fending off, neutralizing, or defeating social forces that would change corporations in directions thought to be desirable by the broader society. On the positive side, a corporation taking a responsive view of its surroundings is more likely to bend in desirable social directions than one that has no social response machinery in place. Even in the best cases, though, the great likelihood is that the social response, particularly when the directive force of the reform movement is partially or even largely controlled by the corporation that is under social attack, will still be made well within the established framework of traditional enterprise where economizing is dominant over other social values.

Much the same result is produced by relying on public policy to curb undesirable corporate behavior. As first developed, this approach was thought to offer a more democratic and a more public basis for judging business performance than could be had by relying either on a vaguely formulated notion of social responsibility (CSR_1) or by leaving corporate response in the hands of a managerial elite (CSR_2). This public policy thrust might have produced more fruitful clarification of normative issues but for two factors.

Public Policy's Shortcomings. One was timing. Much of this literature appeared in the mid-1970s, just as Gerald Ford was lighting the fires of deregulation and just as the business community was becoming more effective in defending itself against social and governmental pressures. Jimmy Carter fanned the deregulatory coals for a while and then Ronald Reagan stoked them into a raging bonfire. By 1981, public policy had become the province and expression of a right wing conservative Republican philosophy, whereas the public policy advocates had been nourished on a diet of liberal to moderate Democratic political traditions and programs. Perhaps never was a theoretical initiative so unfortunately timed, for Ronald Reagan's ascendance to the Presidency was to the liberal public policy approach what that iceberg was to the Titanic. The episode demonstrates the hazards of emphasizing means without adequate consideration of the ends being sought, or capable of being sought, by those who are hostile to liberal conceptions of social, humane, and democratic values.

A second problem with the public policy solution to corporate social responsiveness was the reluctance of its advocates to acknowledge or emphasize how thoroughly saturated the public policy process is with value-laden phenomena. They had hoped to escape the subjectivity and vagueness of CSR_1 philosophizing by substituting a more objective (and hence a more value-neutral) basis for measuring and judging business's social performance. According to this view, if business adhered to the standards of performance in law and existing public policy, then it could be judged acceptably responsive to society's expectations.

But public policy, whether liberal or conservative in tone, is shot through with values and value conflicts. How public policy could ever be imagined to provide an objective, "value free" basis for formulating social performance guidelines for business, or how it could be thought to escape or to deflect the normative issues that dogged the CSR_1 pioneers, remains a mystery. Public policy takes its central meaning from the values and philosophy advocated by its chief participants. Too few public policy scholars have taken this perspective. An exception is Rogene Buchholz who has said, "For business to participate meaningfully in the resolution of public policy issues, it must learn ethical language and concepts and deal explicitly with the ethical and moral dimensions of these arguments."

So, after a highly fruitful decade during which corporate social responsiveness theory was hammered out by the second wave of pioneers, the business-and-society field stands about where it was at the beginning of that period concerning the normative aspects of business operations. CSR_2 thinking has unwittingly come to reflect the dominant values of corporate culture, thus becoming a defensive rationale for the corporate status quo. The field has compounded its normative dilemma by putting its faith in a public policy process that, since 1980, has been taken captive by the forces of reaction, authoritarian rule, and a thinly veiled religious naivete that would be quaintly amusing if it were not so threatening to some of the central values and norms of American society. Whether one relies on the self-induced social responses of corporate managers or on the felt pressures of public policy to guide corporate actions, the outcome is the same. If the post-CSR_2 corporation still possesses the power to do great harm or great good within the social order, as originally posited by CSR_1 thought—if, in other words, it has been only tamed and not conquered by social forces— then all of the normative questions about corporate behavior are still on the table and still largely unanswered.

The Culture of Ethics

Obviously, if one sets out to answer normative questions, one needs a normative anchor, a set of normative guides, a normative platform from which to judge whether any given group or organization is acting in desirable ways. The social-issues-in-management field has never been very clear about its normative role and function because it has lacked a clear vision of the values that underlie and undergird its work and inquiries. The quality of social criticism produced by any normative science is just as good as—but no better than—the values upon which the discipline rests. It is these values that need to be brought to bear upon the normative dilemmas occurring at the business-and-society interface. *Therefore, the major task that lies ahead for this field of inquiry is to formulate a conception of the values that are in contention as business interacts with society.* Such a theory of value can then form the basis of normative judgments about business behavior and practice.

In searching for the value sources that underlie the business-and-society discipline—those that would permit a systematic critique of business's impact upon human consciousness, human community, and human continuity—one finds what is best called a "culture of ethics." Embedded within humankind are moral meanings and conceptions of what is felt to be ethical. Great systems of thought have captured portions of these moral meanings. These moral notions—they could be called moral archetypes—comprise the most fundamental, deeply felt value orientations of humankind generally. Each society varies its emphasis upon the rudimentary moral meanings but each returns over and over again to the basic structure of morality inherent in human interactions. Human behavior occurs within a web of such moral meanings and cannot escape being judged in terms of such a culture of ethics.

To be sure, within this culture are many overlapping, interwoven, and even contradictory streams of morality. But one should not overlook the United Nations Declaration of Human Rights or the Sullivan Principles or the Helsinki Accord's principles of human rights. These normative documents symbolize some of the core values of the culture of ethics on which there is an increasing amount of societal agreement (see **Year 1991** chapter below).

Here, within the culture of ethics, is the referent to which business behavior is to be properly related if judgments about its morality are to be made. Here is the group of moral principles that was just beyond the grasp of the CSR_1 pioneers who, haltingly but with true normative instincts, spoke of the need for greater responsibility and accountability of business to society. Here are the standards for defining responsive social performance that is more broadly moral in meaning and scope than the dominant values of corporate culture or those to be found in extant public policy. Corporate social response surely must take its meaning from this broad context of moral notions and not simply from the needs of any given corporation and its associated stakeholders or from the ability of some groups to excel others in influencing public policy for their own advantage. *The basic normative referent for corporate social response is the core values to be found in the culture of ethics.*

CSR_3 = Corporate Social Rectitude

Here, too, within this culture of ethics, is the key that will unlock the door to another phase of business-and-society thought which, for convenience, might be called CSR_3. In this usage, the "R" stands for rectitude.

Corporate social rectitude embodies the notion of moral correctness in actions taken and policies formulated. Its general value referent is that body of sometimes dimly or poorly expressed but deeply held moral convictions that comprise the culture of ethics.

One criticizes United States companies for doing business in South Africa because they directly or indirectly contribute to a system that immorally denies basic human rights to a majority population. In doing so, these companies lack rectitude. One is aghast at the carelessness that can produce a Bhopal tragedy for it suggests a callousness that is unacceptable in any society, contravening a basic moral principle of humanity that life itself is precious. Such a company does not act with rectitude. The public applauds swift corporate actions that remove dangerous products from the shelves because the innocent and the uninformed are thereby protected in a moment of great vulnerability. One wishes to recognize and reward corporate rectitude, the sense of moral goodness, and the respect for others that is manifested in such episodes.

In viewing the social performance of corporations, we look for more than mere responsibility and more than mere responsiveness. We want corporations to act with rectitude, to refer their policies and plans to a culture of ethics that embraces the most fundamental moral principles of humankind.

A CSR_3 corporation would

- acknowledge that ethics belongs at the core, and not just the periphery, of management decisions and policies,

- employ and train managers who accept and practice the central role of ethics in their everyday work,

- possess sophisticated analytic tools for detecting, possibly anticipating, and coping realistically with ethical problems affecting the company and its employees, and

- attempt to align its current and planned future policies with the core values to be found within the culture of ethics.

A Strategy for Achieving CSR_3

A business system based upon these traits of social rectitude can be encouraged if management scholars and corporate practitioners act strategically within their own spheres.

What Management Scholars Should Do:

- Acknowledge values and ethics to be an explicit, indispensable part of every inquiry. This step would place normative judgments at the very center of research, rather than pretending that such studies can be "value free."

- Identify the contending values that are at work in every business-and-society issue studied, so that the moral issues can be clarified and various alternative moral choices can be outlined. In this way, both business and society would be better informed about what is at stake and they would be better able to understand how various alternative proposed actions would affect the society's central values.

- Expand the value sources upon which business-and-society studies are based, to include the fundamental moral principles embedded in the culture of ethics. This broader normative anchor would be expressive of a wide range of social needs and outlooks and could incorporate much of the moral discourse created by religious thinkers, philosophers, and business critics.

- Draw together the best that can be found and known about the management process, the corporate institution, the actual behavior of managers, the organizational systems that sustain business, and above all *the values that are embedded in management practice.* The resulting integrated picture of corporate management and the business process can then be used, not merely to enhance the strategic planning and policy goals of the corporation, but to understand why the goals of business and the needs of society are so often at odds with each other.

- Work more closely with philosophers who approach the normative issues of business through ethics theory. This rich, fertile heritage of philosophic thought can be used to clarify some of business's ethical dilemmas. Unfortunately, the existing division of academic labor has produced philosopher-ethicists with insufficient knowledge of business, and management theorists innocent of the finer points of ethics reasoning. Contrary to popular belief, managers do not always resist being told by others what is morally correct, but they are more likely to accept such information if it comes from someone whom they see as both credible and knowledgeable. Philosophers and management theorists must join forces and pool their expertise if ethical analysis is to make headway in the executive suite.

- Help create techniques and programs that can encourage business to move beyond CSR_2 and into a CSR_3 posture. The germ of these initiatives is present now in social forecasting, social auditing, environmental scanning, issues management, ethics training programs, the design and implementation of ethics codes, and other types of social technology. Here, too, is where public policy activism (e.g., serving as expert witness or consultant to governmental bodies) can help those in business, government, and the general public to grasp the normative significance of public issues.

What Corporate Managers Should Do

- Adopt an ethics strategy whose purpose would be to enhance and improve a company's ability to cope with ethical problems and issues. *Central to this strategy is an understanding of the dominant values of the company's culture.* Those values will determine how successful an ethics strategy will prove to be.

- Study existing models of successful corporate ethics programs, which can provide valuable lessons in what can be accomplished, as well as pitfalls to avoid. Additional help can be obtained from the Washington-based Ethics Resource Center.

- Establish an ethics outreach activity that goes beyond the company's normal involvement in such important programs as the United Fund, Junior Achievement, and similar community ventures. The ethics frontier has moved on to such matters as the community impact of plant closings, on-the-job drug use and abuse, preparing youths for work in a high-tech society, and the multiform issues rooted in transcultural corporate operations (guerrilla warfare, terrorism, hostage taking, religious boycotts, and other assorted ethical headaches.).

- Join the ethics debate rather than holding back from it. Rubbing shoulders with academic philosophers and management professors who teach business ethics has its rewards. A good place to start is the annual business ethics conference held at Bentley College, which draws top-level managers, government officials, public interest leaders, and prominent academic figures. A corporate membership in the Society for Business Ethics or the Social Issues in Management Division of the Academy of Management would put practitioners in direct and continuing contact with the leadership group of academics who teach and do research on ethics problems.

- Listen to university-based philosophers who have been wrestling with professional ethics, including business ethics, for the past two decades. Ethics theory is not a bottomless pit of vague abstractions. On the contrary, it is a source of analytic tools that can cut to the core of many ethical dilemmas faced by business every day.

- Listen to management scholars in business schools who are working with philosophers to convert many of the abstractions of philosophic theory into managerially meaningful action principles. These academics have moved on beyond the point of finding fault with questionable corporate practices to an approach that seeks realistic alternatives for the harried but ethically concerned manager. They, too, like their philosopher colleagues, are a resource to be used, not an enemy to be avoided.

A Normative Manifesto

Those who study problems at the business-and-society interface, in spite of their diverse approaches and views, share a core of beliefs about their work and its normative significance. A deep enough look into the field's literature—whether CSR_1, CSR_2, or CSR_3—will reveal these beliefs, expressed in one way or another:

- That the claims of humanizing are equal to the claims of economizing

- That the obligations of human beings to one another are greater than the obligations imposed upon human beings by systems of power and dominance

- That claims of legitimacy in corporate life must have as their referent a concern for human consciousness, human community, and human continuity such that human rights may be protected and social justice promoted and preserved

- That the enduring significance of corporate management is found in its ability to harmonize the multiform interests of a pluralistic society

- That the most important meaning freedom of enterprise can assume is the liberation of humankind from the bonds of poverty that restrain body, mind, and soul.

These sober and profound truths are the business-and-society scholar's central message to managers, to colleagues, and to students. They are what this field of study is all about—its sustaining values, its normative manifesto, the framework of philosophic concerns that define and justify the role and function of business-and-society scholarship.

These normative orientations remain as vital today as ever. They are beacons to guide corporations in a world which is fiercely insistent on business policies that conform to socially acceptable ethical norms.

YEAR 1987

[Public confidence in business: 31%]

FROM BHOPAL TO BOESKY:
WHY GOOD MANAGERS DO BAD THINGS

Setting the Scene. By the mid-1980s, business school researchers had begun building an understanding of the psychological and organizational factors responsible for a company's CSR performance, or lack thereof. Such empirical knowledge could, if understood by corporate leaders and government officials, become the basis of initiatives intended to promote responsible business behavior. That was the motive for presenting these surprising research findings to an audience of Pittsburgh business leaders. Little could they have known then that the lessons learned that day would ring true two decades later as another generation of business leaders struggled to comprehend the unethical excesses symbolized by Enron and other major corporations.

Those two words—"Bhopal" and "Boesky"—have won a permanent niche in the business lexicon. "Bhopal" stands for an industrial tragedy of almost unimaginable proportions: over 2,500 deaths, 300,000 people requiring medical treatment, 40,000 permanently sickened, and hundreds of children orphaned. "Boesky" stands for Wall Street conspiratorial scheming, lying, cheating, stealing, and what appears to be unbounded greed.

Unfortunately, Bhopal and Boesky do not stand alone as exemplars of questionable business behavior. E. F. Hutton pleaded guilty to defrauding banks by using other people's money without paying for it. In some circles, that would be called stealing. Bank of Boston and twenty-one other banks acknowledged taking part in a massive money-laundering scheme which probably helped criminals hide illicit revenues from gambling and drugs. General Electric and General Dynamics admitted they deliberately overcharged the government for work done. A. H. Robins sold IUDs that were alleged to have caused the death of some women and sickened thousands of others. Manville Corporation endangered the lives of its asbestos workers by not giving sufficient warning of the risks entailed. The list could go on and on.

This kind of behavior is not limited to business. All one has to do is look around. Ethical dilemmas and scandals abound. A U. S. Senator withdrew from the presidential race after admitting that he plagiarized others' speeches. On the campus, we call that stealing other people's ideas. One of the senator's opponents—another prominent politician who aspires to be President—acknowledged that his campaign staff had leaked the damaging evidence to the press. At the same lofty levels of government, trusted White House officials have freely admitted lying to congressional committees and destroying evidence of their misdeeds, while concurrently they conspired to evade several laws.

Readers of the sports pages know that baseball players use corked bats to get longer hits, while pitchers try to foil them by using balls they scuff with sandpaper hidden in their gloves. Professional football and basketball players live in a world riddled with illicit drug use. High school and college players accept large illegal payments and so-called "scholarships" while coaches look the other way.

As anyone knows who has followed the PTL scandal, televangelists Jim and Tammy Bakker preached the gospel about driving the money changers from the temple—and then we learned they apparently had not driven them much further than PTL's multimillion dollar religious theme park.

Nowhere do ethical puzzles bristle with greater threat to our very concept of humanity than in the health care field—from when life should be ended to when it begins, from who should receive organ transplants to who should give them, from how a new life should be conceived to who is a "true" parent, and from a physician's or nurse's obligation to treat the incurably ill to the moment when such treatment might itself threaten to end the health worker's life.

So, in considering some of the ethical problems of business, it is worth remembering that no single sector of society has a corner on either ethical or unethical behavior.

The Research Picture

Thanks to the efforts of research scholars, much is known now about the factors that lead to unethical business behavior. Taken as a whole, their studies represent leading-edge research in the ethics field. They are empirical studies, not armchair theorizing. In other words, these scholars have gone into the field where the action is; they have observed, questioned, recorded, measured, calculated, and analyzed business behavior. Each has used the most sophisticated, reliable, and valid methods available for investigations of this kind. They are the authentic voices of authoritative experts.

Their research gives deep insight into ethics in the American corporation, especially the following dimensions:

- The *causes* of unethical business behavior
- *Company conditions* that encourage corporate white-collar crime
- The *effectiveness of proposed reforms* intended to curb unethical and illegal business practices.

The results revealed by this research are often surprising and well worth knowing.

Character Failure?

Most popular accounts of unethical business behavior lead one to believe that the root of the problem is a failure of personal character. We tend to ask, What is it about Ivan Boesky's personality and background that led him astray? How can we account for a David Levine or those E. F. Hutton managers or the Yuppie Five (all enjoying six-figure affluence well before their overreaching began) if not by greed, selfishness, and an insatiable ego? These popular explanations of ethical failure do find reinforcement in management theory which tells us that *the personal values of corporate managers* play a central role in making business decisions. So, a thoughtful observer might well conclude that unethical behavior stems from bad personal values. Correct those values, or root them out of the company ("get rid of the few rotten apples"), and the problem is solved. But research tells another and far more interesting story.

One example comes from the research of James Weber who tracked the personal values of a large group of corporate managers to see what those values are. Could their personal value commitments be linked to the policies of business firms faced with such typically controversial decisions as plant closings, foreign bank loans, and diversification of capital investments from steel to oil and gas? Corporations have repeatedly been charged with unethical and socially irresponsible behavior for taking these actions. Surely, here would be an opportunity to demonstrate how the personal values of managers differ from the personal values of their critics, thus uncovering the so-called "bad" or unethical values that are supposed to drive the managerial cadre.

FIGURE 1

PERSONAL VALUE DIFFERENCES
(1987)

TOP-RATED VALUES		
Managers	**Union Members**	**Activists**
Self-respect	Family Security	Honest
Honest	Freedom	Helpful
Family Security	Responsible	Equality
Responsible	Honest	Courageous
Freedom	Happiness	A World at Peace
Capable	Self-respect	Family Security
Ambitious	Courageous	Self-respect
LOWEST-RATED VALUE		
Managers	**Union Members**	**Activists**
Obedient	Social Recognition	Pleasure

But the empirical evidence revealed another side. Figure 1 shows that the *personal values* of managers *do* differ from the values of two of their most vocal critics: union members and community activists. Managers rank **Self-respect** first; union members believe **Family Security** should come first; while the activists put **Honest** at the top of their personal value scale. Of the three values held in common—**Self-Respect, Family Security,** and **Honest**—each group ranks them differently. Whereas the activists believe in **Equality, Helpfulness**, and being **Courageous**, corporate managers subscribe to being **Capable** and **Ambitious**. Interestingly, managers and unionists share more values in common—five out of the top seven—than do the two groups (unions and activists) who have been critical of business performance.

The *primary value orientation* of each group, as shown in Figure 2, also reveals differences among the three. Managers tend to favor **Personal Achievement**, union members **Personal Maturity**, and activists **Personal Comfort**. We also see an expected managerial focus on **Self-respect**, a union emphasis on **Comfort**, and the activists' orientation towards **Equality**—none of these unexpected.

In spite of these value differences, *a remarkable consensus emerged*

FIGURE 2

PRIMARY VALUE ORIENTATION
(1987)

Managers	Union Members	Activists
Personal Achievement Self-respect A Secure, Humane World	Personal Maturity Comfort A Secure, Peaceful World	Personal Comfort Equality A Secure, Humane World

when considering the totality of values that were included in the study. Of the thirty-six values examined, about one-third were closely shared, including **Family Security** and **Self-respect**; the importance of being **Honest, Forgiving, Responsible,** and **Broadminded**; and fostering **True Friendship, Freedom,** and **Inner Harmony.** So each group's vision of the kind of world that is valued turned out to be essentially the same, as shown in Figure 2.

Two common beliefs are jeopardized by this research on the personal values of managers. First, the values held most dear by managers and by some of their most persistent critics show so much overlap and consensus that the observed differences are not big enough to separate the groups on issues of public and corporate policy. The second myth debunked by this research is that managers' *personal* values play a direct role in shaping their *business* decisions and policies. No *logical* connection could be found between the professed values of managers and the range of issues that so often separate corporations from their social critics, such as plant closings, foreign investment, and diversification of capital from one industry to another.

Do Company Goals Drive Managers' Values?

Faced with these unexpected findings, perhaps the research approach had the relationship between managers' values and company policies reversed. Could the causal flow run *from* the business policies *to* the values used by the decision makers? In other words, certain business needs might activate the values that can produce the desired policy decision.

Support for this linkage comes from a 1975 study made by George England of the personal values of managers (see Figure 3). **Operative Values** are those most likely to influence a manager's decisions. This exhibit shows that these values are company-oriented and company-supportive. **Adopted Values** also cause a manager to act in the company's behalf; England discovered that managers adopt and act on such values even though

FIGURE 3

**VALUES OF U. S. MANAGERS
(1975)**

Operative Values	Adopted Values
Customers My company Organizational efficiency Ability Achievement High productivity	Craftsmen Stockholders Aggressiveness White collar employees Change Property
Intended Values	Weak Values
Me Trust Loyalty My co-workers Honor	Tolerance Obedience Equality Compassion Security Autonomy

they may not personally accept them as guides in their own off-the-job lives. In other words, a manager may not *prefer* to interact with "craftsmen" as a group, especially if they are unionized, but will do so if the job calls for it. As the saying goes, "they go with the territory." So the values that are going to be used by managers on the job are the ones shown on the left side of Figure 3. The **Intended Values** of managers may well be blocked from usage by the company's needs and objectives; or in some cases, they may be allowed or encouraged to guide company decisions. It will depend largely on what is required to help the company attain its objectives. **Weak Values,** on the other hand, seldom find expression in the workplace. Although a manager might arrive at work holding these **Intended Values** and **Weak Values,** he or she would normally not be able to bring them to bear on job decisions. In other words, the company context seemed to be shaping the use of managers' values, rather than the other way around.

Organizational Climates—Ethical and Unethical

If, then, a company's internal climate can have a powerful influence on a manager's thinking and decision making, is it possible to identify *the ethical climate* that is present in a company? And is the ethical climate of a business firm different from the ethical climate of other kinds of organizations? The answer to both of these questions turned out to be "yes."

FIGURE 4

COMPONENTS OF ORGANZATIONAL ETHICAL CLIMATES
(1987)

	PERSON	COMPANY	SOCIETY
SELF-CENTERED REASONING	Self Interest ***	Company Interest **	Economic Efficiency Interest *
GROUP-CENTERED REASONING	Friendship	Team Play **	Social Responsibility
PRINCIPLED REASONING	Personal Morality	Organizational Rules *	Law or Professional Code *

* Dominant components of business ethical climate

** Derivative components of business ethical climate

*** Inferential component of business ethical climate

Two business school researchers, Bart Victor and John Cullen, found distinctive ethical climates when they observed business firms, military organizations, and academic institutions. Their system for classifying ethical climates had a total of nine possibilities. The organization's climate could emphasize the person, the company, or the society; and it could favor self-centered reasoning, group-centered reasoning, or broad-principled reasoning, as shown in Figure 4. An ethical climate might be composed of any combination of the resulting nine basic, generic components.

The *dominant traits* of the ethical climate in business were found to be represented by three of these cells: **a self-centered interest** in economic efficiency, **a company-centered focus** on following organizational rules, and a tendency to look to the **law and professional codes** as a societal justification for the company's actions. Beyond this research finding are two further interpretive inferences. First, we know from other research that most companies place high importance on having their employees promote the company's interest and be a good team player. Second, the individual employee soon learns that his or her own on-the-job self interest is best promoted by being seen as economically efficient, a good team player, working for the company's interest, playing by the organization's rules, and not getting the company in legal trouble. So there will be a tendency to incorporate these two behavioral inferences into the firm's ethical climate.

Left out of this typical business ethical climate—or greatly downplayed—are **Friendship, Personal Morality,** and **Social Responsibility** (see Figure 4). In other words, an employee or manager with a strong sense of personal morality, social responsibility, or a caring attitude toward others will not be encouraged to express these values in making business decisions. Nor will such an organization be inclined to recruit this kind of individual, because he or she would not fit into the company's ethical climate. As a result, the company increases its chances of taking actions considered by the public to be morally objectionable, socially irresponsible, and uncaring about others.

Moral Reasoning in the Workplace

Given this strong grip of a company's culture on its employees, how in fact do people in business cope with a moral conflict on the job? When you have an employee who is to be let go in six months because of a reduction in force, do you tell the employee now or wait until a day or so before giving out the pink slip? Or when a valued and talented employee who works for you is qualified for a better job at higher pay that opens up in another division of the company, do you block that move? When others are padding their expense reports, do you do so, too?

Researcher Robbin Derry, set out to discover what kind of moral reasoning is used in such situations. She knew that moral development theory holds that men and women use different ways of thinking their way through ethical issues, and she tested that theory in a Fortune-500 corporation. According to accepted theory, men's concept of morality and justice is based on the performance of duties and responsibilities; they take a *principled* approach to a moral dilemma. Adherence to principle is uppermost in their minds. Women, on the other hand, are theorized to base their moral reasoning on *empathetic caring* for others. Organizational principles and rules are less important to them than the pragmatic, immediate needs of people. For women, morality and justice mean caring for others. For men, morality is acting out well-defined duties and obligations and adhering to such principles.

But Derry's research demonstrated that these differences do not hold up at work. Men *and* women managers and business professionals used the same kind of moral reasoning when faced with a work-related ethical dilemma. Uppermost was the belief that *everyone should adhere to orga-*

nizational rules and should carry out one's expected work duties and obligations. Moral reasoning that involves caring for others was only rarely found. In fact, the only manager whose moral reasoning was predominantly based on a caring principle was a man, not a woman as established theory had predicted.

This researcher also discovered that fully one-third of the corporate managers in the study claimed never to have faced a moral dilemma at work. Given the nature of their jobs, this claim was difficult to square with the facts. On further probing, she concluded that some of these see-no-evil managers defined "good" as following the company's rules and "bad" as breaking them; so as long as they were good team players and obeyed the rules, there could be no moral conflict for them. Others realized that the company discouraged its employees from raising on-the-job moral issues, so they did not "see" them when they occurred. Still others appeared to believe that moral responsibility either has no place at work or was someone else's responsibility.

Once again, empirical research—as contrasted with theory or common-sense intuition—tells us that the values, inclinations, and even the moral reasoning used by people in business are shaped and largely determined by the company, its culture, its objectives, and the general climate that prevails there.

The Real Culprits

All of the above findings confirm earlier research (see Figure 5) that unethical business behavior is encouraged by the example set by one's organizational superiors ("If he does it, why shouldn't I?"); by a company's ethical policy or lack of it ("If the company doesn't care, why should I?"); by general practices in the industry ("If my competitors are doing it, I have to do it, too."); and by the actions of one's colleagues ("If they are raking in the gravy, I'd be a fool not to do so.") Less important, according to this study by Steven Brenner and Earl Molander, were society's moral climate and one's personal financial needs.

To this point, we have seen that an entire stream of research leaves little doubt that popular explanations of unethical business practices are misleading at best and wrong at worst. The culprit is not personal values but the values embedded in an organization's culture. Not a failure of character but a flawed ethical climate. Not just a selfish grab for a larger share of life's goodies but a subtly-conditioned urge to promote a company's goals regardless of the negative consequences for others. The problem is compounded when a manager or an employee has so completely identified his or her own

FIGURE 5

MANAGERS' REASONS FOR BEING UNETHICAL
(1977)

Reason for Being Unethical	Rank
Behavior of superiors	1
Formal policy or lack thereof	2
Industry ethical climate	3
Behavior of one's equals in the company	4
Society's moral climate	5
One's personal financial needs	6

personal interests with those of the company that personal values and company values become one and the same thing. At that point, moral reasoning and company reasoning have merged into a single phenomenon. Such an "ethical automaton" or 'ethical eunuch" not only acts *for the company* but believes that these very acts *are* what is meant by "ethical."

White-Collar Crooks

White-collar crime costs business *and* society billions of dollars each year. Some of these crimes are directed *against* business firms—for example, embezzling, padding expense accounts, and conflict-of-interest relationships. These crimes tend to reward the individual lawbreaker at the expense of the company. But many white-collar crimes are committed *on behalf of* the company, thereby helping or supporting the firm—for example, price fixing, evasion of pollution regulations, or advertisements that misrepresent the product and mislead customers. This type of white-collar crime is called "organizational crime."

Two business school faculty members, Philip Cochran and Douglas Nigh, wanted to know if there is some connection between these pro-business organizational crimes and the characteristics of the law-breaking companies. In other words, do certain kinds of companies tend to break the law more often than other kinds of companies? Is there something about *the company itself*, rather than its individual managers and employees, that is responsible for corporate crime?

They began their study with the idea that a company's organizational rules and regular routines—what they called its standard operating procedures (SOPs)—could either *encourage* or *discourage* law-breaking. A company's customary routines might actually mandate illegal behavior or simply permit it to occur without penalty to the employees involved (or perhaps even rewarding them for breaking the law). This might occur, for example, when the marketing division secretly agrees with competitors to fix prices. Or a business firm might knowingly fail to establish SOPs that could curb or prevent criminal behavior by its employees. For example, the company might simply look the other way when some of its employees do some 'midnight dumping" of hazardous wastes. In other words, you look for the kind of SOPs a company has if you want to know whether it is likely to break the law. The focus here is on the company's procedures and rules, rather than the individuals taking the actions.

So, under what conditions do you find companies with SOPs that either directly encourage illegal behavior or that, by their absence, fail to deter crime? The researchers studied the record of 434 Fortune-500 corporations from 1975 and 1976 and found that 42 percent of them had broken the law. "Law breaking" meant that enforcement actions, including sanctions, were taken against the companies by one or more of twenty-four federal agencies. Companies that broke the law and had no formal action taken against them were not counted, nor did the study include state and local law-breaking, so the reported figures are quite conservative.

What they found is shown in Figure 6. The chances of corporate crime increase under these four conditions:

- *Lower profits of the company.* In order to improve profits, managers would be more likely to institute SOPs that permit illegal acts, or fail to establish SOPs that prevent law-breaking.

- *Larger size of the company.* Big companies are more complex. SOPs that can effectively cover the entire operation are more difficult to establish and police.

FIGURE 6

CORPORATE TRAITS ENCOURAGING ILLEGAL ACTIONS
(1987)

Lower profits of the company

Larger size of the company

Higher growth rate of the company

Greater product diversity of the company

- *Higher growth rate of the company.* Companies that grow at a fast rate may outrun their older SOPs, thus increasing the likelihood that legal controls will be weakened.

- *Greater product diversity of the company.* The more diverse the company, the harder it is to establish SOPs that work the same for everyone. Communication is more difficult.

They also expected that illegal behavior would increase as *industry* profits increased, as a company's liquidity deteriorated, and in companies with extensive multinational operations. But they found no such relationships.

Their findings are not entirely unexpected. It is true that the research does not address some important questions, such as the possibility that some companies are high-profit performers *because* they break the law and get away with it. Other companies may be too small to be a target of the enforcement machinery. Nevertheless, the research tells us something we need to know. There *is* a link between certain corporate conditions and the prevalence of organizational white-collar crime.

Will Board Reform Improve Ethics?

When corporations came under strong attack in the 1960s and 1970s for being socially irresponsible and unethical, it was believed that the way to improve social performance was to reform the board of directors. Legal scholars and other critics pointed out that most boards had become isolated and insulated from social forces because they were dominated by company officers, had no minorities or women as members, and were typically peopled by old WASPish men who held their lucrative posts at the pleasure of the board chairman. A better check-and-balance system was needed. The solution was to increase the size of the board, bring more outsiders (especially minorities and women) to the board, put outsiders on the nominating and audit committees, and beef up the number of lawyers who served as board members.

A pair of business school researchers, Frederick Gautschi and Thomas Jones, decided to see how well these reforms had fared. Had the reforms, in fact, reduced the incidence of unethical and illegal corporate behavior? Does the structure of the board of directors really make any difference?

The answer is: Yes, it does matter but not as predicted by the reformers. By looking at the record of legal actions taken against 100 Fortune-500 corporations, they found that (see Figure 7):

FIGURE 7

CORPORATE GOVERNANCE AND LAW-BREAKING
(1987)

PROPOSED REFORM	RESEARCH FINDING
Larger boards of directors	**More** law-breaking
More outside board members	**More** law-breaking
More outsiders on audit committee	**More** law-breaking
More lawyers on the board of directors	**Less** law-breaking

KEY FINDING OF THE RESEARCH	
More inside company officers on the executive committee of the board	**More** law-breaking

- *Illegal behavior actually increases as the board grows in size.* A possible explanation is that large boards are unlikely to be involved in deep discussion of policy decisions, and therefore a larger board does not act as a check on the decisions of top officers of the company.

- *Putting more outsiders on the board is associated with an **increase**, not a decrease, in corporate illegal behavior.* Using outsiders to monitor the practices of companies does not seem to be working.

- *Not even appointing more outside board members to the key auditing committee of the board reduces the incidence of law-breaking.* The watchdog function at this most sensitive post does not produce the needed results.

- *The only reform that seems to have some effect on corporate law-breaking is to increase the number of attorneys serving as board members.* Their expert knowledge and legal judgment, when applied at policy levels in board deliberations, apparently can moderate the amount of law-breaking that occurs.

- *But perhaps the most important finding of this research is that a higher incidence of corporate crime is associated with a higher number of inside directors on the company's executive committee.* It is the executive committee that acts for the entire board between meetings. It may not matter that a board has more outsiders, more women, or more minorities, if crucial decision-making powers are simultaneously delegated to an insider-dominated executive committee. The inference is obvious: Putting more outsiders on the executive committee may reduce law-breaking by corporations.

This research also seems to be saying something that is consistent with the previously expressed idea that the core elements of a company's culture are implicated in the commission of corporate crimes and other unethical actions. If structural reforms of a company, however well intentioned and planned, do not influence the company's ethical climate, or its embedded organizational values, or the single-minded drive of its managers to achieve organizational goals regardless of the consequences for others or for the law, such reforms will amount to little of lasting significance.

Are Codes of Ethics the Answer?

Of all the research stories told here, the most interesting is about codes of ethics adopted by corporations. It may also be the most depressing for anyone interested in improving business's ethical performance.

A university researcher with a marvelously apt first name, Cash Mathews, wanted to know whether corporate ethics codes can be an effective self-regulator of business behavior. If so, there might be less reliance on government regulations to police the private sector.

She wrote to 485 Fortune-500 manufacturing corporations and asked for a copy of their code of ethical conduct. It was already known that many U. S. companies, during the mid-1970s, either initiated or rewrote codes in the aftermath of Watergate and the revelation of questionable political payments made both here and in foreign countries. One-third of the companies did not respond, about 100 said they had no code, and just over 200 corporations sent her a copy.

She then matched these 200 companies with the number of civil and administrative actions taken against them by four federal government agencies: the Food and Drug Administration (FDA), the Environmental Protection Agency (EPA), the Consumer Product Safety Commission (CPSC), and the National Highway Traffic Safety Administration (NHTSA).

Her first finding (see Figure 8) was that the codes were designed to protect the company more than the public. The great majority of the codes cautioned employees and managers to protect the company in dealings with U. S. and foreign governments and with customers and suppliers. Three of every four codes had provisions regarding conflict-of-interest relationships between employees and other parties. A similar proportion focused on the importance of honest internal record keeping. Both of these provisions pro-

FIGURE 8

CONTENT OF CORPORATE CODES OF ETHICS
(1987)

BEHAVIOR PROTECTING THE COMPANY		
Provision	**Included**	**Not Included**
Relations with U.S. government	87 %	13 %
Relations with customers/suppliers	86 %	14 %
Relations with foreign governments	73 %	27 %
Questionable payments	85 %	15 %
BEHAVIOR HARMING THE COMPANY		
Provision	**Included**	**Not Included**
Conflict of interest	75 %	25 %
Integrity of books and records	75 %	25 %
Divulging trade secrets	44 %	56 %
Insider trading information	43 %	57 %
BEHAVIOR PROTECTING OR NOT HARMING THE PUBLIC		
Provision	**Included**	**Not Included**
Product safety	9 %	91 %
Physical environment	13 %	87 %
Product quality	21 %	79 %
Consumer relations	23 %	77 %
Civic and community affairs	25 %	75 %
Health and safety of employees	37 %	63 %

tect the company against harmful actions that might be taken by its employees and others. Considerably less frequently mentioned were actions that might be harmful to the public. These results suggest that it might be naive to rely on corporate codes of ethics to curb *antisocial* business practices. Rather, the codes tend to check *anti-company* behavior.

But what about the connection between the codes and illegal corporate practices? Do codes help? Using several sophisticated statistical techniques, this researcher could find no association between the existence of a code and a reduction in law-breaking by the companies. In fact, just the opposite relationship was revealed: Having a code is linked to *more*, not fewer, violations. Then, realizing that law-breakers might adopt a code *after* being caught (thereby making it *appear* that codes and law-breaking are linked), she analyzed her data to see if that had happened. It hadn't; the finding was that violations do *not* lead corporations to adopt codes of ethics.

Those companies whose codes put an emphasis on having employees sign compliance ("read-and-sign") affidavits or that spoke about "employee integrity" were found to be greater violators than others. The same thing proved to be true of codes that waxed eloquent about "the reputation of the corporation": those companies were more likely to be law-breakers.

Overall, Mathews found that codes of ethics have less influence on law-breaking than the type of industry involved and the size of the company. The bigger the company, the more violations reported. She also found that higher violations were associated with three industries: food, drugs, and medical instruments and supplies, all regulated by the FDA. This relationship may mean only that the FDA is a more vigorous protector of the public than the other three regulatory agencies.

An Ethical Compass for Business

Having begun with Bhopal and Boesky, what lasting lessons does all of this research teach about those two infamous ethical lapses?

No Bhopal can occur, nor Boesky operate, unless the organization that surrounds the actors permits or encourages their ethical excesses. The corruption symbolized by these twin tragedies is rooted more deeply within the respective *organizational systems* than in the psyches and egos of Union Carbide employees or Ivan Boesky. It *is* possible for an entire system to go to sleep. A company can be so focused on its own internal goals that managers and employees lose sight of broader and more profound ethical principles. When we face ethical uncertainty, what we need is an ethical compass. And if we are to get our bearings, that ethical compass must point toward the fundamental truths that reside *outside* of ourselves, in the broader realm of humanity to which all of us belong. The task is to build bridges from our cloistered existence within our own organizations outward to the broader reaches of humankind. In that direction lies a brighter prospect for improving ethical performance in business.

YEAR 1991

GLOBALIZING CORPORATE ETHICS

Setting the Scene. CSR went global in the mid-1970s as the multinational enterprise—the transnational corporation—rose to prominence. Corporations around the world, not just in the United States, became targets of social protestors and host countries. It soon became apparent that CSR aims overlapped national boundaries and that multinational companies might be held to common CSR standards. This convergence of universal CSR values—a culture of ethics—had its roots in the 1948 United Nations Universal Declaration of Human Rights and then found expression through other well-known international compacts.

Moral guidelines for corporations may be found embedded in several multinational compacts adopted by governments since the end of the Second World War. Taken as a whole, these normative guides comprise a framework for identifying the essential moral behaviors expected of multinational corporations. Corporate actions that transgress these principles are understood to be *de facto*, and in some cases *de jure*, unethical and immoral. This set of normative prescriptions and proscriptions embodies a moral authority that transcends national boundaries and societal differences, thereby invoking or manifesting a universal or transcultural standard of corporate ethical behavior. Although this remarkable development has not run its full course and therefore is not yet all embracing, it is well enough along for its main outlines to be evident and its central normative significance to be clear.

Landmark Multinational Compacts

The four decades between 1948 and 1988 have been remarkable for the proliferation of intergovernmental agreements, compacts, accords, and declarations that have been intended to put on the public record various sets of principles regulating the activities of governments, groups, and individuals. The core concerns of these compacts have ranged from military security to economic and social development, from the protection of national sovereignty to specifying acceptable actions by multinational enterprises, from condemnations of genocide and slavery to the regulation of capital flows and the transfer of technology, from the political rights of women to the movements of refugees and stateless persons, and numerous others. They reflect the many kinds of problems and issues that have confronted governments in the last half of the 20th century.

This chapter focuses on six of these intergovernmental compacts, which by their nature, purpose, and comprehensiveness might well be considered to be the most generic or archetypal of such agreements. Collectively they proclaim the basic outlines of *a transcultural corporate ethic*. This ethic effectively lays down specific guidelines for the formulation of multinational corporate policies and practices. The six compacts and their respective dates of promulgation are:

- The United Nations Universal Declaration of Human Rights (1948)

- The European Convention on Human Rights (1950)

- The Helsinki Final Act (1975)

- The OECD Guidelines for Multinational Enterprises (1976)

- The International Labor Office Tripartite Declaration of Principles Concerning Multinational Enterprises and Social Policy (1977)

- The United Nations Code of Conduct on Transnational Corporations (not yet completed nor promulgated but originating in 1972).

The first two compacts are clearly normative in focus and intention, emphasizing human rights, but they are not addressed specifically to multinational enterprises. The principal emphasis of the Helsinki Final Act is the national and political security of the signatory governments, although this accord and its successor protocols carry strong messages concerning human rights and environmental protections, which do concern business operations. The last three compacts are aimed primarily and explicitly at the practices of multinational enterprises across a wide range of issues and problems. While three of the six accords issue primarily from European-North American governments, the other three represent the views of a much wider, even global, range of governments.

Normative Corporate Guidelines

By careful reading of these six intergovernmental compacts, one can derive a set of explicitly normative guides for the policies, decisions, and operations of multinational corporations. These guidelines refer to normal business operations, as well as more fundamental responsibilities regarding basic human rights. They include detailed and specific standards for employment practices and policies, consumer protection, environmental protection, political payments and involvement, and basic human rights and fundamental freedoms.

Human rights and employment conditions are clearly the leading guideline categories, while consumer protection and corporate political activity appear infrequently. The collective weight of the guidelines is more important than the absence of some of them from specific international agreements. Clearly their inclusion across the board would strengthen the case for a global normative system intended to guide corporate practices.

These normative guidelines have direct implications for a wide range of specific corporate programs and policies. They include policies regarding childcare, minimum wages, hours of work, employee training and education, adequate housing and health care, pollution control efforts, advertising and marketing activities, severance pay, privacy of employees and consumers, information concerning on-the-job hazards, and, especially for those companies with operations in South Africa, such additional matters as the place of residence and free movement of employees. Quite clearly , the guidelines are not intended to be, nor do they act as, mere rhetoric. Nor do they deal with peripheral matters. They have direct applicability to many of the central operations and policies of multinational enterprises.

The Normative Sources of the Guidelines

These guides for the practices and policies of multinational companies seem to rest upon and be justified by four normative orientations. Given sets of the guidelines can be tied directly to one or more of these moral sources.

National sovereignty is one such source. All six compacts invoke the inviolability of national sovereignty. In acting on the compacts' principles each nation is to take care not to infringe on the sovereignty of its neighbors. Hence, preservation of a nation's integrity and self-interest appears to be one of the moral foundations on which such multilateral accords rest. Multinational enterprises are urged to respect the aims, goals, and directions of a host country's economic and social development and its cultural and historical traditions. Companies' plans and goals should not contravene these components of a nation's being and sovereignty. Nor should they interfere in the internal political affairs of host countries through improper political activities, political bribes, or questionable payments of any kind made to political candidates or public officials.

Social equity is another normative basis underlying some of the specific corporate guidelines. Pay scales are to be established in ways that will insure equity between men and women, racial and ethnic groups, professional and occupational groups, host-country nationals and parent-country expatriates, indigenous employees and migrant workers, and those well-off and those least-advantaged. The same equity principle is advocated for job opportunities, job training, treatment of the unemployed, and the provision of other work-related benefits and services.

Market integrity is yet another source of moral authority and justification for some of the guidelines, as well as other restrictive business practices, the transnational flow of capital investments, the repatriation of profits, the rights of ownership, and similar matters. Among the normative corporate guidelines, those tinged with the notion of market integrity include restrictions on political payments and bribes that might inject non-market considerations into business transactions, a recognition of private collective bargaining (rather than government mandates) as a preferred technique for establishing pay scales, working conditions, and benefits for employees, and some (but not all) of the consumer protections sought in the accords.

By far the most fundamental, comprehensive, widely acknowledged, and pervasive source of moral authority for the corporate guidelines is *human rights and fundamental freedoms.* This concept is given eloquent expression in the United Nations Universal Declaration of Human Rights. It is then picked up and adopted by the framers of four of the other five accords. Only the OECD Guidelines for Multinational Enterprises fail to invoke the specific language or the basic meaning of human rights and fundamental freedoms as the normative principle on which these accords are erected, although the OECD Guidelines incorporate some of these rights and freedoms as specific duties and obligations of multinationals. As previously noted, a number of OECD members are signatories to the European Convention on Human Rights, thereby subscribing to the basic principles of the UN Universal Declaration of Human Rights.

Essentially, the United Nations Universal Declaration of Human Rights proclaims the existence of a whole host of human rights and freedoms, saying that they are inherent in the human condition. "All human beings are born free and equal in dignity and rights." "Equal and inalienable rights" are possessed by "all members of the human family" who also manifest an "inherent dignity." Other language speaks of "fundamental human rights," "the dignity and worth of the human person," "the equal rights of men and women," and "fundamental freedoms." These rights and freedoms exist "without distinction of any kind." They are understood as a common possession of humankind, not dependent on membership in any particular group, organization, nation, or society.

This invocation of human rights, as a philosophical principle, owes much to Immanuel Kant. In effect, the Declaration of Human Rights posits the Kantian person as the fundament of moral authority. The human person is said to possess an inherent worth and dignity, as well as inalienable and equal rights and freedoms. This being true of all human beings, correlative duties and obligations are thereby imposed on everyone to respect and not to interfere with the rights of others. No one person is warranted in using another as a means to promote one's own ends and purposes, absent a freely-given informed consent. Hence, a deceptively simple algorithm based on rights and duties sets the stage for the specification of normative rules of conduct for governments, groups, individuals, and—for present purposes—multinational enterprises.

As powerful and compelling as the human rights principle is, it does compete with the other three normative sources—national sovereignty, social equity, and market integrity. This means that human rights are conditioned by political, social, and economic values. Rights do not stand alone or outside the normal range of human institutions, diverse as those institutions are around the globe and from society to society.

Rights everywhere are hedged in by such political, social, and economic features of human society. The behavioral guidelines for multinational corporations seem to have been woven, not from a single philosophic principle, but by a blending of normative threads. At the pattern's center stand human rights and fundamental freedoms, for in the international compacts reference is found most frequently to this normative marker. But the strands of national sovereignty, social equity, and market integrity are woven into the overall pattern, coloring and giving form to the expression of human rights. Thus are human rights conditioned by societal factors.

One important trait is responsible for the normative dominance of the human rights principle. The human rights spoken of in the Universal Declaration of Human Rights are *transcultural*. As a principle, human rights span and disregard cultural and national boundaries, class systems, ethnic groupings, economic levels, and other human arrangements which for a variety of reasons differentiate between individuals and groups. Human rights are just that—human. They inhere in *all* humans, regardless of imposed societal classifications and exclusions. They can be defied, disregarded, or violated but they cannot be eradicated.

Except for the human rights principle, all other normative sources that undergird the multinational corporate guidelines are culture bound, unable to break out of their respective societal contexts. By contrast, human rights are seen to be transcultural. They are the glue or the linchpin that holds the entire normative system together in a coherent international whole. While conditioned by desires for national (or socio-ethnic) sovereignty, social equity, and market integrity—thus finding their operational meaning within a societal context—human rights express attitudes, yearnings, and beliefs common to all humankind. In that sense, they form the core of a global system whose normative aim is to regulate the practices of multinational corporations.

This rights-based normative system finds justification in two ways. One is through deontological obligations implicit in human rights. Here, the philosopher speaks to us. The other justification is more directly operational, taking the form of lessons learned from human experience about the formation and sustenance of human values. These lessons are taught by social scientists. Each of these rationales calls for further elaboration.

Rationale I: Deontological Norms

The normative corporate guidelines may be seen as extensions and manifestations of broad deontological, i.e., duty-based, principles of human conduct. These principles provide a philosophic basis for defining the duties and obligations of multinational enterprises.

The concurring governments, in the several compacts mentioned here, are saying to multinational enterprises:

- Because your employees have rights to work, to security, to freedom of association, to healthful and safe work conditions, to a pay scale that sustains them and their families at a dignified level of subsistence, to privacy, and to be free from discrimination at work, the managers of multinational corporations incur duties and obligations to respect such rights, to promote them where and when possible, and to avoid taking actions that would deny these rights to the corporation's employees and other stakeholders.

- Because humans and their communities have rights to security, to health, and to the opportunity to develop themselves to their fullest potentials, corporations have an obligation to avoid harming the ecological balance on which human community life and health depend, and a positive duty to promote environmental conditions conducive to the pursuit and protection of human rights.

- Because consumers have rights to safe and effective products and to know the quality and traits of the products and services they need to sustain life, companies are obligated, i.e., they have a duty, to offer such products for sale under conditions that permit a free, uncoerced choice for the consumer.

- Because human beings can lay claim to a set of human rights and fundamental freedoms enumerated in the Universal Declaration of Human Rights, multinational corporations are duty-bound to promote, protect, and preserve those rights and freedoms and to avoid trampling on them through corporate operations. The corporations' Kantian duty is implied in the Kantian rights held by all.

A moral imperative is thus imposed on corporations. The source of this deontological imperative is the rights and freedoms that inhere in all human persons. The corporation is bound, by this moral logic to respect all persons within the purview of its decisions, policies, and actions. In some such fashion as this, the Universal Declaration of Human Rights serves as the deontological fount, the moral fundament, that defines a corporation's basic duties and obligations toward others. The Declaration's moral principles have been extended to many if not most of the multilateral compacts of the past 40 years, many of whose specific provisions take the form of normative guides for corporate actions across a large range of issues. So goes the moral logic of the accords and compacts.

Rationale II: Experience-based Values

Respect for persons, respect for community integrity, respect for ecological balance, and respect for tested human experience in many spheres of life can be understood both deontologically and as *adaptive human value orientations*. As value phenomena, they are compatible with the needs and experiences of the world's peoples in a technological era. The need to proclaim many of the rights that appear in the Universal Declaration of Human Rights grew directly out of the gross violations of human rights during the pre-war and war periods of the 1930s and 1940s. Those experiences inspired most of the world's governments to take collective action, in the form of a proclamation, to define an acceptable number of such rights and to urge all to nourish and safeguard them.

Since that time, societies around the globe have felt the bite and seen the promise of technology spawned and applied by multinational corporations and governments. They have experienced the benefits, and have often borne the costs, of business operations undertaken without much regard for environmental, human, and community interests. These experiences have been as compelling, if not as traumatic, as those of the pre-war and war years when human rights were trampled. They have generated widespread agreement and belief in a network of experienced-based values that sustain the lives of individuals, their communities, and their societies. It is these values that have found their way into the several multilateral compacts and accords discussed here. Corporations are urged, not just to attend to their deontological duties but also to support, and not to override, the values that have been found through experience to undergird human flourishing.

Speaking of the role played by experience in formulating value standards, sociologist Robin Williams reminds us that "values are learned [and] developed through some kind of experience. Value orientations, repeatedly experienced and reformulated by large numbers of persons over extended periods, will eventually become intellectualized as components of a comprehensive world view." Such a comprehensive world view of morally acceptable behavior by multinational enterprises is found in the normative guidelines of the several compacts and accords. Humankind is speaking the language of philosophically inspired rights and duties, as well as the language of a social-scientific conception of experienced-based, adaptive human values. The outcome in both cases is movement toward a transcultural corporate ethic, which is manifested in the six multilateral compacts or codes of conduct.

Where nations have been able to identify and agree upon common ethical principles and common values that reflect the experience of even the most diverse cultures, a moral minimum has been established. This minimum—the international common morality, this "common nexus of humane practice," this "planetary perspective"—stands as a benchmark to be striven for. While it exists, no corporation, domestic or multinational, can legitimately claim the right to operate without referring its policies and practices to this basic moral standard, this morality of the commons that has been writ large upon the global scene.

Reservations and Qualifications

Four objections might be raised to the derivation of these normative corporate guidelines.

First, it can rightly be said that the six compacts are agreements among *governments* (except the ILO whose members include enterprises and employee associations). Multinational enterprises themselves are not parties to these accords and thereby are not *directly* bound by their terms and principles. The multinationals were not the authors of these guidelines, did not themselves agree to them, and did not pledge to honor them in practice.

This objection can be offset by noting that all persons, groups, and organizations falling into the sovereign jurisdiction of the concurring governments are bound also by the agreements made by their governments. In this sense, it does not matter that the signatory parties are governments and not enterprises. The UN Universal Declaration of Human Rights asserts that "every organ of society" should promote and secure the human rights proclaimed by the Declaration. "Every organ of society" is obviously broad enough to encompass business corporations.

A second difficulty is that all six accords rely on voluntary compliance by the signatories, since there is no all-embracing international legal authority to enforce the principles, which are recommendatory and expectational, not obligational, in character.

However, more important than formal legal pressures to conform to the agreed principles is the manner in which normative, ethical, and moral forces exert their influence on human perceptions and actions. Compliance with moral standards occurs most frequently when there is self-awareness of what others believe to be morally correct. Research has shown that most people register an apparent desire to hold values, and to be seen as holding values, that are consistent with others' values. Other research reports that value commitments and various types of moral reasoning are strongly influenced by social interactions and social learning experiences.

Without this psychological and socially induced strain toward moral consistency, it is unlikely that governmental coercion by itself would be able to secure compliance with socially acceptable moral standards. This is what is usually meant by those who say that "Morals cannot be legislated." Compliance is more a matter of social learning and an understanding of the worthwhileness and serviceability of given moral standards than an acceptance forced by an authoritarian source. Hence, the widespread declaration of moral principles founded on voluntary acceptance may symbolize a type of moral commitment that is conceivably stronger and more effective than the use of government police power to secure compliance with moral directives.

A third difficulty arises when arguing that normative corporate guidelines form the core of a transcultural corporate ethic. The guidelines are not subscribed to by all governments, and even some of the signatory governments may override or ignore them in some circumstances. Thus, the guidelines fall considerably short of representing a universal world view of what multinational corporations should do.

However, a modicum of hope may exist in the very *process* of trying to achieve consensus, prickly as it often is. If nations can agree on procedural rules for determining a fair distribution of the benefits and costs of joining with others in multilateral compacts, more international collaboration might be forthcoming. It is worth remembering that corporations remain remarkably attuned to public perceptions of their images and reputations, displaying an often surprising sensitivity to public criticism of their policies and actions. The reasons are frequently self protective, rather than stemming from altruistic or socially responsible motives. Even so, the hovering presence and repeated expression of moral principles seemingly accepted by large public blocs and their governments may influence corporate behavior towards voluntary compliance with these normative standards.

A fourth difficulty is that the normative guidelines are obviously an incomplete set of moral instructions to enterprises. They do not cover many important matters and issues related to multinational corporate operations. In spite of the relatively limited moral compass of the six major accords, an impressively diverse range of issues has been evident in several other multilateral conventions, codes, and treaties during the 1970s and 1980s. They attempt to establish guidelines concerning product liability, safety of consumer products, protection of privacy and personal data, transnational movement of hazardous waste materials, distribution and use of pesticides, business operations in South Africa, elimination of various forms of discrimination, protection of employees from workplace hazards, and reduction and elimination of chlorofluorocarbons.

The argument here does not require that all possible issues be included nor that all parties accept all of the provisions of the compacts. It is not claimed that we are witnessing more than the bare beginnings of a globally oriented system of normative principles governing corporate behavior. The only claim being made is that the general outlines of such a system are now discernible and partially operational.

Lessons for Policy Makers

Those who set policies, whether for public or private institutions, can find some important lessons in these multinational codes of conduct.

The most compelling lesson is that highly diverse governments and societies have been able to reach a workable consensus about some core normative directives for multinational enterprises. That should send a strong message to corporate leaders everywhere that the world's peoples, speaking through their governments, are capable of setting standards intended to guide corporate practices and policies into morally desirable channels. Failure to agree on everything should not be allowed to cloak an achieved consensus on many issues.

Wise corporate leaders will be able to interpret this consensus as a framework of public expectations on which the policies of their own companies can be based. Global stakeholders have set out their positions on a large range of problems and issues that matter to them. In effect, corporations are being offered an opportunity to match their own operations to these public expectations. The best ones will do so. The others may wish they had if, in failing to heed the normative messages, they encounter rising hostility and increased governmental intervention in their affairs.

For public policy makers, these agreements betoken a growing consensus among the world's peoples about what is thought to be morally desirable action by governments. It would be as perilous for political leaders to ignore this rising tide of global agreement as for corporate policy makers to turn their backs upon it. The authority and legitimacy of these central economic and political institutions are frequently at risk. Therefore, it will be vitally important for those charged with making institutional policies to guide their respective societies in ways acceptable to their citizens.

Acting to promote this normative consensus can be encouraged if policy makers understand both the philosophic roots and the experience-based values from which these international agreements draw their meaning and strength. The philosophic concept of the human person that one finds in these multilateral compacts, and the human and humane values that grow out of shared global experiences, are no mere passing fancy of a planetary people. Building policy on these twin foundations will bring government and business into alignment with the deep structure of human aspirations.

Beyond Multinationals: The Culture of Ethics

The transcultural corporate ethic described here is only one part of a much more comprehensive, universal moral order whose shadowy outlines are only partially apparent. This broader 'culture of ethics" includes all of those fundamental values and moral orientations that have been proven through long experience to contribute to the sustenance and flourishing of human persons within their communities. It will be increasingly apparent that all economic enterprises, public and private, domestic and multinational, are bound to acknowledge the moral force of this culture of ethics and to shape their policies and practices accordingly. This moral dimension of economic analysis and corporate decision making can no longer be set aside or treated as a peripheral matter. As human societies are drawn ever closer together by electronic and other technologies, and as they face the multiple threats posed by the unwise and heedless use of these devices, it will become ever more necessary to reach agreement on the core values and ethical principles that permit a humane life to be lived by all. Such planetary agreement is now visible, though yet feeble in its rudiments. This broad-scale culture of ethics draws upon many societal, religious, and philosophical sources. It is a great chorus of human voices, human aspirations, and human experiences, arising out of societal and cultural and individual diversity, that expresses the collective normative needs of a global people.

PART III

NATURE AND CORPORATE MORALITY

Corporate social responsibility has long been thought to be enhanced—or spurned—by a combination of personal character (usually the CEO's) and a corporate culture attuned either towards or away from ethics. This twofold explanation—character and culture—began to be vastly supplemented by advances in the natural sciences. Care for the natural environment became a public policy priority, as business sought socially responsible ways to reconcile economic and ecological demands. Corporations themselves were seen as complex adaptive entities obeying the laws of nature as fully as cultural custom. Could social contracts that lie at the heart of market exchange and arbitrate so much of what is thought to be just and fair be a product of Darwinian logic? Perhaps the moral perplexities of corporate life arise from nature itself. Could the unprecedented torrent of corporate corruption that ushered in the new millennium be the unwanted gift of a hardwired executive brain, run amok with greed and power seeking? Blaming it all on character failure and a flawed corporate culture may overlook nature's role in shaping the networks of deceit and criminality found among top-level corporate managers and their confederates.

YEAR 2000

[Public confidence in big business: 29%]

THE CORPORATION:
NATURE'S BLACK BOX

Setting the Scene. The central message of Values, Nature, and Culture in the American Corporation, published in 1995, is that business values, the corporation's moral standing, and its moral dilemmas are the outcome of natural evolutionary forces interacting with corporate culture. The present chapter extends that picture by focusing on the actual functions performed by the modern corporation, arguing once again that they, like the values they express, are another manifestation of nature at work.

Nature plays an enormously important role in business life. Hurricanes, floods, tornadoes, snow storms, and other natural disasters cause immense property damage, disrupt vital services, reduce business profits, and sometimes bankrupt insurance companies. Drouths and unseasonable weather cycles bring financial ruin to farmers, lower the demand for seasonal farm workers, and drastically raise supermarket prices of consumables. Attempts to reduce environmental pollution and global warming, whether through government regulation or industry initiatives, impose costs, delay the adoption of new technologies, and ban useful products from markets. Pharmaceutical and health care companies are required by law to test drugs and medical devices for efficacy and safety, while many food products require quality checks and nutritional labeling to encourage optimum diets. Personal computers come with instructions and warnings about proper posture and periodic rest breaks so as "to reduce the risk of nerve, tendon, or muscle injury." Sick- building syndrome has felled countless office workers and required large remodeling investments by firms.

Health care costs alone, borne directly or indirectly by corporate benefit programs, are a dramatic marker of how biology and business interact, not to speak of the growing number of health maintenance organizations whose task is to find an acceptable balance between economic return and the health needs of their subscribers. Then there is the rush of firms eager to cash in on the growing number of patentable gene therapies and other genetic miracles that offer the lure of better health, or improved farm crops, along with enviable financial returns to the patent holders.

These intersections of nature and business—where biology impinges upon finance, weather cycles make or break agribusiness, health needs challenge for-profit HMOs, and atmospheric chemistry constrains car makers and their designers—are only the most obvious signs that nature has a direct impact on the bottom line. In a more subtle yet comprehensive sense, nature also operates within almost every nook and cranny of the business firm. The profits, the losses, the competitive drive, the high levels of economic productivity, the explosive global diffusion of business culture, the mergers and acquisitions that continue to build corporate behemoths, the onrush of technology—all of these and much more are the end result of natural forces at play in human affairs.

In what follows, the arguments for nature's activist role are vigorously pursued. Business motives are linked to the physics of cosmic evolution—a bold thrust but believable in the end. The yardsticks that measure business success, such as market domination, return on capital, exorbitantly lavish executive salaries, bonuses, and stock options, are attributed to innate biological urges. The socially disruptive swirls of new technology, along with the innovative miracles of productivity they inject into the business system, are traced to synaptic connections and neuronal firings lying deep in the human brain. The way business employees and managers are organized into levels of command and control, into complex hierarchies of technical sophistication, into teams, task forces, coalitions, alliances, assembly lines, cubicled ranks—these too are shown to owe their traits and patterns to expressive cerebral codes long ago implanted in the brains of our Stone Age ancestors. And the business practitioner's urge to control what happens, to direct the firm into chosen channels, to measure outcomes with precision, and to assure a long life for the enterprise will be shown to stand on shaky ground, undercut by nonlinear ecological forces that defy the practitioner's rationalistic urges and linear mindset.

Using nature to interpret business behavior is unusual and potentially off-putting because we are accustomed to believe that a combination of economics, psychology, and politics can tell most of the story. Self-interested pursuit of profits, modulated by a political system supportive of private property, has long constituted the ideological infrastructure and the central plot of Western market economies. For many of Adam Smith's current followers, it seems to explain enough without resort to natural causes, although Smith himself argued that supply and demand are natural laws expressive of natural sentiments. Nor have the many and diverse social critiques of market economic theory—Marxist, socialist, institutionalist, socioeconomic, feminist—ventured into the naturalist realm to any significant degree. Nature has been left to one side.

Now, however, it is possible to think in naturalistic terms because of the great upwelling of information and new insights being generated by natural scientists in many fields. One observer labels this gush of scientific discovery and interpretation as a "third culture," the work of a loose collection of scientific theorists who are exploring everything from cosmic origins to language origins, primate behavior and its possible relation to human behavior, evolutionary biology, the meaning of consciousness, gene-directed human traits, computer-simulated neural networks, genetic algorithms of emergence and self-organizing systems, ecological diversity and species extinctions, and the neurobiology of both normal and abnormal behavior.

Why not make use of these scientific riches, if any of them can help clarify or improve business performance? Doing so is the central thrust and inspiration of this chapter. It will carry the reader along new pathways, broader and more inviting than the usual dry economic explanations, and less ideologically argumentative than those offered by business's many critics.

If business is surrounded and shaped by nature, what are the practical effects? Wouldn't one have to show that nature has the power to make the bottom line either a plus or a minus? Or that nature is able to control the direction and pace of a company's strategic planning? Can nature actually override a manager's decisions? Where free markets rest on initiative, personal autonomy, consumer choice, and decentralized decision making, any claim that an impersonal, unfeeling nature is in charge of economic and business affairs will meet great resistance. Free enterprisers work to free themselves and their companies from all fetters imposed by government regulators, employee unions, or social protestors. They won't like to be told that natural causes are a newly discovered constraint. Some entrepreneurs, however, have an easier time seeing nature as a co-investor and working partner when new business opportunities, such as recycling industrial wastes to produce useful products, create both jobs and profits. It seems possible, then, that the practical effects of the nature-business bonding may run in two directions, one possibly channeling or constraining the range of business decisions, the other opening the way for business to collaborate with nature and therefore to dampen some of nature's negative impacts on human affairs—and of equal importance, lessening the damage done to our natural earthly home by some kinds of business operations.

The main message is that nature matters. It matters in the way business is done and how well it achieves its purposes. Nature also makes a difference to the people who work in business, what they give to it and what they take away from it. Perhaps more important than any other aspect of the nature-business bond, nature matters regarding the larger purposes and ultimate meaning sought by human communities around the globe. That ancient unending personal search is now subject to the burgeoning power and influence of a business order that reaches into the remotest, innermost recesses of human existence—once by transistor radio, now by the Internet. Business has indeed thrust itself, without full knowledge, into that poignant human space that tradition has reserved for the contemplative search for life's meaning. It is there, in stark and simple ways, that one comes to terms with life, death, and nature. Nature does matter. And business matters because it has been drawn into a deep, lasting, and profoundly close relationship with nature and natural forces.

To explore these business-and-nature ties, both practical and philosophical, four major, overarching questions are posed. Each question raises an issue vital to the successful operation of any business firm, whether large or small, international or local, for-profit or not-for-profit. In each case, nature plays an indispensable part in shaping the firm's bottom line. The four questions are:

- What motivates or drives the business firm?
- What generates business productivity and innovation?
- What shapes business organization?
- What enables the achievement of business goals?

The four key concepts here are *motivation, productivity/innovation, organization,* and *goal achievement,* and the plan is to demonstrate how nature affects and shapes each of these central processes of the typical business firm.

Nature's Black Box

The metaphor Nature's Black Box suggests that much of what goes on inside the business firm is of naturalistic origin and is either unknown or appears to be mysterious and remote to observers who are on the outside looking in. The "black box" image has frequently been used to describe any reasonably complex, specialized process or activity that may be admired for what it does but whose internal functioning is not fully understood. Could there be a better example than today's personal computer, especially laptops whose main processor is literally a black box and whose miraculous inner workings are out of reach of most users? The same image can be applied to an organization or institution, such as a hospital, a university, a religious organization, or a legislative body, where internal expert knowledge and skills are required but run well beyond the average person's grasp. To the outsider or neophyte, the hospital may do a marvelous job of caring for patients, or the university may graduate a stream of well educated students, or a church may reach many communicants with its message, or a legislature may govern a society in compelling ways—but just what happens and how these feats are accomplished may be a mystery. For all practical purposes, the organization is an opaque-sided black box, not unlike one's personal computer.

In the same way, today's businesses employ a daunting array of specialized technology, complex financial analysis, advanced marketing research, accounting and cost controls, computerized production and inventory systems, human resource and benefit plans, competitive intelligence systems, and (for the largest companies) the managerial equivalent of satellite-based global positioning systems to calculate the rate and timing of their capital investments, new market ventures, and alliances with other firms and governments around the globe. Most corporate insiders themselves seldom see or understand more than a fraction of the company's overall operations, while outsiders can only guess what goes on behind the corporate walls. For this reason, the idea of a "corporate black box" that does something but whose inner workings are invisible and not readily accessible seems to fit today's business firm.

Now go one step further and imagine that the forces driving and influencing business activity have a natural origin. In other words, put nature inside the black box and let it represent the source of the box's output. Getting inside to see how nature works, that is, explaining how nature causes business to be what it is and to do what it does, is the goal. The guiding vision of Nature's Black Box is that the business firm itself is little more than a feature of the natural landscape.

Some may object on theoretical and aesthetic grounds to the mechanical image invoked by probing the innards of a square, opaque, six-sided box. Putting a spontaneous, unpredictable, evolving nature inside such a mechanical contraption will strike some as wrong-headed and contradictory of nature's dynamic, flowing character. More imaginatively, one might take a page from current cosmological theory where constantly evolving "bubble" universes are said to be created in an endless procession, with passageways called worm holes theoretically allowing travel from one bubble to another. As a metaphor, "bubble" might work as well as "black box" and would certainly convey more vividly the evolutionary, untamed character of business and business change. However, setting aside the speculative, unobserved (and probably unobservable), untested tenets of cosmology's bubbles, there is a certain comfort and well understood stability in the notion of a "black box" with inner workings that need clarification, so that is the vision to be used here.

So, shall we gingerly lift the lid of Nature's Black Box?

Looking Inside the Black Box

Inside Nature's Black Box natural forces of great complexity and stunning power generate all the behavior we recognize as business practice. The Black Box's output *is* business. The power generated deep within that Box takes on phenomenal, even cosmic dimensions, whether the box is large, as in today's global corporate behemoths, or small sleek-lean-and-agile entrepreneurial firms. All of them do business suspended in a force-field that oscillates and pulses to rhythms set deep within cosmic time and space.

One of the first things you notice when peeking under the lid of the Black Box is the clustering of components. Although complex, the contents are not a total mess. Maybe they resemble your own desk—it may look like total chaos but you know where everything is among heaps of stuff stacked everywhere. A little bit of poking and tinkering reveals these component-clusters are linked together. That tells us that what one cluster does must affect the others. When it beeps or hums, it can make others do the same. If these interconnecting pathways were to be lighted up the way those computerized brain scans are, we would be able to see the signals each gadget-cluster sends out and where they go. Fortunately, each cluster-component bears a label, which gives a broad hint about what it does.

Keep in mind that we're talking about business here—plain old commerce, making money, trying to earn a profit, finding ways to get enough people, money, and materials together to turn out products or services that other people might want to buy. It's not very romantic but can be exciting, not the stuff of Nobel prizes but not entirely ignoble either. In one way or another, it keeps all of us going by creating and generating what is needed to get through the days and years.

When we first pried the lid off, you might have noticed how old-looking, how very ancient the entire thing seemed to be. Still strong, it reeked of old age. Something about it hinted at times long past and worlds no longer seen. It was as if those component-clusters had been humming and clicking, sending out those impulses to one another for untold centuries, long before the centuries themselves were known—out to the edge of time itself. That's because everything inside the Box—*everything!*—is a little fragment of space-time, primordial, molar, basal, as original as the initial elements of the Big Bang. We're talking fundamentals here in a big way, the biggest that can be fitted into the human imagination, and that's saying a lot. But it's not saying that Adam Smith's capitalism or Karl Marx's communism were "present at the Creation." One now extinct, the other globally regnant, they have been only small wrinkles on the face of galactic evolution. The Black Box as we know it today cannot be invented anew because it was never invented in the first place. As we shall see, it houses natural rhythms that owe everything to forces that long antedated the conscious shaping of anything. The Box and its contents are nature emergent, a "becoming" process, one still evolving, as full of surprises as ever, which is why it is so incomparably valuable. What we call business is nothing less than a natural substrate of cosmic forces.

The Nature of Business

Now to the clusters. What are they? What do they do? Four in number, they are labeled **Motivator, Creator, Organizer, Enabler.**

What motivates or drives the business firm? The natural **Motivator** of all business and economic activity is thermodynamic entropy, which is one of the most pervasive physical processes in the entire cosmos and is probably *the* most basic life-generating force in all of organic nature. Entropy—the relentless tendency of all energy to disperse toward an equilibrium that renders the energy unavailable or useless for work—drives organic life's economizing activities that attempt to stem or delay the arrival of thermodynamic equilibrium conditions where all life would cease. The first appearance of life was necessarily an economizing act, for it meant that organisms, however simple and rudimentary they may have been, had begun to capture and preserve, however temporarily, enough energy to offset its entropic flow toward thermodynamic equilibrium. Economizing organisms are catch basins of life-sustaining energy. The initial acts of economizing laid the basis for the evolution of all subsequent organic life. In today's highly elaborated and extended evolutionary world, this core economizing function is performed by business and economic institutions, as well as by myriad forms of organic life. Hence, modern business rests on, and finds its societal rationale in, an ability to forestall the entropic rush of energy toward a condition of lifeless and formless equilibrium. Business practitioners of whatever stripe share a common motivation—to economize, to capture energy, to channel it in self-protective and self-promoting ways so that they and their firms may survive, grow, and develop within the potentials offered by their own personal DNA and within the constraints set by the societies where they do business. Their motives are forged in one of nature's most fundamental furnaces, where entropy and economizing are fused to drive the business system and human society away from thermodynamic equilibrium. In this sense, economizing is the supreme motivator of all business activity.

What generates business productivity and innovation? The natural source of business knowing, creativity, and innovation—the **Creator** component of Nature's Black Box—is the human brain as it interacts with its environment. Composed of several billion neurons (nerve cells) interconnected so that they form an astonishingly complex network, the brain generates symbols or images or representations of what it senses. It might aptly be called the restless brain for it is in constant motion as the axons and dendrites of each nerve cell both send and receive electrochemical impulses or "firings" to and from other neurons. The human brain never sleeps, as everyone knows by the nighttime dreams it manufactures as if an endless video tape depicting strange, wonderful, and weird events and stories. When fully awake and when its circuits are plugged into the circuits of other people, as in a business firm, even more wonderful things can and do regularly happen. The cerebral codes flow together, mix and mingle, creating new and unforeseen blends and patterns. There one finds the fount of creativity and innovation, the source of unique combinations, new inventions, startling insights never glimpsed before, vistas of an emerging future, new markets, novel products, emergent technologies. Recognizing creativity's source in the human brain is equivalent to acknowledging that business innovation is the product of a biological process, a brain-and-environment interaction. Cognition and creativity are not the full story of either business innovation or of the human brain, for environment plays a role though a curious one that is difficult to disentangle from the brain itself.

Adding fascinating detail—and perhaps innovative energy—to the whole neurobiological process is the presence of what some have called the emotional brain, paired with the cognitive, calculative brain, both of them active agents in business strategy, structure, and goal seeking. The **Creator** component undergirds and makes possible all business activity, for if escape from entropy's grasp drives business to economize, knowing how to do it depends on the creativity and innovativeness that spew out of the human brain's neurological circuits.

What shapes business organization? Organization in business is the agency of biological process. That means that the **Organizer** component of

Nature's Black Box is an extrusion of the natural forces that undergird and give life to the business firm. Business organization is built upon three biological bases. One is neural networks mediated by symbolic language. Another is the power-and-dominance hierarchy so common to business firms. A third is systems of social exchange moderated by reciprocal altruism. Each of these organizational patterns is grounded firmly in one type or another of biological process that has proven to have selective advantage through evolutionary time; hence, they are the most substantial, basal, molar organizational elements upon which business firms can be built.

Being organized means being linked to others. In business, those linkages induce cooperation among specialized professional practitioners to achieve the firm's purposes. Person-to-person and group-to-group networks exist, and these networks *are* the firm's organization. At a biological level, they consist of neuron-to-neuron, brain-to-brain, synapse-to-synapse, electrochemical-firing-pattern to electrochemical-firing-pattern linkages and the resulting flow of cerebral codes back and forth between members of the firm and between the company and its stakeholders. In the most basic sense, the substance of business organization is an interconnected flow of symbolic quanta, or packets of meaning, activated as multiple human brains interact with each other. Organization exists only when neurons are interlinked in purposive exchange patterns.

From ethology and primate studies, we learn that organizational form among those creatures most closely related to humans has evolved mainly as a power-and-dominance pattern where alpha males dominate other males and have the widest access to food and females. Of unquestionable genetic origins, this organizational pattern is imprinted widely through other evolutionary lines, including the human species where it prevails across a broad spectrum of human endeavor. The business firm is one of those behavioral realms where the linkages between employees, managers, and owners are mediated by and through a power-and-dominance model. Its biological-genetic-evolutionary base is obvious and irrefutable.

From evolution, the **Organizer** component embraces yet another natural trait. Social exchange, upon which market exchange is based, is an ancient human practice etched deeply into the neural circuitry of Ice Age Pleistocene people and probably owing no little to their even more ancient proto-human ancestors. Accompanying that impulse to exchange was a guardedness to insure if possible that the exchange was perceived as appropriate for the parties to the transaction. Modern game theory offers explanations of the tit-for-tat exchange strategies intended to achieve social reciprocity, thereby avoiding the potential social instability that can arise from unequal or unfair exchanges. A second biologically embedded group practice is found in reciprocal altruism, which ensures genetic continuity through self-sacrificial acts of individuals in behalf of close kin. By extending reciprocal altruistic acts beyond immediate kin to non-kin individuals and groups, a basis is laid for the emergence of a rudimentary moral system. The combination of these two biologically derived behavioral systems—social exchange modulated by game theory strategies, and reciprocal altruism that supports generational continuity by self-sacrificial acts—creates a naturalistic organizational infrastructure contributory to market exchanges and to strategies for resolving moral issues arising from this kind of social exchange among humans.

Thus, the organizational sinews of modern business firms owe much to nature: the neural networks literally join business practitioners together within their firms and into bonding relationships with their stakeholders; the power-and-dominance impulses structure the principal hierarchical organizational systems of the typical business firm; and the linked systems of social exchange and reciprocal altruism govern the organizational dynamics found within today's business corporations. At all points, nature is the foundational element, revealed by the sciences of neurology, ethology, and evolutionary psychology.

What enables the achievement of business goals? To understand the **Enabler** component of Nature's Black Box requires a brief journey into ecosystems and the ways they operate. All organisms live within ecosystems that are composed of sets of interrelated plants and animals and their physical surroundings. Their lives are affected by the niche they acquire and can hold. Their niche is their life base while the niches of all others in the ecosystem comprise their environment. Within that niche base, the organism economizes and in doing so comes in contact with other organisms also economizing in *their* respective niches. In this way, an ecosystem consists of a vast network of interlinked life forms, where each affects all the others and the totality affects the smallest unit. Mutual benefits abound, along with dire threats from competitive or predatory agents. Throughout the ecosystem, internal change is constant as life ebbs and flows among the niches, although the ecosystem itself tends to remain stable over long periods of time.

It is within such ecosystems that business is conducted. The business firm itself is an integral part of the ecosystem. It is composed largely of individual organisms (its employees, managers, and owners), each one an economizing life form seeking and attempting to hold onto a supportive niche. So too is the firm itself a larger life unit—a complex adaptive system charged to economize in economically productive ways. It too seeks a niche within markets and as part of an economy where others do the same.

Like all organisms, business enjoys and seeks to promote mutual benefits with others, while suffering the slings and arrows of vigorous competition from others who covet its niche. As all now realize, change is constant within business ecosystems, as firms jockey for position and advantage. The landscape on which these struggles occur is a test of survival fitness and can be the scene of exultant triumph or disastrous failure. The alert companies search ceaselessly for the keys to competitive success, spurring a drive for economizing efficiency and technological innovations.

Business is enabled to economize, to be creative and productive, and to organize people and resources by the naturalistic traits of the ecosystems in which the firm operates. From the self-seeking behaviors of many firms there emerge strong supportive mutual advantages for all participants. That may sound like Adam Smith speaking but it isn't. It's the voice of nature. Mutualistic economizing occurs all the time: competitive alliances, coalitions, mergers, regional compacts to regulate trade, and international agreements to control transnational pollutants. These arrangements allow business to go forward by finding ways that are beneficial to many parties, and in that way they reveal their kinship with all kinds of biologically based mutualisms found widely throughout the organic world.

It is in such a nonlinear world of ecosystem dynamics that business is conducted, a realm where the shortest distance is frequently not the best route, clear goals blur as they are approached, carefully crafted strategies miss maddeningly elusive targets, yardsticks and benchmarks swell and shrink, and the future is but a phantom shadow of present experience. Faced with such nonlinearity, it is understandable why modern business minds have found so alluring the seeming stability of the precision, measurement, and predictability offered up by accountants, financial experts, economists, and computer analysts. But it will not be until they grasp that their businesses are irretrievably subsumed within unpredictable, unmeasurable, imprecise nonlinear ecosystem dynamics that they will be fully enabled to practice the business they seek and to promote the kind of business the world needs.

Many questions remain. Business practitioners will want to know what practical difference it makes to know that they are beholden to and perhaps even driven by natural forces. Are they thereby ensnared within a natural cage that provides no outlet for individual judgment, making them mere captive automatons responding passively and obediently to nature's demands and whims? Do business plans, strategies, initiatives undertaken, carefully crafted analyses, innovative organizational systems, clever marketing programs count for nothing? Has an indifferent nature programmed each firm's actions, set each manager and employee on a predetermined course, and left the outcome to be decided by nature's own fickle, fluctuating, and sometimes ominous powers? More fundamentally, does nature rule the bottom line?

And what of human culture? Does it have a role? Is nature all, or is it only part of the story? Have we not learned that a corporation's culture is key to its success or failure? Have not many corporate mergers foundered on the shoals of incompatible cultures? Does culture regulate, moderate, and redirect nature's powers toward humanly sought ends?

Then there is the question of moral governance. Can nature's own governors—the moral safeguards offered by social exchange and reciprocal altruism—be trusted to do the job? Are the natural forces that drive business conduct powerful enough to overwhelm the moral, aesthetic, humanitarian dimensions favored by societies everywhere? More intriguingly and optimistically, can a governing and humane morality perhaps be found within nature itself?

These are the questions. Some of the answers are found in the next chapters of Part III, but let me say this now to business practitioners: Nature can be your powerful ally if you get to know its ways. Its grip on you and your firm is not unyielding or inescapable. Nature's realm is infinitely variable. It provides opportunities galore for those who value freedom of enterprise and individual initiative. Nature is the fount of productivity and innovation sought by every business firm. Tapping and releasing the vast store of organizational energy found within a company's employees, managers, and supportive stakeholders can be achieved only when mindful of people's natural proclivities to self-organize and self-direct. Business itself is one of nature's creations. If it is to find its way toward the goals of its directors and managers, if it is to fit successfully and effectively within its natural surroundings, and if it is to be both admired and sought as a valuable, indispensable feature of society, then practitioners must become as familiar with the natural forces that shape the firm as with the shape and form they seek to impart to it by their goal-seeking decisions.

And I add this note to business scholars, teachers, and researchers: You teach, study, and write of nature whether you know it or not. The behavior, the motives, the organizational systems, the strategies, the goals, the outcomes—all bear the mark of nature's processes, are indeed themselves nothing but nature speaking the language of business while insinuating its subtle influence deep within the business mind. Business is not merely *like* nature. Business *is* nature.

YEAR 1998

[Public confidence in big business: 30%]

CORPORATION AND COMMUNITY:
BONDED BY NATURE

Setting the Scene. Complexity theory carries some discomforting messages alien to the rationalist theory of management. Rather than being "managed," large-scale systems such as corporations have a way of "managing" themselves according to the laws of nature. Corporations' social role—their social and moral responsibility—is an outcome of these uncertain and unpredictable natural forces, which can only minimally be rationally directed towards socially desirable goals and purposes. What then becomes of the quest for CSR? Confronted with this puzzle—indeed, this powerful challenge to the very concept of acting responsibly—I soon realized that the puzzle's solution lay in the very nature-based values that sustain human life and induce socially cooperative attitudes and actions. CSR is itself, sui generis, an expression and manifestation of nature.

The major goal here is to present a naturological account of corporation-community relations. A *naturological* explanation draws on natural science for description, evidence, and verification. By contrast, a *culturological* explanation proceeds from a base in social science to describe, verify, and provide evidence of theoretical hypotheses and research propositions.

This new naturological way of thinking is centered in complexity theory, a variant of chaos theory which explains the organizational and evolutionary dynamics that occur as complex living systems interact with each other and with their environments. The overarching theme will be that both corporation and community are natural systems interacting and coevolving in response to biological and physical processes. The corporation is hypothesized as a complex adaptive system and the host community as a dense interactive network of diverse adaptive systems. The goal is to find and describe the role that the corporation plays, and should play, in its interactions with the host community.

The solution emerges from the *naturalistic base* that sustains both business and community through evolutionary time. Within that base, one finds the value sets that drive corporate decisions and policies, as well as the community's preferred values. At times, these value sets compete; at other times, they work in harmony. However, at all times, they are in constant motion and constant tension. In this view, the normative relationship between corporation and community, while stabilized by the value commitments of each system, remains open to continuous change and redefinition over time stemming from the dynamics of the two complex living systems and the relative strengths of the ever-shifting values found in each.

Such a natural science approach to business-and-society relationships opens up an imaginative, and possibly fruitful, way for organization theorists, strategic management scholars, corporate practitioners, and civic officials to understand their respective roles in shaping the decisions, policies, and practices of corporations within their host communities.

Using Nature as an Explanatory Variable

Naturological explanations of human (and business) behavior are not as popular or as well known as culturological ones, especially among social scientists and those with derivative social science backgrounds found throughout the business school. Natural science approaches tend to create a decided sense of disciplinary discomfort such as the professional risk of venturing into an unfamiliar discipline, as well as the ideological unease and fear of endorsing uncontrollable behavioral constraints and thereby surrendering personal autonomy.

In spite of these sometimes well-founded reservations, it becomes increasingly difficult to ignore nature's beckoning calls when thinking about the modern corporation and global economics. El Nino alone has revealed the scope of economic havoc wreaked by natural forces—from California's battered coasts, to Canadians ravaged by a massive ice storm, to Indonesia's forest fires so vast their smoke blanketed much of Southeastern Asia, to Papua New Guinea's devastating drought and destructive tidal waves, to African climatic shifts that spell future trouble, and brutal heat waves that shrivel farm crops here and elsewhere. Even in more "normal" times, floods, earthquakes, volcanic eruptions, tornadoes, hurricanes, monsoons, red tides, snowstorms, avalanches, sand storms, and other natural disasters disrupt settled life and the economic prospects of business and agriculture. Then there is the well-known list of environmental threats—global warming, rain forest depletion, acid rain, declining ground-water tables, creeping desertification on one-quarter of earth's land area, salinization of fresh-water supplies, radiation perils, industrial pollution, arable land erosion, chemical runoffs from industry and agriculture, etc., which make inroads on corporate earnings and require new corporate strategies. Add to this the genetics revolution that threatens to supplement, if not displace, the culturological explanations of human behavior on which all management and organization theories are founded.

At some point, one must ask, Can business scholars afford to ignore nature or pretend that it falls outside the normal scope of corporate operations? Can we continue to act as though a pesky Nature will sooner or later go away, thereby allowing us to spin out our theories in a culture-centered, nature-free way? The risks of doing so are great. More importantly, they can be avoided by embracing, not ignoring, what the natural sciences have to say about human behavior, including business behavior.

Culturology's View of the Corporate Social Role

During the last half of the 20th century, business-and-society scholars have offered three solutions to the question of business's community role.

Social Responsibility. Beginning in the 1950s, the most popular, though hardly the most effective, proposal has been that corporations should voluntarily shoulder many social burdens, largely through philanthropic support and/or lending executive expertise to community agencies, schools, art institutions, local government, United Way, and other such non-profit community groups. Here, business's civic role is like that of any public-spirited citizen. A somewhat expanded version of social responsibility has become prominent in the 1990s, known as the stakeholder theory of the firm, which requires corporations to pay some attention to everyone in the community who has a "stake" in what the company does.

Government Regulation and Public Policy. When voluntary social responsibility proved too weak and ineffectual during the 1960s and 1970s to confront and solve troublesome social problems attributed to business—racism, sexism, consumerism, pollution, war-and-peace, etc.—government and politics were called upon to put the social reins on Big (and small) Business. So, business's community role was to be defined by public policy guidelines, laws, and regulations, all enforced by the courts.

Business Ethics. With the ethics scandals of the 1980s (Wall Street junk-bond kings, the savings & loan debacle, rampant "Me"ism), business ethics was thrust forward as yet another approach. The idea here was to school, or retool, top-level executives in workplace ethics, giving them a stronger regard for human rights, fairness, and justice, and reminding them that their own role behavior could set an inspiring ethical tone for all employees. Training in virtue ethics was to develop ethical character, with the presumption that such corporate leadership would improve a company's relations with the public.

Something can be said for all three approaches, and there is an impressive research literature supporting each way of defining and operationalizing business's social role. However—and this is the reason for rehearsing this history—*to date there is no resolution of the basic issue— no "Eureka!" Fifty years of top-flight scholarship has not produced a satisfactory, or even an approximate, answer.* There is still no point at which one can say with confidence that the community role of business is X or Y or Z—or that business's civic responsibility is discharged when it does A or B or C. Communities and corporations throughout the world now confront a range of daunting issues involving corporate practices and community welfare, while consensus on the respective roles of corporation and community remains elusive. Conventional culturology has yet to find its way towards clear answers.

The contrasting naturological argument is made in three parts. The first outlines the essential elements of complexity theory. The second argues that the corporation is a type of complex adaptive system driven by nature-based value clusters. The third section defines the community as a dense network of diverse, complex adaptive systems. A concluding section presents a naturological answer to culturology's 50-year-old (unanswered) question: What is business's social role in the community?

Complexity Theory: An Overview

In its initial and purest formulation, complexity theory's language was and remains mathematics—not your garden-variety mathematics but non-linear differential equations, three- and four-dimensional graphics, and other numerical exotica. Its original "applied" venue was meteorology, arising from the uncertainties and frustrations of trying to predict the weather. Biology and biological change followed closely after, as attempts were made to model evolutionary change.

Complexity theory is a variant or offspring of Darwinian evolutionary theory. Darwin argued that biological evolution occurs through natural selection as organisms interact with an environment presenting both opportunities and threats. Those traits, behavioral, morphological, and physiological, that help an organism survive are "selected for" through a constant interplay of organism and environment. The result is a "fit" between the two as an organism finds an adaptive environmental niche. Such fit organisms then pass their fitness traits along to their offspring, while less fit ones are weeded out over the long term.

Darwin's successors in the 20th century—called neo-Darwinians—added the wrinkle of genetic change to the evolutionary story. They say that the genes (DNA) that reside in each organism's cells are the driving and guiding force of evolution. By determining organic processes, physiology, structure, and behavioral impulses, the genes in effect make the organism behave in ways that guarantee *the genes'* own replication. Thus, genes are said to be "selfish," centered on their own replication and survival. For neo-Darwinians, no trait will survive the natural selection process unless it serves its genetic masters. This proposition has become highly controversial in societies that value freedom, autonomy, and flexibility. Most people resist the idea of being a genetic calculating machine and therefore may welcome the openness and implicit optimism of complexity theory's main thrust.

Complexity theory takes one step beyond Darwinism and neo-Darwinism and is a kind of overlay on or supplement to them. *Its principal contention is that organization arises spontaneously and is adaptive.* That means that organic life emerged spontaneously, then adapted to its environment, and survived to reproduce itself. The same principle or process operates in all forms of organic life, including humans, plants, and animals. Another more dramatic and comprehensive way of stating the idea is that *organic order is built into the universe—it emerges without external guidance.*

Four Core Concepts Anchor Complexity Theory

In the abbreviated account given here, four leading concepts are featured. The first is *Self-Organization*, a spontaneous ordering process that can occur in organisms and in non-living material components as well. The self-assembly can take place at the atomic, molecular, and cellular levels.

Self-assembly is the hallmark of all organic life. Cells, when provided with energy in the form of light or heat or other nutrients, spontaneously move into combination with other cells to form organs and to regulate vital processes. A developing embryo self-assembles, once the egg is fertilized. A tree self-assembles from the seed. A tadpole spontaneously becomes a frog, a larval worm a butterfly. While genetic encoding sketches out the general pathways to be followed, the genetic imprint is activated by interactions among the many cellular and molecular components involved. The encoded order blooms under the influence of the spontaneously interacting parts. More important for present purposes, this self-organizing tendency is also a potential presence in all forms of human organization, including corporations. The ubiquity of self-organization throughout nature hints at some kind of subtle, hidden, innate order.

This kind of self-organization is greatly assisted by one of those jaw-breaker terms complexifiers love to use—*Autocatalysis*. The idea, if not the term, is simple enough. It means that the parts being combined speed up the combination or the self-assembly process. There is an active feedback process going on, so that what one cell does stimulates action by other cells, and then those other cells interact with the original cell, and on and on in an accelerating process. As we shall see, autocatalytic change in self-organized systems can lead to very, very rapid rates of change and varying directions of change, until a state of chaos is threatened.

Third is the idea of a *Complex Adaptive System (CAS)*. When self-assembly occurs in living systems, the result is the formation of an interrelated and usually *complex* set of cells, atoms, molecules, organs, etc., that collectively have the ability to *adapt* to the environment in a *systematic* way. Every living organism, whether mosquito, orchid, kangaroo, or human being, is a complex adaptive system. So too are organized groups of organisms, e.g., a beehive, a pride of lions, a church, a corporation. In one way or another, each CAS manages to adapt to the surrounding conditions it finds—or conversely it may not adapt.

Whether it will be successful depends on its skills in maneuvering around, through, and across what is called a *Fitness Landscape*, which is the fourth core concept. Picture a broad landscape composed of mountains and valleys, hills and plains of varying height and expanse. Getting around is a test of an organism's ability to fit in or adapt. Scaling the highest peaks symbolizes good fitness. Some get to the top, others settle for the lower slopes, while still others take up abode in the valleys and plains. Fitness landscapes are dangerous places—one misstep is all it takes. A fish swimming too close to the water's surface becomes an osprey's lunch. A maker of buggy whips—or Apple computers? [Oops!]—soon joins the jobless ranks. A command-and-control economy loses out in the competitive global race. To avoid this fate, each CAS seeks out a secure niche within the particular fitness landscape that is its home. Vigilance, cleverness, flexibility, and creativity are the qualities that maximize its chances of success.

The kinship of these four concepts to Darwinian evolution is too obvious to miss. Only the language is new. Living forms emerge, evolve into more complex forms, adapt to their environment, and the fittest ones survive. But there is a fork in the evolutionary road. Complexity theory takes the unfamiliar path.

The Edge of Chaos

Complex adaptive systems (CASs), when moving around on their fitness landscapes, face another problem of profound importance—so profound that it involves nothing less than their survival. This time, the threat comes from the internal dynamics of self-organizing systems. Because they are autocatalytic systems subject to rapid and unpredictable change, CASs are potentially unstable. They may evolve so rapidly and in such diverse ways that they self-destruct. In other words, self-organization may lead to self-destruction. An organism's self-assembly may produce poor adaptive skills—there is no Darwinian guarantee written into the process. Or autocatalytic change may get out of control and drive the CAS to destroy itself, as with cancer or AIDS. Or a better-assembled competitor with superior autocatalytic abilities may push another CAS out of its niche.

CASs that change in this way enter a zone of random-like behavior verging on chaos. Too far into that zone, their wild movements and gyrations appear to be completely out of control—or as organizational theorists would say, they become unmanageable. Their ability to find a niche in the fitness landscape disappears in a flurry of uncontrollable, dizzying oscillations. They have gone over the edge of stability into the chaos zone *and beyond*. They die. A plant closes down. A savings & loan defaults. A nation's economy plunges into misery. Stock markets crash. The jobless go hungry, or riot, and sink further into poverty.

The idea of chaos, in the hands of complexity theorists, takes on a special meaning. In spite of outward appearances, it does not mean totally out-of-control behavior. *Within the chaos zone*, a hidden order may be concealed beneath what looks like utter randomness. These latent regularities are difficult to discern because chaotic change usually occurs in the form of branching, chain-reaction, accelerated movement. The more branching-points (they are called "bifurcations") there are, the more complex and potentially catastrophic the changes become. Chaotic change within an organization thus occurs in these branching layers or bands and can quickly lead to precipitous, catastrophic decline and disorder.

For the best CASs there may be a way to escape this fate. The key to survival turns out to be the latent and subtle orderliness lurking within the chaos zone. Once having gained a foothold on one of those fitness peaks, a CAS has demonstrated its skill in adapting to its environment. If it can channel its own autocatalytic tendencies just enough to stay there and possibly even inch up higher, it may enjoy a long life rather than plunging into the abyss of utter randomness and decay.

The trick is to hover between too rapid, directionless change and too little change, where it might be overtaken by unfriendly environmental forces. Its best chance occurs at the *Edge of Chaos* (EOC). Evolution carries each CAS to a zone or region between order and disorder called the Edge of Chaos, which is the CAS's point of maximum fitness and adaptability. It is the CAS's "best of worlds"—and its potentially worst nightmare. Poised on this evolutionary edge, one critical misstep can unleash a cascade of disastrous events. If a corporation (i.e., a CAS) clings too tightly to the factors that helped it attain its present niche, it will be overtaken and pushed out by a more determined CAS (i.e., a competitor firm). But if the company can step right up to the edge of chaos—in other words, if it can let its autocatalytic forces generate new adaptive skills (e.g., technological innovations for the firm), then and there is where it maximizes its future possibilities and can realize its inherent potentials.

Getting to that critical point and staying there depends on what complexity theorists call a "strange attractor." It is the key to fitness success when a CAS faces a chaos/beyond-chaos choice.

Strange Attractor

Of all the bizarre, exotic ideas to be found in complexity theory, none tops the notion of *Strange Attractor*. Nevertheless, its meaning and significance can be made reasonably clear.

A CAS's strange attractor "does" two things. It describes the CAS's movements through time and space—the many pathways the CAS takes from day-to-day, month-to-month, and year-to-year (if it lasts that long). *These pathways are never exactly the same and are not precisely predictable.* In a sense, any CAS associated with a strange attractor continually explores the terrain of its fitness landscape, seeking new footholds that may boost it up to higher levels on the fitness peaks. Innovation is a built-in quality of any strange attractor because of the differential orbits it prescribes for the CAS. Who knows what it will encounter on these unpredictable journeys—perhaps risks and dangers, perhaps novel opportunities?

However, while generating variety and diversity of adaptation, the strange attractor also literally "attracts" or pulls the CAS toward a broad *range* of behaviors. It is drawn toward an inertial state but displays a dynamic one. A strange attractor permits change while providing order. Aha! That must mean that it can lead a CAS (i.e., an organization) just up to the Edge of Chaos but hold it back from plunging over the edge into extreme, destructive, disordered behavior. This means that an organization's (a CAS's) key to survival and continued fitness success is to be found in its strange attractor.

The Corporation's Strange Attractor

The corporation's Strange Attractor—the component that permits change within constrained limits—is its value system. The main corporate value clusters—economizing, growth, power-aggrandizing, technologizing, etc.—originated in nature and continue to express nature's powerful influence on corporate operations, practices, and culture. Together, they hold the corporation to a recognizable order—organizational roles, standard operating procedures, permitted information flows, short-range goals, allocation of work responsibilities—while opening the company to innovations, new explorations, and new discoveries that carry it along in diverse, varying, and unpredictable directions. The push and pull of its value clusters ultimately determines the corporation's fate—its success in balancing between order and disorder, adaptation and decline, self-organization and entropy, service to humankind and an inward-looking, power-centered self-interest.

But this natural history of the corporation is not yet fully told, for the fitness landscape on which it maneuvers is likewise sculpted by natural forces. Scholars are accustomed to calling that economic, social, and political landscape "the community." Is it possible that nature has hidden the key to business's social role somewhere within the community itself?

Community as Ecosystem

The classic question posed by business-and-society scholars has been: What is a community and what is the proper way to define the relations between corporation and community? *Culturological* explanations of community have emphasized the personal and institutionalized ties between people living in proximity to one another. Communities are seen as collections of political, governmental, societal, ethnic, tribal, religious, and cultural institutions, each with a history, a loyal following, and a stakeholder status justifying claims to ethical treatment by corporate decision makers.

A *naturological* explanation emphasizes that a community is not a group, not a collection of institutions, not simply a legal unit, not a society nor a culture, people, or government. Nor is the community a bounded geographical space. A community may *contain* all of these things but it cannot be defined as any one of them or all of them added together.

A community is an ecological system—an ecosystem—consisting of interlinked organisms living within an abiotic (non-living) setting. It has no center and no edges. All communities are ecosystems open to the widest range of external influences. They are dynamic, coevolving populations of people, plants, animals, bacteria, etc., linked together by natural processes, responsive to each other and to the forces that stitched them into a collective, coherent whole.

A community's dynamic is driven by the ceaseless, persistent economizing activities of its resident organisms as they respond to thermodynamic energy fluxes that penetrate all levels of the ecosystem. Each organism is a complex adaptive system entirely dependent for its life on all of the other organisms within the ecosystem.

A community exhibits an enormously complex overlapping interplay among diverse CASs. Each CAS has its own strange attractor—its own preferred value set—pushing it towards the edge of chaos but holding it back from unbridled turbulence. *The corporation is one of these community CASs.* So too are governments, schools, mass media, transport systems, mail services, utilities, hospitals, museums, religious bodies, civic organizations, families, individuals, non-human animals, plants, bacteria, and all other forms of living matter. What appears to the naked eye as a single entity—the community—is revealed as *a mosaic of interacting values.* As much as anything else, a community is a great staging arena where values meet, collide, clash, compete, and blend. Or, as complexity theory would say, a community is myriad CASs hitched to diverse and sometimes competing strange attractors.

The stunning complexity can be sensed by realizing that the fitness landscape of each CAS consists of all the other CASs in the ecosystem plus the non-living environmental forces of nature (climate, geology, gravity, solar energy flows, etc.). This tangled yet strangely patterned fitness landscape constantly shifts, presenting each CAS with a never-ending challenge to adapt or perish. The fate of each one is bound up in the fate of all. Internal autocatalytic change generates a constant stream of novelties. Techno-symbolic forces create new opportunities and new threats. Physical environmental processes—volcanic eruptions, earthquakes, droughts, massive floods, etc.—de-form and shift the fitness landscape. Value change within society modifies the force of strange attractors, increasing some, diminishing others. New competitors riding new strange attractors threaten to dislodge established CASs from their environmental niches. Amidst all of this turbulence, some scale the peaks and find a niche among their neighbors, while others lose their footing and are replaced.

As complexity theory maintains, the future of this community ecosystem cannot be predicted. Both corporation and community are nonlinear systems, linked together, driven by their respective and intertwined strange attractors, their behaviors indeterminate, unpredictable, and largely uncontrollable though not "out of control." One further conclusion is obvious: corporation and community are, if not one, then surely tied inseparably together. Business does not stand apart but is an integral piece of the total community ecosystem. Nature teaches this profound lesson: *There is no boundary between business and society.* Their fates are as intertwined as the doubled helical strands of DNA that give life to us all.

The CSR Puzzle Solved

After this long journey through complexity land, the long-sought answer is now at hand. Complexity theory allows us to see that *nature drives the social role of business.* Corporation and community are engaged in a highly dramatic dance, a kind of grand ballet. It is not a *pas de deux*—a duet of company and community—but one that encompasses the entire *corps de ballet*—all members of the community—in a kind of wild orgy of swirling, dizzying, chaotic rhythms and patterns. Nature choreographs this dance of life, setting each member of company and community free to dance to the music composed by its own Strange Attractor.

But patterns are discernible, just as they are within any system of deterministic chaos. The relations between a company and its host community reflect past history. Some began with a company-town relationship—the company *was* the town, and vice versa. Or an industrial-financial complex predominated, as in Pittsburgh in the 19th and early 20th centuries. Or a mushroom-like growth of high-technology firms in the Silicon Valley created a different set of "initial conditions" (a critically important feature of complex systems). The launching of these ties was all-important in setting the pattern of future relationships in each case and could bring either strength or weakness. Pittsburgh's initial conditions left it economically and socially vulnerable following the collapse of its steel industry infrastructure in the 1980s, while California's high-tech beginnings underwrote high but sometimes unstable rates of economic growth and job creation.

Because corporation and community comprise one large coevolving, nonlinear system, business's civic role is ever-evolving, always indeterminate, a moving target. The corporation's *mission* is set by its value clusters: economizing, power-aggrandizing, technologizing, and the many individual-personal-ethnic distinctions of its workforce. They push the company into varying orbits, always striving for a fitness niche on its always-changing landscape. *The corporation's civic actions thus are a function of the interplay of its own strange attractor values and the values of others in the ecosystem.* All people within the community also economize, organize and seek power, are part of an ecological system, display X-factor values in great abundance and variety, and explore the environment (i.e., the fitness landscape) in techno-symbolic ways. Although all embrace the same general kinds or types of values, hence giving rise to order and stability in a given community tradition, the ways of realizing them can vary greatly from person to person, group to group, and company to company, thus giving rise to almost infinite variety. This corporation-community system is complex and chaotic, therefore both self-organizing and open to infinite possibilities. The system contains its own instability and its own sense of order. Corporation-community relations become a push-pull among attractors, stable and unstable, dynamic, relativistic, turbulent. The "boundary" conditions between corporation and community are inherently uncertain, unpredictable, and potentially chaotic but not often destructive of either party.

Given the innate indeterminacy of corporation-community ties, it is little wonder that *the* social role of business has eluded scholars, corporate policy makers, and civic officials for so long. There are *many* civic roles for business. They vary from time to time, from community to community, and are entirely a matter determined by the interplay of natural forces that are themselves unpredictable and uncertain.

The Lessons of Mutualism

Recognizing that business has no single societal role is not equivalent to walking away from the many perplexing issues raised at the corporation-community interface. The essence of ecology—the trait that marks every ecosystem—is the presence of *mutualisms*, those symbiotic bonds that shelter and secure life for cooperating organisms. These mutual-aid bondings include not only the coordinated support found among the ants in a colony or the chimpanzees in a clan but extend to cross-species networks of mutual support—the bees that pollinate flowering plants, the bacteria that help digest our food, the photosynthetic organisms that provide oxygen to all aerobic creatures.

Business is learning this central lesson that nature teaches. The Montreal Compact, the Rio Conference, the Kyoto Protocol, the Caux Principles, and the CERES-Exxon Valdez Principles testify to business's sometimes begrudging but newly-awakened ecological conscience and a willingness to think beyond the economizing bottom line. Mutualistic thinking is slowly but surely seeping into the executive mind. Whether induced by social responsibility, government regulation, or a rising ethical awareness matters little, so long as the community impulse is there.

There *is* a tangible community role for managers that carries them beyond the barebones economizing process, and it begins at home, *within* the corporation. It requires great moral courage and creative moral leadership to face up to the tensions that nature breeds within corporate value systems. Here is a partial list of what might be done by managers to improve relations between corporation and community:

- Distinguish between productive economizing growth and the bloat of expansionist glory

- Accept the ecological limits set by nature as a constraint on bottom-line urges and marketing impulses

- Know that technology can pulverize some as it liberates and enriches others

- Release the latent self-organizing, innovative impulses within the company's workforce, thereby allowing this discretionary energy to flow into productive channels

- Nourish, honor, and shield the personal values held by the corporate citizenry who devote their skills to achieving the company's goals

- Acknowledge the presence and power of the covert spirituality quest concealed within the hearts and minds of employees and managers

- Overcome the moral muteness so prevalent within the corporate workplace

- Blend and harmonize the corporation's economizing mission with the strivings of others, not dominating, disrupting, trampling on, or destroying its community neighbors in the name of its own mission but seeking a niche mutually advantageous to corporation and community.

Taking these steps can only fructify, magnify, and enrich the life opportunities of all CASs within any community ecosystem. They become in effect the corporation's naturological responsibilities, defined by a nature long evolved and anciently patterned by the hidden order lurking within nonlinear natural systems.

But the story does not end there. The community, too, along with its leaders, must face up to nature's demands. The public is beginning to grasp and absorb some of nature's hard lessons. Indeed, it must, as the global ecosystem expands to envelop ever-widening spheres of daily life, from the U.S. heartland to the remotest Indonesian village (or as the Indonesians might say, from the Indonesian heartland to the remotest U.S. village). New fitness demands are being placed on all the world's CASs by the onrush of new electronic technologies and the shifting economic fortunes of nations. New skills are being created and must be learned. New industries emerge and must find resilient community homes. Within this boiling, bubbling, roiling global stew, each "local" community must find its way, secure its niche, know and accept its diverse values, and plug in to the global network. To do otherwise within this rapidly self-organizing system is to forfeit one's place on today's fitness landscape. Tapping nature's sometimes latent secrets of self-organization and coevolution is now a prime responsibility of community, as well as corporate, leaders.

As the 20th century closes down, nature is treating the world to one of its grandiose upheavals. That is the way of complexity, to push corporation and community to the edge of chaos while discovering mutually supportive values, a blend of strange attractors holding all back from the abyss, where none possesses an *a priori* claim of precedence and all can seek a secure niche.

But complexity theory is no magic bullet. It has little or nothing to say about the specific values, or combinations of values, that can bring corporation and community together. Such a theoretical task not only has not been undertaken but it does not appear to have been seriously contemplated by the main body of complexity theorists. The claim made here that *strange attractors embody and enact the core values of each and every complex adaptive system* is an initial, tentative step toward resolving that larger normative question. When values are understood to be the driving adaptive force of all complex adaptive systems, one can better appreciate their tenacity and persistence—and indeed their necessitous nature. Their regulative function of holding an organism, a person, a corporation back from the pitfalls of total chaos gives hope. Their interwoven interdependence that creates life-support networks throughout any ecosystem community hints at common normative threads among the many diverse patterns making up the whole.

Accepting this view could mean something of overriding importance for corporate decision makers and strategic planners, for organization theorists and management scholars, for civic officials charged with community responsibilities, and for the general community citizenry. Together, they might then one day find and put in place the nature-based values of mutualism and cooperation that in the end will and must sustain both corporation and community.

YEAR 2002

BUSINESS, BIOLOGY, AND MORALITY

Setting the Scene. In April 2002, the theme of the Ruffin Lectures sponsored by the Darden School at the University of Virginia was Business, Science, and Ethics. Primatologist Frans de Waal, evolutionary psychologist Leda Cosmides, management theorist Paul Lawrence, and philosopher Edwin Hartman lectured, as did I. My lecture, presented here in condensed form, expanded on naturological themes developed in the two preceding chapters (__Year 1998__ and __Year 2000__), and concluded that reaching CSR goals may be far more difficult than anyone has realized.

The business firm, called here the Evolutionary Firm (EF), is proposed as a natural entity. The firm's motives, organization, productivity, strategy, and moral significance are a direct outgrowth of natural evolution. Its managers, directors, and employees are natural agents enacting and responding to biological, physical, and ecological impulses inherited over evolutionary time from ancient human ancestors. Their decisions and policies are molded, sometimes haphazardly, other times effectively, by complex environmental natural forces over which they exert little or no direct rational control but which require highly attuned pragmatic skills. The normative significance of the EF—its moral deficits and credits—is understood only after peeling back the successive organizational and behavioral strata laid down through evolutionary time to reveal the values, ethics, and moral precepts left standing by natural selection.

An Overview of the Evolutionary Firm

All business firms—large or small, domestically sheltered or globally exposed, giant corporation or neighborhood proprietor, prospector for minerals or producer of complex software, hawker of goods or provider of services—are Evolutionary Firms. They are made so by responding to

Figure 1

THE EVOLUTIONARY FIRM'S FIVE CORE FUNCTIONS

- **MOTIVATOR/DRIVER**

  The central motive of business operations

- **INNOVATOR/GENERATOR**

  The source of innovation and productivity

- **ORGANIZER/COORDINATOR**

  The firm's organizational systems

- **ENABLER/STRATEGIZER**

  Strategic management to achieve business goals

- **MORALIZER/VALUATOR**

  Moral impulses operative within the firm

insistent, unyielding pressures of nature that impel them to be what they are and to do what they do. Natural selection has implanted motives deep within the firm's core structure, has given it the gift of creativity and productivity, has laid down organizational pathways, has enabled it to maneuver (though perilously) across competitive landscapes, and has imbued it with a troubling, vexatious moral impulse.

The Evolutionary Firm (EF) displays five principal operations and core functions (see Figure 1). The **Motivator/Driver** function conditions all activities and features of the EF, while the **Moralizer/Valuator** function expresses the EF's moral stature. The other three functions, **Innovator/Generator, Organizer/Coordinator,** and **Enabler/Strategizer**, also affect the firm's moral status in important ways.

Lying behind, supporting, and activating each of these five functions are distinctive, identifiable natural processes.

- **Thermodynamics** defines and sustains the principal business motive of economizing.

- **The brain's symbolic/neural circuits** drive business productivity and innovation.

- Two natural components—**symbolic language networks** and **coercive power systems**—shape the firm's organizational architecture.

- **Complex ecosystem dynamics** dictate the firm's search for a sustainable strategy.

- **Embedded neural algorithms** (the brain's "hard-wiring") activate conflicting moral impulses within the firm.

The firm's organic core is a coalition—an alliance, a collective, a team—of biological agents (i.e., people) who act collectively and symbolically as an adaptive unit, displaying a suite of organic behaviors, interacting with environment as do all organisms, and thus subject to natural selection. The human members of the coalition include owners, directors, managers, employees, and others who enable the firm to do its work. In most firms, especially the larger ones, multiple coalitions exist, often with overlapping memberships; ideally, they cooperate in pursuing the firm's goals but frequently compete with each other. As biological agents acting in behalf of the firm, these human (organic) coalitions are subject to natural selection pressures.

To anticipate much of the following discussion, the central thesis can be expressed this way: *The confluence and contradictions among these underlying natural forces produce the distinctive, peculiar moral proclivities and ethical dilemmas of the Evolutionary Firm.* This claim is not equivalent to saying that nature defines morality or is itself moral. Moral value (and its converse) is a human conceptual invention, an assigned quality, made possible by human judgment which is itself a natural process. Morality is not in nature but emerges from judgments about natural processes that affect human welfare. Morality is in this sense a reflexive relationship between natural process and human judgment. Evolutionary change produces biologically adaptive (and maladaptive) behaviors whose consequences are judged by humans to be either moral or immoral. In addition to these moral proclivities associated directly with organic adaptation are the many ethical themes generated by human experience as lived in highly diverse sociocultural settings. However, these cultural themes, too, are subject to a natural evolutionary calculus, as discussed later.

The Firm's Motivator/Driver Function

Outwitting entropy through economizing. The primary natural force responsible for business motives is found within the operation of thermodynamic laws. These physical processes set the basic conditions under which all living organisms exist and sustain themselves over time. All life entities must acquire and process sufficient energy to begin life, build their basic cellular structure, and develop whatever growth potential is present in their genetic makeup. By capturing energy and incorporating it within themselves, living beings are responding to nature's thermodynamic laws.

Using energy always converts it into some less useful form. This tendency of energy to be degraded until it is no longer available to do work is called "entropy." All life entities, including the business firm, are driven to find and use energy. In doing so, they produce entropy in the form of degraded energy, wastes, and pollution. Within the living space firms occupy, their constant need is to absorb energy, using it to build and maintain an organizational structure, and letting the energy drive the firms onward, striving to stay ahead of the entropy wave that they themselves are helping to create. Entropy constantly bears down upon all living entities. Evading or avoiding or postponing it is essential.

The firm's search for energy to exceed entropy and for organizational order to repel disorder and dissolution is ceaseless because entropy carries the danger of increasing faster than the firm can absorb and use energy to do its work. The only way a firm can sustain itself over time is to have a favorable energy-to-entropy ratio. *To achieve such a favorable ratio is the central driving force—the core motivator—of business activity. Economizing* is an attempt to acquire enough energy (in the form of capital, technology, natural resources, people, information, skills) to produce something of marketable value (goods, services, information), using revenues (and borrowed funds) to build and maintain an organizational structure and expand the firm's operations, while minimizing costs.

The larger significance of business economizing, aside from its importance for each individual firm, is that the societies who host such firms depend upon this vital process if there is to be human collective life. In this regard, it is possible to say that the economizing business firm is one of nature's most brilliant, though flawed, inventions.

The growth imperative. A thermodynamic specter haunts the lives of all who occupy places within or interact with the Evolutionary Firm: its directors, managers, employees, stakeholders, and dependent communities. Because the EF, as a successful economizer, may generate entropy in proportions equaling or even exceeding the levels of incoming energy, information, and order, it feels the pressure of thermodynamic selection keenly. It risks having its pollutants outrun its production, its costs exceed its revenues. As technology and information seem to lift it out of the entropic slough, the firm's organizational systems may (and often do) impede the acceptance of the new technologies, while information overload (e.g., a torrent of e-mail messages) clogs communications and usage channels. Order and regularity may slide toward disorder and chaos. As economizing flags and entropy looms, excess personnel are let go ("downsized"), inefficient plants are closed or moved to low-cost nonunionized areas or Third World locales, services are outsourced, budgets are trimmed, managers are put on notice to reduce costs—or else.

Entropy is a voracious beast with an unlimited appetite. Feeding its maw is a case of hope struggling against fate. Vaguely but uneasily aware they are up against an implacable enemy, the EF's managers must search for ways to enhance productivity while reducing or foregoing costs. They turn first to expansive growth. Their laboratories and product development departments bring out new products; their marketing programs seek to undercut rivals by increasing the firm's market share; their global strategists explore and exploit ever-widening markets around the world; they flog their suppliers to reduce costs and speed deliveries ("just-in-time"); their shrewd financial analysts identify ways to diminish competitive pressures by merging with or acquiring competitors, or to expand through technology-sharing alliances, market-sharing joint ventures, let's-not-compete partnerships, or government bail-out deals. Presumably, though often dubiously, such expansive arrangements are claimed to enhance the firm's productivity, profits, and overall economizing. While the true verdict may be long in coming, the firm enjoys a peaceful and joyous interregnum when it is believed that the entropic monster has been sated, at least until its stomach is heard to rumble again. Expansive growth in this sense is an unavoidable extension of the EF's basic economizing impulse. Stasis risks decline and eventual dissolution.

Growth of the EF can be greatly enhanced if ways can be found to discard its ever-increasing entropic load into the environment of the communities in which it operates. As its growth creates jobs and produces new products and services—thus improving the firm's and the community's economic stature—so too does the community become the EF's sink for degraded energy, setting up a two-way exchange between firm and ecosystem: energy in, energy and entropy out. The EF's borders, its outer boundaries, its membranous outlines are entirely porous and non-confining, and in this sense the firm is an open system able both to engulf energy and belch out the degraded forms remaining after its economizing efforts, which are welcomed by all. Business and society are thus locked in an inescapable embrace enjoyed by both in the short run (jobs and growth) but by neither in the longer run (when new technologies displace employees and disrupt communities, and the firm encounters the limits of entropic disposal). This flow, this firm-environment exchange literally keeps the firm viable while simultaneously showering its sphere of operations with both life-supporting jobs and new products, as well as life-diminishing entropic wastes.

Discipline and renewal. Undergirding and reinforcing the centrality of economizing as the EF's **Motivator/Driver** is the training and disciplining of the business professionals who together make up the directing and controlling coalition. Corporate culture is honed, shaped, and cultivated in ways that drive home the necessity of possessing, displaying, and improving high levels of cost consciousness, a dedication to the firm's well-being even at cost to one's own self, displaying an enthusiasm for and a loyalty to the firm's policy goals and strategic moves, and on occasion concealing, distorting, and falsifying information detrimental to the firm's on-going operations.

The list lengthens of companies successful in inculcating such values in coalition members: Enron's go-go culture was enthusiastically embraced by employees throughout the company. Arthur Andersen's auditors were key players in preparing less-than-fully-truthful financial reports for a number of firms and ordering the destruction of files sought by government investigators. Xerox, World Com, Dynegy, Global Crossing, Lucent Technologies, PNC Financial Services, Tyco, and between 150 and 200 other companies have "restated earnings" under pressure from regulatory officials, meaning their loyal, disciplined employees falsified earlier reports.

Such attitudes and values supportive of corporate culture are not infrequently found to be highly prized in management training schools of universities—a kind of MBA boot camp—where tomorrow's elite corporate soldiery ("a few good men") are sought by a company's "recruiters." In this way, fresh sources of energy flood into the lower levels of the EF, where they will be channeled to promote the company's central economizing purposes (see **Year 2005** chapter in Part IV. below).

The Firm's Moralizer/Valuator Function

The modern large-scale business corporation—the Evolutionary Firm—is an expression of natural forces that embed a moralizing function deep within the firm's structure and being. In thus showing a moral face, the EF draws on three distinct but overlapping kinds of innate brain-based circuitry. Evolutionary psychologists and cognitive neuroscientists often call these hard-wired circuits "algorithms," which are problem-solving or sense-making procedures. Sometimes, they are labeled "neural modules," which are groups of interacting neurons that are activated when certain distinct kinds of environmental situations arise. Those hard-wired modules most prominent in defining the firm's **Moralizing/Valuator** function are *economizing algorithms, symbiotic-moralizing algorithms,* and *emotive algorithms.* A fourth set of algorithms expresses power-dominance predispositions that support a wide range of normatively questionable corporate actions.

A company's coalition members—its directors, managers, and employees—draw upon a suite of these algorithmic possibilities, some impelling them towards economizing goals, others seeking cooperative-symbiotic actions, and still others evoking a range of strong emotions that condition, channel, and solidify decisions taken in behalf of the firm. From this mélanges of interacting, overlapping, algorithmically-driven behaviors emerges the moral substrate of the EF upon which it judges itself and is judged by others. Whether it will be considered to be acting in morally acceptable ways or, to the contrary, to be partially or grossly immoral depends largely (but not entirely) on the particular ideological-sociocultural context from which such judgments are launched. More fundamentally, the basis on which the EF can be seen to display moral content is its effect on the survival, adaptation, and qualitative efflorescence of those people and communities who come within its orbit.

The moral traits, features, habits—and ultimately the moral problems, puzzles, and dilemmas—of the Evolutionary Firm are a product of contradictions embedded in diverse neural algorithms that motivate and activate the behavior of the firm's coalition members and thence, through them, the firm's aggregate operations. For these reasons, the EF is not only its own worst enemy but cannot avoid moral condemnation by others both inside and outside the firm. The firm is reflexively immoral for reasons beyond the control of its participants while simultaneously preserving and promoting what is arguably the central moral principle—economizing—on which all life depends. Nature has indeed played a cruel trick on humankind. Just how it was done takes us deeper into the business firm's **Moralizer-Valuator** function.

Evolutionary Algorithms

Leda Cosmides, frequently collaborating with John Tooby, has been the leading advocate of the view that modern human behavior owes much to our ancestral past, especially the experiences of hunter-gatherers who lived during the Pleistocene (Ice Age) era from 2 million years ago to 50,000 years ago. During this period the modern human brain took shape and became the powerful computational tool we now possess. In confronting and resolving the many different kinds of survival and adaptive problems that arose, the hunter-gatherer brain became specialized, developing domain-specific neural algorithms that matched the challenges presented by the Pleistocene environment. Our modern brains bear the deep imprint of our ancient forebears. We are wired for Pleistocene times while living in the Age of the World Wide Web. The peculiar moral problems of the EF are one result.

The three major sets of neural algorithms inherited from ancestral times that activate the **Moralizer-Valuator** function in the modern business corporation are the following ones.

Economizing algorithms. The energy required for adaptation, survival, and outwitting entropy in ancestral times was sought by hunting, gathering, and scavenging. Social systems in the form of family, clan, band, and tribe extended humans' economizing reach. Faced with real problems, risks, and dangers requiring judgment, skills, prediction, and cause-and-effect understanding, pragmatic reasoning schemas emerged as sense-making and problem-solving methods. Each of these three economizing modes—energy capture, social system building, and pragmatic reasoning—was a response to one or more environmental challenges. Over long periods of evolutionary time, brains capable of confronting and resolving such challenges evolved. *It is that same brain that drives the economizing actions and motives of the coalition members of the modern business corporation.*

Symbiotic-moralizing algorithms. Behavior that draws people together in common cause through cooperation, mutual defense, nurturance, caring, and sympathetic bonding has long been typical of the human experience. *Care-bonding* of parent and offspring, while not found among all living creatures, is presumed to have been selected for among many mammalian groups, thus leading to the formation of human family groupings. Kinship bonds that produce an *inclusive fitness* for close kin are present among the social insects and other organisms, as well as humans. *Reciprocal altruism*—acting to promote the reproductive interest of others, even against one's own similar interests, and even for unrelated strangers—is another form of mutualistic behavior appearing in the ancestral record. So too is mutually advantageous *social exchange* an ancient practice among humans, leading to the emergence of *social contract algorithms*, primitive trade, early markets, and eventually modern market exchanges. All of these symbiotic linkages find additional reinforcement in a whole host of other *ecological mutualisms* (see **Year 2004** chapter that follows this one).

Over long stretches of evolutionary time when ancient peoples repeatedly encountered environmental situations favorable to the activation of these symbiotic-moralizing impulses, and especially when they carried

adaptive and reproductive advantage, brain circuitry to support such cooperative, symbiotic behaviors emerged to become a part of Pleistocene (and
subsequently, modern-day) brains. Behavior that acknowledged the dependence of individuals on one another to promote their own and their collective interests thus entered the human realm very early. Only at a much later
time did it acquire the label of "moral" behavior. Today's Evolutionary
Firm harbors traces of these ancient symbiotic-moralizing algorithms, even
in the midst of furious, intense economizing that often overrides and rup-
tures their mutualistic tendencies. It is precisely at that algorithmic cross-
roads where one finds the most intractable moral dilemmas of today's
Evolutionary Firm.

Emotive algorithms. The human brain houses a set of emotive algorithms formed during ancient times as our ancestors interacted with an
environment filled with dangers, threats, and unforeseen risks as well as
opportunities and potential windfalls that could boost survival and reproductive chances. Their presence within the modern human brain would
have to mean that such emotions are potentially capable of becoming a part
of everyday life in the modern corporation, expressed by members of the
firm's human coalition as they interact with each other and as they come in
contact with others outside the firm. If they originally emerged and were
selected for their functional usefulness as survival-and-reproductive capabilities in ancient times, do they continue to do so today in the actions of
corporate directors, managers, and employees?

Emotions cue and condition almost every aspect of a firm's work
life—from goals to motives to rules to values and to the many behavioral
and attitudinal subtleties of corporate culture. A wide range of emotions—
rage, fear, lust, and panic, as well as care, play, and exploratory curiosity-
seeking—surge through the ranks of the corporate citizenry unceasingly,
affecting channels of communication through which the firm's work is
done.

The Evolutionary Firm's instrumental economizing and its moralizing
impulses are thus orchestrated, even directed, by emotive algorithms of
ancient lineage. For example, the pride and confidence stemming from
authoritative knowledge-based skills and accomplishment can be offset or
cancelled by the exultant hubris generated by holding and wielding *authoritarian* dominance power. Or the joy and comfort found when cooperative
team efforts pay off can quickly sour and turn into anger, frustration, disappointment, and cynicism when a power hierarchy's demands or a bureaucracy's smug sluggishness take precedence.

Similarly, the pleasures of achieving goals fade into bitterness and
anxiety in face of layoffs and downsizing demanded by a faceless com-

mand structure seeking to preserve its power and domination through ever more effective economizing. Rage, anger, fear, panic, disgust, vengeance flicker through the corporate structure like small bolts of lightning, while executives find reasons and passions to justify decisions made in the name of economizing and power-holding. No better example exists than Enron. Hence, evolution's legacy in the form of emotive algorithms takes its toll on the very people who carry them and whose behavior they cue and orchestrate.

On a more positive note, corporate managers have been urged to recognize and accept the emotional nature of employees when planning major organizational changes, recruiting rather than denying their feelings and emotional needs. Another study demonstrates that a deliberately induced policy of encouraging emotional interactions with customers creates positive attitudes about a company and pays large economizing dividends. What has been called "emotional intelligence" helps organizational members adapt to change, and an organization's "emotional capability" is one measure of its strategic success, so say other researchers.

Algorithmic moral contradictions. In these several ways, the modern corporation confronts the moral dilemmas and the moral opportunities posed by nature's ways—a veritable tangle of overlapping, inconsistent, and ultimately contradictory neural algorithms lying at the heart (and in the brain) of today's business practitioners. Economizing algorithms sometimes tear asunder a community's symbiotic linkages. Symbiotic-moralizing circuits impel coalition members towards cooperative, mutualistically supportive organizational behaviors that clash with and often lose out to the dominant economizing impulses and its managers' self-aggrandizing behavior. Emotive circuits cue a range of adaptive reactions to the risks and dangers presented by a high-velocity competitive market environment, stirring up intense emotional storms that can and do threaten both the achievement of economizing goals and the organizational acceptance of mutualistically advantageous symbiotic operations.

These nature-induced moral contradictions embody the EF's central ethical dilemma. Two million years of human evolution and genetic embedding have laid them at the corporation's doorstep and implanted them in the modern business mind. They must be recognized for what they are and for the behavioral constraints they bring to a search for ethical resolutions.

How the Evolutionary Firm Makes Choices

Is there a priority system that sorts out and regulates the inevitable tensions among the urges and impulses generated within the minds of business practitioners? The answer is yes, bound up in the evolutionary process itself. Nature does seem to play favorites in evolution. Here is how.

The Evolutionary Firm has an array of algorithmic possibilities on which it can draw. Those with positive thermodynamic effect will be favored by natural selection. *In the case of the Evolutionary Firm, economizing algorithms are consistently selected, i. e., favored,* and they thus have emerged as the dominant motivating force behind the firm's and the coalition's decisions, operations, strategies, and policies. Moralizing algorithms appear to be selected only when producing an economizing effect for the firm or when their entropic drag is slight. Emotive algorithms occupy a somewhat middle ground inasmuch as they may cue behaviors conducive to economizing outcomes, and thus be selected, or they may in some instances orchestrate actions that plunge the firm into passionate controversy, conflict, and possible dissolution.

The EF's consistent focus on economizing ("profits before people," "greed before good," "good ethics is good business"), along with the subordinate position it assigns to morality ("moral muteness," "codes of ethics"), plus strenuous efforts to abolish emotional expressions from the workplace ("love," "lust-sexuality," "displays of temper")—all are strong hints of an algorithmic priority system set by nature itself, and which constrains and moderates the choices made by business practitioners.

Those who despair of this state of affairs can take comfort from the variations that occur around the EF's top priority norm of economizing. The **Moralizer/Valuator** function of any particular business firm varies with the diversity of its biological agents who, though not entirely free agents, are nevertheless inheritors of variable genetic traits and the predispositions they engender (these variations are called "X-factor" values at other points in this book). The algorithms passed on through evolution represent statistical averages and probabilities generalized over many generations. They induce predispositions to behavior, not precise behavioral regimes. They outline possibilities, not certainties or rigid routines. For any given person, their operational effect is therefore unpredictable except in a very general sense. When multiplied by the numbers and types of people found within any given business firm at any given point of time, the lack of predictability of their moral state is magnified by several orders of magnitude. The inner core of the EF's dominant coalition—the directors, executives, and managers—may itself display a diversity of algorithmic inheritance that can cause the firm to lurch from one strategic (and moral) stance to another. Most employees are kept in line by training and disciplined supervision, but because they too are the inheritors of neural algorithms they can be a rich source of independence, creativity, moral

imagination, resistance, and even rebellion, including an occasional whis-
tle-blower. Primary stakeholders—suppliers, dealers, consultants—bring
additional attitudes and inclinations that may fit uneasily and roughly (or
well) into the economizing grooves gouged out by nature.

For all of these reasons—each one itself a product and expression of
natural algorithmic impulses—the EF's strict economizing focus may be
constrained and redirected by some varying combination of moralizing and
emotive algorithmic forces. After all, Malden Mills CEO Aaron Feuerstein's humane decisions at a moment of financial crisis reflected a different proportional mixture of economizing, moralizing, and emotion than
those made by Enron CEOs Jeffrey Skilling and Kenneth Lay and CFO
Andrew Fastow whose self-aggrandizing decisions brought a powerful firm
to the brink of financial disaster. Longtime students of corporate social
responsibility recognize the difference between Johnson & Johnson's life-
saving decisions during the Tylenol contamination crisis when consumer
welfare ranked higher than short-run profits, and the more recent defective-
tire fiasco at Ford-Firestone where the economic and legal standing of both
firms seemed to outweigh concern and regret for the loss of human lives.

The lesson here is not that innate predispositions can be summarily
denied or that human agents are completely free to pick and choose among
the algorithms that nature has implanted in their genomes. Natural selection
has set a probabilistic pattern, created a framework, designed a system, and
assigned priorities to the work of the Evolutionary Firm. Business practitioners are bound to act, make decisions, and set policies guided by these
broad evolutionary guidelines, especially where (or because) economizing
tends to dominate corporate operations. The diversity that is reflected in the
varying algorithmic patterns of the firm's biological agentry is the source—
a kind of moral escape valve—that registers whatever degree of decision-
making latitude one finds among those who occupy key positions in the
collective whole.

The Moral Force of the EF's Other Nature-Based Functions

The centrality of economizing as the principal driving force of business creates a great wash of moral dilemmas for those both inside and outside the firm. These are the most wrenching, most intractable ethical
problems posed by the Evolutionary Firm. However, the story does not end
there, for the EF's other functions also carry moral weight.

The **Innovator/Generator function** is derived from an underlying
natural process: the spontaneous generation of symbolic representations by
the human central nervous system, particularly the neocortex that houses

the brain's principal cognitive, calculative capability. From that neurological seat arise the tools, language, and behavioral guides that enable the firm
to economize, innovate, and achieve a productive output. Here too resides
the brain's "wild card," the source of new insights, the fount of creativity,
the imaginative intelligence that generates new ways of seeing, thinking,
and solving problems. These cerebral symbolic processes are the leading
edge of human adaptation, the principal means we have of surviving and
flourishing in an evolving world. As a human generative force housed
within a corporate shell, this uniquely creative symbolic pulse gives the
Evolutionary Firm its principal moral and social justification. Its never-ending innovations—from silicon chips to World Wide Web, from cell phones
and DVD to pacemakers and computers-on-a-molecule—energize and viv-
ify an essential economizing process, greatly amplifying the adaptive range
of life options available to the human species. Turned outward towards the
burgeoning needs of a global society, rather than being focused exclusively
on the EF's own goals, this generative force holds great moral promise for
a better human future. Take note, those who would redesign the Evolutionary Firm.

The EF's **Organizer/Coordinator function** is based upon two underlying natural features. One is a power-dominance natural impulse that is
emotively driven; the other a system of linguistic linkages *cognitively driven*. Power-dominance organizes the firm as a vertical status hierarchy; language and data flows organize it technologically and horizontally. Both
systems tie the firm's coalition members together and help coordinate their
workplace activities. The resultant network focuses power, information,
and decision making in a managerial elite that seeks to aggrandize its interests and (where possible) those of the firm.

Some of the most intransigent moral dilemmas of the Evolutionary
Firm center on the use of dominance and power by a corporate elite that
often is unmindful of the needs, interests, and welfare of others within and
outside the corporation. Even a company's economizing goals are often
made to yield to the self-aggrandizing urges and impulses of top-level executives, hence undermining the principal adaptive morality of the firm itself.
Executive insiders of now-defunct Global Crossing cashed out $1.3 billion
of their personal holdings in the company as it slid toward bankruptcy and
ruin, even outdoing Enron's insiders who dumped about $1 billion worth of
that company's stock under similar circumstances. As his company was
collapsing and its stock losing value, Enron's CEO sold $20 million of
Enron stock *back to the company* while telling other investors and Enron
employees that their own holdings would soon have "a significantly higher
price." In another case, Enron Broadband executives spent $2 billion of

Enron money setting up high-speed transmission cables across the U.S., but as one source later reported, "Enron Broadband was a colossal [financial] catastrophe." However, Broadband's CEO got $72 million by selling off his stock, and the firm's president took in $35 million the same way. Another Enron subsidiary lost $17 million in 2001's third quarter, then it was put up for sale at a $200 million loss, while its chairman walked away with $75 million from stock sales.

In all likelihood, the radical conflicts of interest between executives and their firms reveal the active presence of a fourth kind of neural algorithm driving the business mind: a power-dominance circuitry that predisposes to the capture, retention, and magnification of power and influence, to be wielded first for personal gain and secondarily for the company's benefit. Evolutionary psychologist Denise Cummins traces this behavioral predisposition to ancestral times, where in a social world organized along dominance lines, the keys to success and survival came in two different forms: obliging others and guile. Guile apparently won the day at Enron, Worldcom, Tyco, et al.

An **Enabler/Strategizer function** reflects the complex, nonlinear ecosystem landscape on which the EF must maneuver if it is to survive, adapt, and expand its sphere of economizing influence. Mutualisms—life-supporting symbiotic linkages—abound within all ecosystems and they literally define what an ecosystem is at its core. A firm's economizing success depends almost entirely on identifying, forming, and developing mutually beneficial ecological alliances with others, whether firms, governments, or institutional stakeholders of all varieties. Its economizing goals are achievable only through such ecologizing strategies. Finding, keeping, and expanding an economic niche calls for pushing back the chaotic disorder that is typical of such environments and for developing pragmatic intelligence to match the competitive challenges encountered. Complexity theory's "strange attractors" (see **Year 1998** chapter above) that orient the EF within an ever-shifting competitive marketplace are nothing more nor less than the firm's values and moral/immoral commitments, and these will determine whether the firm survives at the edge of chaos or plunges into uncontrolled chaotic-entropic disorder. This possibility alone should motivate an active search for values that sustain not just the EF but all others whose fate is tied to its fortunes.

In the end, it is worth remembering that the modern Evolutionary Firm remains one of nature's ongoing evolutionary experiments—a mere 200+ years in the making—with the long-run outcome not yet clear. The average life expectancy of a typical large-scale corporation today is 40 to 50 years; only a handful have lived more than a century. Configured as it is, the Evolutionary Firm's long-run prospects do not seem too promising. It may not be important that the Evolutionary Firm as we know it today lives to see the end of the present century, but if it fades away nature will need to replace its several functions with equally vigorous ones housed in another organizational shell because in its present form the EF sustains huge swaths of humanity through its economizing vigor, even though it often does so with grievous moral consequences.

Whatever Happened to Culture?

In this account which has leaned so heavily on nature for an explanation of business behavior, it is reasonable for one to ask: But what about culture? Should we not heed the anthropologists who, for almost as long as Charles Darwin, have explained human behavior as a manifestation, not of biology or physics but of culture? Has not the concept of corporate culture, now well into its third decade of use, proved to be a valuable way of tracking, understanding, and perhaps even improving business behavior?

To this challenge, there are two answers. The standard social science model that favors a *tabula rasa* (blank slate) concept of human learning, behavior, and development is being seriously eroded by the research of cognitive neuroscientists, evolutionary psychologists, geneticists, evolutionary biologists, primatologists, and paleontologists. Human behavior is now understood to be a function of natural systems: brains, genes, climate, geography, ecology, and anciently embedded ancestral impulses including the basic grammars of language, the comprehension of music and artistic-aesthetic expressions, mathematical intelligence, and other traits once explained in purely cultural terms. The 20th century saw the rise, domination, and decline of culture as an analytic tool. The palette from which scholars now paint a human portrait is far richer in color, depth, and perspective than previously possible. The decline of culture and the rise of biology can be seen as an advance, as a filling out of the picture we seek to draw of the human—and business—experience.

The reason that makes it possible to celebrate rather than to regret today's greater reliance on the natural sciences—and this is the second answer to the basic question about culture's relevance—is the close kinship of nature and culture. Cognitive neuroscience now makes it possible to understand culture as an elaboration, an extension, a magnification, an amplification of cerebral symbol-making of almost unbounded human potential. Culture in this view *is* nature. Not only can we now grasp Frans de Waal's point that our primate progenitor-cousins are capable of cultural behavior but we can in that way understand culture's debt to nature, as well as the lack of a clear boundary between the two.

Corporate culture is truly a powerful analytic concept to both understand what goes on in business firms and to help managers do their daily work effectively. However, the Evolutionary Firm's five nature-based functions undergird and comprise the core of its corporate culture. Rather than a cloak that conceals nature's grip on the business mind, corporate culture illustrates the close bond between biological nature and symbolic culture.

Prospects for Corporate Moral Inquiry

Moral inquiry about business must begin with the Evolutionary Firm's **Motivator-Driver** function. Business firms are first and foremost economizing organizations, made that way by nature. All the wishful thinking in the world—even the most sophisticated philosophic speculations—will not make that feature go away. The firm's moral problems arise from contradictions rooted in behavioral impulses of the human psyche interacting with an entropic universe. Human culture and reason can channel, moderate, and reconfigure—but cannot eliminate—these behavioral predispositions. Virtuous character can confront but not seriously deflect the natural course of embedded neural algorithms. Social contracts can design but cannot enforce or guarantee fair exchanges. Stakeholder claims on the corporation cannot exceed or violate the firm's entropic limits. Philosophic principles and ideals not consistent with the firm's natural architecture cannot be expected to prevail.

Moral analysis of business must *begin* with what nature has bequeathed to business and to humanity. Within that bequest, one finds a brain marvelously attuned to meeting environmental challenges and finding ways to adapt, survive, create, experiment, explore, imagine, and expand the quantity and quality of life. That brain has carried *Homo sapiens* to its present state in evolutionary time, far and well beyond our Pleistocene ancestral base. Its very flexibility, creativity, and emotionality hints—and haunts one's hopes and dreams—that it can point the way to a better moral life for the Evolutionary Firm and for human society.

YEAR 2004

[Public confidence in big business: 24%]

SOCIAL CONTRACTS:
ROOTED IN NATURE

Setting the Scene. A compact between business and society, implying obligations of each to the other, is the very essence of CSR. The prestigious Committee for Economic Development had floated the notion—calling it a government-and-business partnership—amidst the anti-business social turmoil of the 1970s (__Year 1973__, __Year 1981__, __Year 1983__ in Part I. above). Even Chase Manhattan's David Rockefeller placed the business establishment's imprimatur on "a new social contract." Thus did Jean-Jacques Rousseau's social vision confront once again Thomas Hobbes' Leviathan, garbed now in an executive suit. It was left to two scholars at the venerable Wharton School of Finance—one a philosopher, the other a legal scholar—to put a modern gloss on the social contract, calling it Integrative Social Contracts Theory. Embracing law, philosophy, and modern anthropological insights, ISCT lacked only mention of social contract's long association with nature itself. Rousseau was right after all: Nature matters, providing the moral cement of business's compact with society.

Social contracts rest upon an evolutionary base of several hundred thousand years of human and even pre-human practice. Hobbes, Locke, Rousseau, Hume, et al., though credited with "inventing" the idea of social contract, were doing little more than capturing for their contemporaries an ancient message written into the genes and brains of *Homo sapiens*. The same can be said for contemporary social contractarians John Rawls, as well as Thomas Donaldson and Thomas Dunfee, the authors of Integrative Social Contracts Theory. Ancient ancestral patterns of biologically-moderated communal behavior preceded and shaped the emergence and form of contemporary culturally-moderated social contracts. Social contracts theory, including ISCT, can be conceptually strengthened by acknowledging the Darwinian evolutionary basis of social contracts and the Deweyan pragmatic character of business decision making.

A Theory of Evolutionary Origins

A theory of evolutionary origins can identify the initiating sources, forms, and functions of human interactions that established the patterns, motives, and *raison d'etre* of social exchanges between human beings. Such ancient behavioral forms of communal interaction have long sustained the evolution of modern *Homo sapiens* and quite possibly appeared in rudimentary form among several predecessor hominid types, including *Homo neanderthalensis, Homo erectus, Homo ergaster, Homo habilis,* and several others who lived between 100,000 and 2.5 million years ago. *The central premise here is that modern socio-economic exchanges (social contracts) owe their logic, form, and purpose to these earlier ancestral forms of communal behavior.*

Figure 1 is a graphic representation of the key **Phases of Human Communal Evolution.** Each phase located around the circular wheel is an evolved form of human interaction, and all have been confirmed by the extensive research of evolutionary biologists and psychologists. The phases may be seen as evolutionary way stations during the long development and emergence of modern human life. Each one promoted human survival prospects and in that sense each was evolutionarily adaptive. Each phase forged bonds of cooperation among humans and helped build communal life. All phases are as "alive and well" today, functioning simultaneously to promote human bonding and communal effects, as they were during their early evolution. In describing them, it is best to begin where all life began.

Adaptation/Reproduction. Today's human beings are the outcome of a natural selection process that favored organic traits conducive to survival, adaptation, and reproduction (S/A/R). Survival required a metabolic ability to acquire, store, process, and use energy for life support. Adaptation meant finding a place or niche within one's environment that permitted genetic potentials to be realized. Reproduction required a kind of sexual reproduction capable of producing genetic variability in offspring and therefore within the species. *Homo sapiens*—today's humans—are the evolved result of this natural selection process.

Inclusive Fitness/Kin Selection. Growing directly out of the S/A/R activities of gene-directed individuals are two interrelated communal behavior patterns. **Inclusive fitness** means that an individual acting adaptively for its own survival needs may, in doing so, also produce similar

Figure 1

PHASES OF HUMAN COMMUNAL EVOLUTION

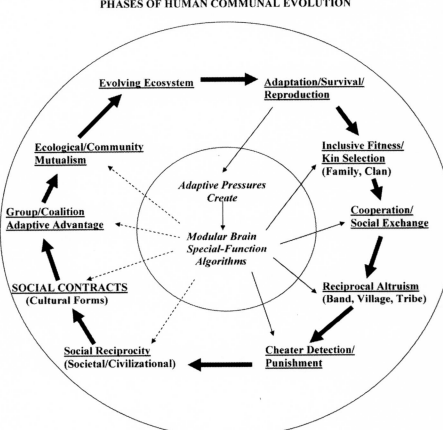

results for others, such as may be found in clans or small hunter-gatherer bands. The individual's "fitness" (survivability and adaptability), measured by its reproductive success, may be assured and multiplied if others it closely interacts with, e.g., in cooperative hunting, also experience S/A/R success. The quality of "fitness" is inclusive of others, not limited just to a single person. Such mutually beneficial adaptive behavior can then spread via natural selection and become established among the members of a close-knit community.

Kin selection is a type of inclusive fitness that occurs among family members and that multiples the prospects of extending one's own genes, as well as those of family members, into the next generation. The closer the kinship, the greater the probability of sharing similar genes with one's relatives. Caring for one's own offspring, for siblings, for cousins, and other kin so that they, too, live on to be reproductively successful maximizes the probability that one's genes, or closely related copies of them, will survive beyond one's own death.

Inclusive fitness and kin selection—built-in, innate, gene-based, hard-wired types of communal behavior—can, and do, powerfully underwrite social cooperation between humans.

Cooperation/Social Exchange. Paleontologists, evolutionary biologists, archaeologists, historians, anthropologists, and evolutionary psychologists affirm that cooperation and social exchange are inherent practices among hominid primates, including *Homo sapiens* and its evolutionary predecessors. In the most basic sense, a minimum degree of cooperative interaction is necessary for sexual pairing and reproduction. Offspring require extended care and close cooperation between parent and infant. Parental investments in offspring are one-half of a long-lasting reciprocal social exchange whose parental payoffs take the form of successful gene transmission (and thereby, generational adaptation of the species) through the children. Adoptive parenting, surrogate birthing, sperm donation, and similar practices are a biological step removed from direct parental transmission of genes through offspring, although the generational (survival, adaptive) effect on the species is identical.

Beyond mate choice, breeding, and birthing lie the range of problems common to human existence and flourishing, all of which call for varying degrees of cooperation and social exchange: finding food, sharing it, fending off predators (i.e., avoiding *being* food), knowing one's environment (plants, animals, weather, topography, circadian and seasonal cycles, astronomical phenomena), securing shelter, making tools, clothing, containers and finding the necessary raw materials, learning and transmitting skills, dealing with illness and injury, encountering non-kin humans and interacting with them, etc. These were the earliest, most rudimentary forms of human communal behavior, necessitated and driven by survival and adaptive needs.

Social exchange, a step beyond cooperation, likely arises from the variability of environmental resources, the differential skills and traits among individuals and within groups, and the perception of how these differences might be manipulated for survival and adaptive purposes and goals. Hence, a skilled hunter's exchange of food for sex by a receptive (and hungry) female; cooperation between hunters in return for sharing the bounty; gathering and scavenging food items and sharing them with family and close kin in exchange for shelter and protection; coastal villagers exchanging fish for vegetables from inland villagers; tropical fruit and spices exchanged for iron, gold, and precious stones mined in northern climes. Some social exchanges are directly instrumental: obtaining or providing food, sex, and protection. Other exchanges serve symbolic functions: acknowledging or wielding status rank, using or acceding to power, and marking or reinforcing group membership. In all social exchanges, humans are drawn together interactively and communally.

Reciprocal Altruism. Any system of social exchange depends on fairness in the minds of the exchange partners. Once the exchange has been completed, each side needs to feel it was worthwhile, i.e., just, fair, balanced, equitable. This is true whether one seeks instrumental or symbolic benefits from exchange. Such reassurances are more likely when the exchange is between family members (kin selection) and, to a lesser extent, between more distantly related clan and tribal members (inclusive fitness). Exchange in this sense is serving two important functions: contributing to the survival/adaptive/reproductive (S/A/R) needs of the exchange partners and doing so in a way that preserves the advantages and security of gene-based communality.

Reciprocal altruism takes the principle of fairness in social exchange a large step beyond the adaptive bonds forged through family ties and clan-tribal membership, by extending the idea to include social exchanges among *non-kin strangers*. Here is the natural seedbed from which the idea of "social contract" grew but only long ages after reciprocating exchanges became embedded by natural selection in the ancestral behavior of hominid primates. Reciprocal altruism is a radical idea: that in an exchange transaction an individual will consciously extend benefits to an unrelated stranger in ways detrimental to one's own immediate well-being. That seems to contradict the very idea of fairness or balance in exchange.

A key to the puzzle is the way evolutionary biologists define altruism. To them, altruism means nothing more nor less than promoting the reproductive interests of someone else while simultaneously diminishing one's own reproductive prospects. That is what looks and sounds like *a very large munificent act of kindness*—but it is nothing of the sort. That would be the way philosophers think of altruism, as consciously intentional beneficent acts. Evolutionary biologists point out that what appears to be a kind but costly act is expected to be reciprocated by the beneficiary *in the future*. In the logic of social exchange, that would be fair. Reciprocal altruism thus produces a fair exchange of favors that enhances the life prospects of *both* exchange partners—one now, the other later—even when they are total strangers. If natural selection were to favor this kind of behavior (because it supports survival, adaptation, and reproduction), it would then spread throughout the population and become yet another phase of communal evolution. The evidence is strong and clear that the human species is hard-wired to reciprocate altruistic behavior extended to them, not just by close kin but even by strangers whom one may never see again.

Cheater Detection/Punishment.   How is reciprocal altruism enforced? What about free riders? Whatever happened to *caveat emptor*? The mechanism that enforces reciprocal exchange and reciprocal altruism is an innate neurological impulse to seek out non-reciprocators (i.e., cheaters) and punish them, and to reward cooperators who impose costs on themselves. Deviants and rule-breakers may be severely reprimanded or even shunned. One type of game theory (the Ultimatum Game), played across a wide range of people from different societies, reveals a strong sense of reciprocity and fairness in distributing benefits, as well as an almost universal tendency to punish those who cheat by not reciprocating a benefit they receive. Research shows that people exact punishment even when it is costly to themselves to do so and when they will never encounter the cheater again. They are acting out the idea of reciprocal altruism and insisting that all members of their community should do the same. "Even when naturally selfish individuals are a majority, the presence of people willing to punish freeloaders can enforce social cooperation in much larger groups," according to evolutionary biologist Ernst Fehr. Finding and punishing free loaders even brings pleasure to the enforcers, as shown by the activation of brain areas that signal reward and emotional pleasure. Under these circumstances, a reputation for fairness becomes a social plus. Free loaders lose social esteem. Communal behavior is strengthened. The idea of social justice is hard-wired.

Modular Brain/Special-Function Algorithms. At the center of Figure 1 and indeed at the core of all communal behavior one finds the modular brain of *Homo sapiens*. A modular brain is specialized to cope with the specific problems it encounters in daily life. The modules are integrated sets of neurons (nerve cells) attuned and positively responsive to perceived problems. The physical design and the sense-making traits of the brain's neurological circuits are, like other physical features of our bodies, the result of a long, long evolution during which natural selection favored structure and behavior that preserved life through adaptation and reproduction. Form (specialized modules) followed function (survival/adaptive/reproductive success).

Today's brain tissue is the outcome of more than 2 million years of interaction between hominid brain and environment. It is truly an ancestral brain, most recently formed into the characteristic modular circuits of *Homo sapiens* around 100,000 years ago, with little discernible architectural change since then. That is why it is often called a hunter-gatherer brain identical to the one possessed by those ancient peoples who lived precariously, but with marvelous ingenuity, in small groups or bands on savanna and forest lands. Their brains and ours possess the same basic circuitry, the same modular specialization, the same environmental awareness, the same overall functional design for two reasons: they have proved themselves over time by meeting natural selection's relentless pruning of maladaptive traits, and the rate of genetic change through mutations and genetic drift has been insufficient to transform the brain's basic architecture.

Neural algorithms are the brain's problem-solving (or in some cases, only problem-*coping*) routines responsive to diverse environmental cues, challenges, and opportunities encountered by our Pleistocene Ice Age ancestors: foraging for food, kin recognition, social exchange, choosing mates, interpreting threats, channeling emotions, nurturing offspring, acquiring and using language, etc. The human brain's 100+ billion neurons are clustered in functional units able to perceive, interpret, and respond to environmental signals in adaptive ways.

As depicted in Figure 1, the modular brain's special-function algorithms—its specialized circuits—are the active biological agent responsible for the major phases of human communal behavior. Inclusive fitness, kin selection, social exchange, reciprocal altruism, and cheater detection/punishment are all built into the brain in the sense that each phase reflects the repeated experiences of ancestral groups whose continued survival, adaptation, and reproduction depended on these kinds of communal interactions. The solid arrows in Figure 1 radiating outward from *Modular Brain/Special-Function Algorithms* to the various phases of communal evolution are meant to show that neural algorithms exist to activate and support these communal behaviors.

Without question, one must acknowledge the stunning differences between ancestral forms of human behavior and the complexity, diversity, and adaptive efficiency found in (advanced) contemporary cultures. Accordingly, the *broken* arrows in Figure 1 radiating from **Modular Brain** to the communal behaviors depicted on the left side of the circle are meant to convey the presence of gene-based neural algorithms that are supportive of *societal and cultural forms* of communal behavior, which are perhaps less obviously (but no less functionally) embedded in a Darwinian evolutionary process than the behaviors on the right side of the circle.

The algorithmic brain that sustained the earliest forms of human exchange and cooperation—the most rudimentary types of communal interaction—continues today to perform its ancient ancestral function, though much elaborated now by more complex cultural patterns of exchange and cooperation. Both then and now, the brain's neural circuits or modules can be considered to be the active mediator of relations between organism and environment.

Social Reciprocity (Societal/Civilizational). One of the most pervasive features of human societies everywhere is the notion of social reciprocity—that somehow or other the relations between people should be balanced, as if behavior is being weighed in a vast scale where an action calls for an equally calibrated counteraction. Social reciprocity takes many forms and occurs in many different contexts. It may appear as formalized social norms; as far-ranging systems of ritual exchange like the Trobriand Islanders' *kula* ceremony; as both formal and informal gift-giving among and between various levels of social class; as ceremonial, pre-market, quasi-monetary systems of exchange; as a way of calculating medieval just prices; as primitive and prehistoric forms of barter, trade and exchange; as early capitalist trade; as crime and punishment; as tit-for-tat strategy in game playing; as a nation's balance of trade; as price equilibrium in economic theory; as fairness, or its absence, in taxation; as reciprocal gift-giving on holidays; as a tension-reducing psychological impulse.

One effect of these many kinds of reciprocating behavior is to conserve, or if possible freeze in place, interpersonal, social, class, economic, and political relationships. Tit-for-tat keeps everyone in place. Another result is to fashion a notion of reciprocal fairness and justice that suffuses wide realms of human culture. At some point in hominid evolution, or perhaps at many different points of time and place, communalism (sharing) came to mean reciprocal fairness in dealing with one's life companions, whether in family, clan, tribe, polity, or civil society. When that transient, shifting threshold was crossed, it became possible for the human algorithmic brain to draw upon eons of evolutionary experience in moderating human relationships and to begin to formulate what we now call "social contracts."

SOCIAL CONTRACTS (Cultural Forms). Contemporary social contracts of any kind or form—whether formal or informal, written or implicit, enforced by law or by custom, domestic or international, civil or economic—rest on an evolutionary base of social reciprocity moderated by an algorithmic brain, as depicted in Figure 1. Five major features of evolutionary social contracts are found in any and all such instruments, regardless of societal or cultural origin or placement. David Wasieleski and I have hypothesized that a social contract is (1) a social exchange relationship, (2) sustained by adaptive biosocial processes, (3) moderated by social exchange neural algorithms, (4) motivated by self-seeking personal and/or group advantage, and (5) bound, channeled, and constrained by reciprocal expectations and obligations.

However, the contract's *precise* form, content, terms, psychological/emotional expectations, interpretation, enforcement provisions, and penalties for breach of contract, as well as the types of contractors involved, are all a function of the particular societies and cultures in which such contracts are drawn up and agreed to. Each will reflect in some degree that society's prevailing and dominant value systems, social norms, fair-play rules, and relevant laws. This sociocultural embeddedness is acknowledged in Integrative Social Contracts Theory, mainly through the concept of micro social contracts.

All modern (cultural) ideas of social contract have appeared only at the near end of a long period of human evolution. They date principally, at least in Western thought, only from the 17th and 18th centuries, reflecting the values, times, and views of Enlightenment philosophers. Even the updated versions, such as that of John Rawls and the ISCT of Donaldson and Dunfee, continue mainly in this same tradition. Until ISCT appeared, social contractarians had been mainly interested in civil/political contracts between citizens and the state. However, ISCT's inventors have departed from this tradition by applying the idea to the modern business corporation and to life in a market economy.

Social contracts, in business or elsewhere, are not a modern "cultural" invention nor a mere product of Enlightenment and later thinking. A time-tested S/A/R evolutionary process has built such arrangements into our very beings. Because they are natural extrusions of the S/A/R impulse, they are not even entirely volitional. Contracting suffuses and pervades today's corporation, which would have a hard time operating otherwise. The firm is indeed a "nexus of contracts" as claimed by economists Michael Jensen and William Meckling and confirmed by business ethics philosopher John Boatright. The reasons are rooted in evolutionary imperatives imposed on the corporation as an economizing entity. If it is to adapt and prove its fitness in the marketplace, cooperative coalitional behavior is essential. That kind of communal action is the heart and soul of social contracting. Absent such contractual agreements, neither the corporation nor the surrounding market economy can be productive. Therefore, social contracts embrace two functions: one is adaptive, the other is moral; both are emergent products of human evolution. This is as true of contemporary social contracts as it was of the ancient communal behaviors that preceded and ultimately spawned them.

Group/Coalition Adaptive Advantage. The benefits stemming from the form of social cooperation that we call "social contracts" accrue to social groups and coalitions as well as to individuals. The idea is so deeply and so long buried within human consciousness as to be secure in most people's minds. What may be worth emphasizing though is that the benefits sought and obtained by social contractors—whether individuals, groups, or coalitions—are entirely a form of self gain. Social contracting is adaptively efficient—i.e., benefits outweigh costs—for each side. No common purpose, no greater good beyond this requirement need enter nor cloud the transaction. This self-gain is, of course, only a manifestation of evolutionary S/A/R traits long ingrained.

The society-wide gains of social contracting are achievable only when the self gain sought by individuals and groups is kept in check by a system of evolutionary morals, whose early (and continuing) forms are inclusive fitness, kin selection, and reciprocal altruism, now reinforced by societal rule-making and laws. There must be a convergence, a consilience, between adaptive need and moral guidance if widespread benefits are to be had.

No one has put the case for a convergence of morals and survival/adaptation more clearly or cleverly than game theorist Kenneth Binmore: "The notion of a game of life and a game of morals being played simultaneously has substantial descriptive validity for the way *homo sapiens* runs his societies. It is the rules of the game of life that determines whether a particular set of behavior patterns can survive. To be viable, a social contract must therefore be an equilibrium [i.e., provide benefits to each contractor] in the game of life. ... we often tell ourselves that we are playing the game of morals and hence choose 'fair' equilibria in the game of life. In doing so, the danger we always face is that of failing to understand the relationship that holds between the game of morals and the game of life. When playing the game of morals, it is easy to forget that it is not the game of life. This does little harm as long as we keep playing a game of morals that has evolved to be compatible with the game of life."

Social contracts, even in today's highly complex societies—and also in the modern corporation—continue to be biocultural devices for coordinating the behavior of people who have need to interact with each other in adaptive ways as they play the (S/A/R) Game of Life. Binmore is telling us that socially constructed moral systems, concepts, and theories incompatible with the coevolved game of life and game of morals may end up diminishing or misdirecting the socially adaptive benefits of social contracts in modern business and society.

Ecological/Community Mutualism. The moral dimensions of human communal evolution converge in the mutualistic traits of ecological networks. Mutual benefits are unquestionably enjoyed by all who reside within any given ecosystem. The benefit is life support on a larger scale than otherwise attainable. The benefit is mutually experienced—that is, shared either directly or indirectly—through the many diverse symbiotic linkages that draw living forms together in reciprocally supportive ways. Social contracts sustained by the moral logic of reciprocal altruism express the spirit of ecological mutualism. Given varying forms in modern culture, these contracts enhance the life chances of the contractors by concerting their respective interests. This is the outcome of the contracts that lace together the diverse groups (i.e., stakeholders) found in today's business firms. The Game of Life is thus propelled onward, guided by a coevolved Game of Reciprocal Morals.

Nevertheless, the human community impulse toward mutual benefit is of limited scope and compass, falling considerably short of embracing the whole of humanity. Species-centered behavior is rare. *Homo sapiens* is a scientific category, just as "humanity" is a literary metaphor. Neither constitutes a comprehensive concerted behavioral reality. We do not act as, or for, our species, i.e., for humanity at large. Evolution and natural selection have programmed us to act for ourselves in survival/adaptive/reproductive ways. Our adaptive loyalties are to the groups and coalitions we identify as our adaptive helpmates, not to "humanity" as a whole. It reminds one of the waggish saying, "I love humanity. It's *people* I can't stand." The Game of Morals does not stretch to the farthest reaches of the human species. The Game's rules, norms, and morals are about fair play in lesser realms of the overall ecosystem. Where those rules are respected and operationalized there can be great mutualistic gain for the groups and coalitions (contractors) involved. *Homo sapiens,* the sole possessor of symbolic culture, has yet to devise a species-wide moral system or code that can operationally capture the behavioral essence of ecological mutualism. The (biological) Game of Life thus far trumps the (cultural) Game of Morals.

Evolving Ecosystems. Ecological systems change through time. Their inhabitants come and go, some succeeding, others failing to meet the S/A/R test. Geological, climatological, and astronomical forces rearrange the physical landscape. Genetic mutations and genetic drift both enable and disable the best of adaptive efforts. Deadly viruses may threaten to decimate entire populations. Invader species enter ecosystems, choking off the life prospects of long-time residents. Global warming, desertification, species-ending asteroid impacts, oceanic thermal oscillations, etc., have the power to transform organic life on a worldwide basis. Ecosystems are seldom "balanced" but are always in transition, as their diverse but interlinked life forms are driven onward by the forces of nature—and culture too in the case of humans. The interplay of these two processes (nature and culture), neither one entirely separate from the other, alters the shape and outcome of today's and tomorrow's ecosystems. They set the stage for the continuing round of survival/adaptation/reproduction activities of humankind and our non-human life companions, thus bringing us back to the initial phase of human communal evolution shown in Figure 1.

The evolutionary theory of origins therefore presents social contracts as a blend of nature and culture. Social contract norms are contemporary extensions and expressions of communal behavior norms forged in the human brain during ancient ancestral times. The more recent, culturally diversified norms found in social contracts simply reflect the adaptive history and experience of peoples living in varying ecological circumstances who bring their pragmatic reasoning abilities (i.e., those specialized neural modules) to bear on solving problems and arranging themselves into livable relationships. Nature's behavioral norms and the derivative sociocultural norms are as fully expressive today as they were in ancestral times. Nature's behavioral norms—**Adaptation/Reproduction, Inclusive Fitness/Kin Selection, Cooperation/Social Exchange, Reciprocal Altruism, Cheater Detection/Punishment**—are the primordial moral infrastructure of social exchange and the moral cement of social contracts, whether ancient or recent. One need only remember that derivative cultural norms, whether of Western or other cultural origin, may or may not be compatible with Binmore's Game of Life. He reminds us that "the rules of the game of morals that grew up [historically] with our species are merely fictions embodied in our culture. People can and do persuade themselves and others to seek to play by different rules that are not adapted to the game of life."

A Theory of Pragmatic Action

Pragmatic philosopher John Dewey's theory of action emerges directly and generically from a Darwinian evolutionary theory of origins. The "action" that needs to be accounted for is business decision making and business practices as we normally understand them.

Dewey's instrumentalist, experiential pragmatism leads directly into the "real world" of the business practitioner by emphasizing the problem-generating, problem-coping, and problem-solving nature of the workplace. It is there where business values and norms are formed and enacted. The test is workability. The approach is experimental and open-ended: use what works, discard what doesn't. The resultant values and norms are entirely contextual and entirely provisional until new insights emerge from newly generated workplace experiences. This kind of norm-generating, experience-based, problem-solving activity is the ground from which operational business values emerge and become behavioral guides for business practitioners. These are values in action, i.e., normative guides for defining, judging, and acting on problems that must be solved if, in this case, the business firm is to move ahead in performing its economizing function within human society.

In this sense, the generation of workplace values and norms bears a remarkable similarity to the survival/adaptation/reproduction (S/A/R) process of human evolution. Both are problem-solving processes—one to economize within the firm, the other to replicate and sustain human life. Both are generic to *Homo sapiens*. Both are directed by a modular brain whose message is the same to both: adapt, i.e., solve problems, or perish. Both produce workable norms of behavior to meet that challenge. In both contexts, cooperative coalitional arrangements emerged as the most effective, most practical, most pragmatic, most workable way to proceed. The coeval, coevolved norms of reciprocal altruism (i.e., fair, just exchange) shape this pragmatic program of problem-coping and problem-solving in both firm and human life generally.

Theories of social contract can easily accommodate a natural, pragmatic theory of action. Nature's behavioral norms are as fundamental to the well-being and sustenance of *Homo sapiens* as any norms could be. They bind human individuals, groups, and communities together in adaptive ways. They also promote pragmatic problem solving and coalition building, both vital to business economizing that sustains broad swaths of the world's peoples.

But then one recalls Binmore's moral fictions that litter human history and that are at odds with the Game of Life. Has natural selection then allowed non-adaptive or maladaptive traits to slip through the S/A/R filter? Whether a behavioral trait is imbued with a S/A/R moral content depends on a pragmatic test based on experience: can human intelligence draw upon past and present experience to discern the adaptive from the maladaptive? An approach that embraces the long-evolved communal values and practices that support human life, and that do so from a workably pragmatic perspective, is preferable to the culturally-bounded meanings given by Western culture to Kantian human rights and Rawlsian social justice.

Origins and Actions: A Summing Up

Homo sapiens is a quarrelsome species, riven by murderous conflict, one of the few creatures to war against itself. One is tempted, as social contractarians have been, to find a way out by appealing to broadly shared principles and motives having a more peaceful outcome, one that offers business practitioners a machinery of moral calculation consistent with managerial decision making.

The search can be enhanced by centering attention on the communal bonding sources that have been handed on a platter to *Homo sapiens* by natural selection. Those bonds go deeper, have been around longer, and

have been tested more often by the lived experience of countless generations stretching back to our Pleistocene ancestors than can be found in contemporary culture-bound, pre-Darwinian formulations of human reason
and human rights. The human moral sense that reveals itself by lighting up
the screens of (f)MRI brain scans and manifests itself in reciprocal bonding with kin and strangers sends an important signal about human possibilities. We bond, we cooperate, we contract, not to the outermost boundaries
of our species but only to those edges where natural selection and lived
experience drives us. Nature-based norms, reinforced by ecological awareness and sensitivity, tug the world's peoples towards common cause
because, while culturally and environmentally diverse, they have all
emerged from evolutionarily similar beginnings and have managed to cope
successfully with common problems.

This nature-enriched view captures the advantage already present in
such social contract theories as the Donaldson-Dunfee Integrative Social
Contracts Theory that enables corporate managers to identify and formulate
pragmatically workable responses to workplace ethical challenges and
opportunities wherever encountered.

However, deeply troubling puzzles remain, even for the best of social
contracts. The human modular brain houses and expresses ancestral
impulses that can contradict and supervene a social contract's reciprocal
morals. They can and do drive human behavior towards power, domination,
aggression, fear, anger, and rage that too often find their way not just into
the workplace but also into families, neighborhoods, major institutions, and
national policies.

The Game of Life as played by business and the Game of Morals as
played by society are intertwined and partially self reinforcing. One can
hope for a convergence, or in Edward O. Wilson's term, a consilience of
ethical standards that sustain human life in all of its cultural and ecological
diversity. That kind of moral consilience, originating in nature and elaborated by culture, is what social contracts are all about. It is a lesson to be
urgently learned by today's corporate decision makers.

YEAR 2005

[Public confidence in big business: 22%]

HARD-WIRED MANAGEMENT MORALITY: COALITIONAL CRIME AT ENRON, WORLDCOM, TYCO, HEALTHSOUTH

Setting the Scene. *The sheer audacity and scale of the corporate corruption uncovered at century's end left the general public—as well as the business community itself—overwhelmed and shocked. Large numbers of executives and companies at the very pinnacle of American (and foreign) enterprise were charged with crimes and civil misdeeds. Public distrust of business plunged to new lows. New laws sought to curb these excesses. Many voices of protest were heard, many explanations offered. This chapter offers yet another, drawing upon network theory, complexity science, neuroscience, and evolutionary psychology.*

Corporate corruption is typically a group activity. Beyond secrecy, it requires the cooperation and active collaboration of an initiator and confederates. The lone embezzler who siphons off illicit gains and the entrepreneurial investment advisor who hoodwinks trusting clients, though numerous, are exceptions to the rule. Corporate misdeeds of the kind discussed here tend to be carried out by corrupt alliances.

This view is at odds with various popular explanations of the great flood of corruption that washed over the U. S. corporate landscape at the turn of the century. Flawed personal character, lax corporate governance systems, executive pay tied to stock options, understaffed regulatory agencies, cozy ties between companies and their auditors, collusion between stock analysts and the companies whose stock they analyze and report on, a market-induced profits-before-people attitude, the "irrational exuberance" of stock market investors, an unprincipled focus on greed and personal gain—all have been advanced as key flaws that need to be "fixed" if business is to recapture the confidence and trust of investors and the general public. While there is something to be said for each, taken together they are little more than folk explanations, lacking a theoretical base grounded in empirically derived data.

This chapter takes a different tack, arguing that corporate corruption is a function of (1) managerial hierarchy, (2) environmental opportunity, (3) dominant values of corporate culture, and (4) executive minds hard-wired for the pursuit of power. The presence of these four conceptual components is demonstrated by interpretive data derived from published sources. The goal is to describe networks of intrigue and corruption that emerged in four of the most prominent corporations involved in the corporate scandals of the late 1990s and the early 2000s: Enron, WorldCom, Tyco, and Health-South.

What the Companies Did

Fraudulent, corrupt actions varied from company to company, but a common pattern can be discerned. These might conveniently be called generic types of corporate wrongdoing that appeared in each of the four companies.

- Lax, compliant oversight by the board of directors, including audit and compensation committees

- Flexible interpretation and use of generally accepted accounting principles

- Issuing reports falsifying the company's financial condition by understating costs and inflating revenues, income, and profits

- Executives receiving and paying unauthorized bonuses and other non-job-related personal benefits from company funds

- Collusion with audit firms to conceal the company's financial condition from, and thereby to mislead, investors, creditors, government regulators, stock exchange commissions, and tax authorities

- Collusive cooperation with stock analysts, brokerage firms, and investment banks to boost the reputed value of the company's stock

These generic forms of fraud and corruption were then multiplied and varied from company to company:

- Manipulation and restriction of energy supplies to boost prices and company profits at **Enron**

- Off-book transfer of assets, costs, and revenues through special purpose entities, for personal profit of insider executives at **Enron**

- Salaries and bonuses unjustified by economic performance at **Enron Broadband Services** and at **Tyco**

- Over-claiming on Medicare payments at **HealthSouth**

- Conflict-of-interest contracts between the company, directors, and executives at **HealthSouth, Tyco,** and **WorldCom**

- Payments-in-kind (bonuses, housing loans forgiven, gifts of company cars, condos, private school tuitions) to cooperating managers and staff members at **Tyco**

- Use of family members and friends to funnel company funds for illegitimate purposes at **Enron** and **HealthSouth.**

The consequences of these modern forms of piracy were far ranging, victimizing literally millions of people and affecting some of the economy's major institutions. The plundering:

- Diminished stock values for individual shareholders, creditors, pension funds, brokerage houses, and other investment institutions

- Destroyed jobs, disrupted career paths, and wiped out retirement reserves of employees

- Reduced sales and revenues of dependent supplier companies

- Through market manipulation, created crisis, uncertainty, and exorbitant prices in energy markets, especially in California, thus greatly burdening state budgets with debt loads

- Exacerbated the debt problems of state governments through false reporting of income, use of off-shore and off-book accounting, and questionable classification of revenues, thereby reducing state tax collections

- Caused the bankruptcy of **Enron, WorldCom,** and **Tyco**, significant financial loss and continuing instability of **HealthSouth**, and dismemberment of the **Arthur Andersen** auditing firm

- Produced a range of new government regulations and stock exchange rules, thereby increasing the complexity and cost of business operations

- Resulted in a massive loss of public trust in corporations and great damage to the image and reputation of business in general.

The Central Propositions

Seven propositions support the central argument that corporate fraud and corruption are group activities initiated by high-ranking executives working collaboratively with company directors, other senior officers, mid-level managers, administrative staff, and various external confederates.

In the four companies reported here, corporate fraud and corruption are proposed as:

P1: *coalitional actions, not individual acts*

P2: *top-down in origin, not bottom-up*

P3: *hierarchically imposed and collaboratively induced, not independently volitional*

P4: *activated by self-aggrandizing executive impulse, not by pursuit of organizational function or purpose*

P5: *habitual, repetitive, and infectious, not a reversible one-time event*

P6: *extra-organizational, not confined within the company*

P7: *opportunistic and episodic, not ubiquitous, and triggered by environmental challenges and energized by aggressive, high-velocity, growth-oriented corporate culture.*

Sources Used

Most of the data reported here were derived from news stories and investigative reports published in the business press. The leading journalistic source was *The Wall Street Journal*; others were *The New York Times, Business Week*, wire service stories, and various on-line newspaper and magazine data banks.

No claim is made for completeness or comprehensiveness of the reported data, especially since investigations and legal ramifications can continue indefinitely. Press reports of unproved charges, legal indictments, court-approved plea agreements, guilty pleas, convictions, and prison sentences have been used to identify and describe the alleged initiators, collaborators, and corruption networks. Unless clearly stated otherwise by legal authority, all such reported charges and legal actions are treated as allegations only. In spite of these qualifications necessitated by fairness to the parties involved, the published data give a reasonably accurate impression of the organizational skeins tying corporate actors together into networks of intrigue, corruption, and personal enrichment.

The focus of this inquiry and report is on actions that can be construed as *unethical*, not whether an individual, group, or firm is found guilty or innocent of a crime or of fraudulent and corrupt behavior that is judged to be *illegal*. Reported unethical actions tend to be far more numerous than prosecuted unlawful acts for the simple reason that the legal process allows, and often encourages, a winnowing down of charges by prosecutorial strategies as a way of securing convictions on those that can be proved in court. Negotiating plea agreements often, perhaps usually, reduces the number of legal grounds on which a final agreement will be based. An example is **Enron's** Chief Financial Officer (CFO) indicted on nearly 100 counts who was allowed to plead guilty to only 2 of the charges to induce his cooperation in naming others. Hung juries, retrials, and mid-trial changes of strategy by prosecutor or defendant can result in abandonment of one or more charges of illegal action. Therefore, news media reports of corporate activities that may eventually produce indictments, trials, convictions, and sentences tend to give fuller accounts of what can be construed as unethical or socially irresponsible behavior than the court record itself.

Webs of Intrigue

Figures 1–4 depict the organizational networks sustaining the corrupt and fraudulent activities at **Enron, WorldCom, Tyco,** and **HealthSouth**. These might usefully be called webs of intrigue and deceit. As the internal auditor who uncovered the fraudulent scheme at WorldCom said, "It was a spider web of transactions, and it was not easy to trace." Corruption in each company was made possible and carried out by four kinds of participants. *Schemers/Drivers* are the originators and the primary source of organizational authority for corrupt actions—the spiders sitting at the web's center, so to speak. In each figure, they are located in the circle. *Functional Enablers*, shown on the left, use their organizational function and authority to advance or reinforce the corrupt scheme. *Staff Cooperators* (on right) "go along" with the scheme, either willingly or reluctantly, by following orders from superiors. *External Confederates* (bottom), though not directly part of the company, provide indispensable aid that both sustains and extends the corrupt scheme's influence well beyond the company's borders.

Knowledge of the corrupt scheme is unevenly distributed throughout the web, so that any of the four—Schemers/Drivers, Functional Enablers, Staff Cooperators, and External Confederates—may or may not be aware of the full extent of the scheme. This would be especially true in any very large corporate structure where operations are far-flung, authority is divisionalized, or board oversight is technically difficult.

Figure 1

THE ENRON WEB

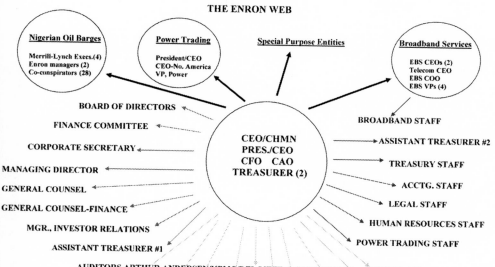

Figure 2

THE WORLDCOM WEB

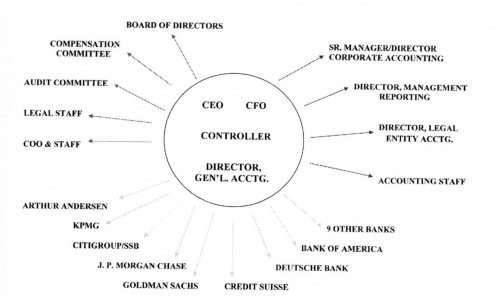

Figure 3

THE TYCO WEB

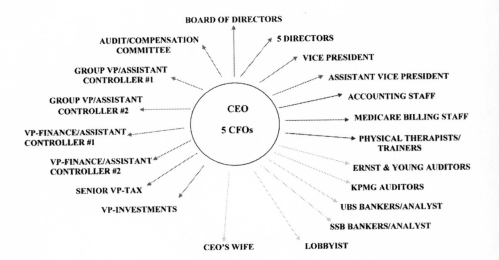

Figure 4

THE HEALTHSOUTH WEB

Support for the Propositions

Proposition 1: *Corporate fraud and corruption are coalitional actions, not individual acts.*

Enron. News reports identify more than 50 people by name said to be involved in corrupt, illegal activities of one kind or another, but this figure does not include a large number of others, including unnamed members of the board of directors; in-house lawyers; miscellaneous staff members in accounting, law, broadband services, treasury, and energy trading; several outside law firms; staff of the Federal Energy Regulatory Commission (FERC); 16+ banks; four auditing firms; close friends of Enron's CFO, as well as family members. Enron's president, as part of his legal defense strategy, asked permission of a federal judge to release the names of 114 co-conspirators, but even that count falls short of the total numbers involved.

Enron's networks of corruption were very extensive, requiring the collaboration and active involvement of many corporate functionaries at many different levels and in many different offices. Fraud was centered in four different areas of company operations: special purpose entities, broadband services, energy trading, and an operation in Nigeria. If one were to picture Enron corruption as a cancer centered in company headquarters, then these four "daughter cells" had metastisized to other locales and organs in Enron's far-flung corporate body.

WorldCom (now MCI). At WorldCom, 14 persons were named as active participants. Others included 12 directors, members of the board's compensation committee, 3 accounting managers, in-house lawyers, 7 miscellaneous executives and their spouses, miscellaneous staff in accounting and law, 15 banks, 2 brokerage firms, and 2 auditing firms. Bankruptcy court examiner Dick Thornburgh reported that at least 40 WorldCom employees knew about the fraud but were afraid to speak out. A former WorldCom CEO stated that the wrongdoing was confined to "fewer than 100" employees.

Tyco. The numbers at Tyco also reveal the presence of a coalitional network. Eighteen persons have been identified by name or position, while others include members of the board's compensation committee; board members identified as "cheerleaders" of the fraudulent operations; in-house lawyers; 51 employees who received unauthorized bonuses; lower-level managers who manipulated accounting rules; miscellaneous staff in accounting and regulatory law; 1 auditing firm; and 1 brokerage firm's vice president and stock analyst. The total number involved probably reached 70 or more.

HealthSouth. Thirty-three persons were identified by name. Others unnamed but involved were the board of directors; members of the board's audit-compensation committee; miscellaneous staff in accounting and Medicare billing; physical therapists and trainers; 2 auditing firms; 2 bankers; stock analysts at 2 brokerage firms; a director's wife; and the CEO's wife. An estimate of 50 or more employees is not unreasonable.

These reported coalition numbers for the four companies are under-counts of the actual numbers of network participants. In no case was the fraud carried out by a single individual or a duo of schemers. Like wolves, corporate crooks conspire and hunt in packs, not as loners.

Proposition 2: *Corporate fraud and corruption are top-down in origin, not bottom-up.*

A stereotypical view of crime depicts a kid putting his hand in the cookie jar while Mom isn't looking. That image doesn't compute in the corporate world, at least not in the companies discussed here. In all four companies, the very topmost executives—chief executive officer (CEO) and chief financial officer (CFO)—were the leaders, the initiators, the drivers, and the schemers. It was Mom, not Johnny, who sneaked the cookies while no one was looking.

At **Enron**, CEO and CFO were joined by several other high-ranking executives, including the CEO of North American operations, Energy CEO, and Telecommunications CEO (2 of the latter), the company's chief accounting officer (CAO), 5 vice presidents, and a chief operating officer (COO). Also implicated were members of the board of directors, especially the board's finance committee, general counsel, and general counsel-finance.

The story is essentially the same at **WorldCom** (CEO, CFO, COO, controller, director-general accounting, board members and board committees), **Tyco** (CEO, CFO, general counsel, compliant board of directors, and board compensation committee), and **HealthSouth** (CEO, 5 different CFOs, board members, board audit-compensation committee, and 8 vice presidents).

Clearly, people who occupied these exalted positions were the organizational elite. Corporate fraud is an elitist activity, originated at the pinnacles of power and authority. Thus the corporation's hierarchical organization that cedes dominant power and decision making to the highest ranking officers contributes to, and makes possible, the formation of elitist coalitions bent on personal enrichment through fraudulent and corrupt means.

Proposition 3: *Corporate fraud and corruption are hierarchically imposed and collaboratively induced, not independently volitional.*

To be successful, high-level corporate defrauders and corrupters must enlist others from within the company. These others—they might accurately be called "gang members"—are recruited for their usefulness in authorizing dubious actions, falsifying company records, devising ways around standard operating procedures (such as generally accepted accounting principles), colluding with auditors or deceiving them, jacking up market prices by artificially restricting supply (as **Enron's** energy traders did), shredding incriminating documents or deleting e-mail files, submitting inflated financial reports, concealing true costs of operations, etc.

Not all gang members sign on willingly or even knowingly. They may be persuaded or ordered to write a financial report they know to be untrue. When a **WorldCom** employee questioned an accounting discrepancy, the company's director of general accounting told him, "Show those numbers to the damn auditors and I'll throw you out the f_____ window." One J. P. Morgan Chase banker told a colleague who knew about **Enron's** fraudulent trading contracts, "Shut up and delete this e-mail!!!!!" **Tyco's** manager of human relations eased the CEO's questionable loans through or around official channels, while the head of regulatory accounting altered internal documents to conceal results from Arthur Andersen auditors. Three mid-level accountants knowingly counted reserves as current expenses for several consecutive quarters. A combination of physical therapists, trainers, and billing personnel at **HealthSouth** cooperated in making false claims to Medicare. One of the healthcare company's vice presidents authorized the filing of false federal and state tax returns, while another overvalued company investments to make the company look good to investors. **Health-South's** assistant controller and four subordinates made false accounting entries and "were afraid to report what was going on," then later pleaded guilty, saying they believed they wouldn't be implicated in the fraud because they weren't actually signing the falsified documents!

The plight and ethical posture of these lesser gang members varies. Some were willing accomplices, amply rewarded for their cooperation by raises, promotions, bonuses, forgiveness of housing and relocation loans, vacation trips, golden parachutes, gifts of company stock and company SUVs, lavish lunches and parties, etc. Others were reluctant to go along but did so anyway, fearing job loss if they did not cooperate. Whether shill or knowing crook, both types were caught up within an organizational system that exerted a powerful influence on their economic well-being: their salary, benefits, health care, and retirement pensions. Many found it easy to "go along if the boss wants it," like good organizational soldiers everywhere. They were also subject to all the pressures one feels in a vibrant corporate culture, not wanting to rock the boat and having little incentive to do so.

Enron's go-go culture was famous for its lavish excesses, employee parties, celebrations, and awards, in one case featuring a baby elephant as party guest. It would have been hard to resist going along with whatever the job called for, even though legally or professionally dubious. Although some employees clearly struggled with their consciences and in some cases openly opposed corrupt actions, most accepted what they believed to be the realities of life in a big organization and became willing accomplices.

Ethical culpability in general is associated with one's level of organizational authority, starting with top-ranked *Schemers/Drivers*, followed by *Functional Enablers* who use their organizational authority to advance or reinforce the corrupt scheme, and then by lesser-ranked *Staff Cooperators* who, willingly or reluctantly, agree to follow orders.

Proposition 4: *Corporate fraud and corruption are activated by self-aggrandizing executive impulse, not by pursuit of organizational function or purpose.*

However exorbitant the executive salaries, however generous the bonuses, however lavish the company-paid personal expenses, however enriching the special-favor allocations of IPO stocks to favorites, however stratospheric their stock-option awards, however many conflict-of-interest deals with directors, however often false reports were filed with regulatory overseers—in all these instances, it was always claimed by the Schemers/Drivers that such actions benefited the company and helped discharge obligations to shareholders, creditors, employees, and other stakeholders. "I did it for the company" was the accused's mantra, and later became a part of their legal defense, at **Enron, WorldCom, Tyco,** and **HealthSouth**.

CEOs at all four companies could point to a phenomenal expansion of corporate assets and markets during their tenure. Stock valuations climbed steadily, boosted by (and boosting) investor confidence. Acquisitions ballooned, creating larger and larger corporate empires with larger and larger revenues. Investment banks poured billions in credit into corporate treasuries. Brokerage analysts touted the companies' stock as a sure-fire thing. Auditors' reports reinforced the judgments of outsiders. Company employees were induced, and sometimes required, to put their retirement funds into company stock. Such all-round confidence from so many quarters certainly seemed to testify that top management was guiding each of the four companies in the best possible way to achieve positive results for all market participants.

The fuller, and more accurate, story is now known. It was not organizational purpose and economic function that drove the key Schemers. Each CEO knew well before anyone else that his company's economic standing, and even its future, was threatened by decisions and actions that profited the Schemers/Drivers, Functional Enablers, and Staff Cooperators, not to say many External Confederates. **Enron, WorldCom, Tyco,** and **Health-South** suffered financially as a direct result of the unethical, corrupt, behind-the-scenes actions initiated by the top-level executives and carried out with the help of others both inside and outside each company.

WorldCom fraud totaled at least $11 billion, the company lost $60 billion in asset value and wound up bankrupt. Of **Enron's** three main fraudulent operations—broadband services, energy trading, and off-book special purpose entities—only energy trading brought money into the company but did so illegally by rigging market supplies and prices. Broadband services never made a penny, and the off-book, off-shore special purpose entities lined the CFO's pockets but not **Enron's**. At **HealthSouth**, the total fraud figure was over $4 billion and, like the other three companies, its stock value plummeted. All four companies turned out to be financial disasters for shareholders, creditors, and employees. None could legitimately claim that their top executives' policies and decisions had produced results beneficial for the company's long-term economic strength.

By contrast, the record shows that executive self-aggrandizement was the central motive at work. Executive Schemers raided company treasuries at will, authorizing out-of-sight salaries for themselves, exorbitant (and in at least one case, extortionate) bonuses, travel allowances, stock options and outright gifts of stock, purchases of artwork, forgiveness of personal loans, gifts of housing and jewelry, multimillion dollar parties (including an infamous one on foreign soil to celebrate a CEO's wife's birthday), sweetheart deals for favored directors, and underwriting executive love affairs with favored staff members.

The chief Schemers' self-magnification quest went beyond mere economic enrichment to include social and political influence. **HealthSouth's** political lobbyist orchestrated political influence at local, state, and federal levels, including friendly relations with Senators Daschle, Harkin, and Hatch, House Speaker Hastert, and President Clinton. Through generous philanthropic gifts, executives at **Enron** and **Tyco** saw their names linked to university halls, sports stadiums, streets, and other public venues. Others were seen and admired as patrons of the arts. An apparent craving for fame fed an endless accelerating cycle of attention-getting activities. As one post-bankruptcy report said, the CEO at **WorldCom** "was allowed nearly imperial reign over the affairs of the company." Another source labeled **Tyco's** CEO as "the captain of corporate piggery," not a coveted title but a suggestive one.

All the evidence points towards a quest for self-aggrandizing executive glory, which subordinated and sabotaged what might otherwise have been policies intended to strengthen and expand their company's core economic mission. This observation is consistent with evolutionary psychology's contention that the modern executive brain reflects the ancestral conditions and challenges of Ice Age hunter-gatherers whose families, clans, and tribal groups were organized hierarchically by dominant alpha males who monopolized sexual access to females and the spoils of hunting. The impulse to acquire and wield power, and to enjoy all of the associated perquisites—financial, social, political, and sexual—appeared to be present in these companies. That the urge might be planted deep within a hard-wired executive brain may explain the persistence with which it appears and reappears in today's corporate world.

Such behavior also supports a picture of corporate culture dominated by two core value sets—economizing and power-aggrandizement—that shape and drive company decisions. This view was developed in the preceding **Year 2000** chapter in Part III. and more fully in an earlier book, *Values, Nature, and Culture in the American Corporation.*

Proposition 5: *Corporate fraud and corruption are habitual, repetitive, and infectious, not a reversible one-time event.*

Once begun, corporate corruption seems to take on a life of its own, becoming virtually unstoppable. Normal checks and balances are corrupted: internal and external audits, board of directors authorization, arm's-length relations between stock analysts and client companies, due diligence by creditors. Top-level Schemers find they must draw in larger numbers of Enablers and Cooperators: quarterly reports must be fudged, anticipated revenue is booked as current income, off-book entities become a dump for burying excessive costs or boosting company revenues, tax and government regulatory reports must be fine tuned to conceal lax compliance, compensation and audit committees are induced to bend the rules or look the other way. Gang membership swells as recruits are drawn from all organizational levels. Secretaries, supervisory staff, accounting underlings, financial analysts, professional staff, public relations managers, health care specialists, and legal staff become knowing partners, or in some cases unwitting ones, in the crimes initiated by their superiors.

Accounting fraud began at **HealthSouth** in the mid-1990s and continued quarterly for nearly a decade. **Tyco's** misdeeds may date as far back as the 1980s, while **WorldCom's** accounting irregularities began in 1997 and its CEO-CFO collusion around 2000. **Enron's** several layers of corruption were laid down mainly during the 1990s. In general, the most active fraud paralleled each company's drive for growth, expansion, and market dominance. As stock valuations climbed higher and higher, so likewise did executive rewards, putting a premium on keeping the curve on an upward slope. Fortunes were being made. The slightest hints of trouble—a slippage of quarterly revenue, a negative earnings report, the loss of an important market segment, failure to get regulatory approval of a new product, government cutback of health care allocations, a Wall Street analyst's skeptical assessment—could bring it all crashing down.

The corruption juggernaut bulled ahead, gathering speed and compounding fraud as it went. Nothing was allowed to block its path—not organizational rules, professional standards, laws, company traditions, uncooperative employees, auditor oversight, government regulations, stock exchange guidelines—nothing! Rules were bent, standards disregarded, laws flouted, traditions disregarded, uncooperative employees fired, auditors deceived or co-opted, regulatory agencies lied to, securities exchange guidelines manipulated. What had been epidemic in the executive suite soon was endemic to the entire culture. The cancer, the virus, the infection invaded all levels, broke down governance immune systems, leapt over corporate walls, infected auditors, bankers, brokers, regulators, friends, and family members. A virtual plague had descended on corporate America. It would not be easy to shake off.

Proposition 6: *Corporate fraud and corruption are extra-organizational, not confined within the company.*

An integral part of corruption strategy is the recruitment of External Confederates. Although varying somewhat from company to company, the usual candidates for gang membership are auditors, investment bankers, brokerage houses and their analysts, outside law firms, cooperative government regulators, and close friends and family members of the chief Schemers. Typically, **Enron** led the way among the four companies discussed here, having successfully recruited Arthur Andersen auditors, several of its partners, and one of its in-house lawyers; 3 other auditing firms; Merrill Lynch as a firm entity plus several senior-level individual officers, and staff lawyers; J. P. Morgan Chase and Citigroup as firms plus senior officers; 14 additional investment banks; several outside law firms; compliant Federal Energy Regulatory Commission regulatory staff; and the CFO's friends and family members, including his wife who also was assistant treasurer. **WorldCom's** reach was somewhat less by comparison, involving only two auditing firms, 3 investment banks, and a brokerage house and its star analyst. **Tyco's** crookedness received support from its auditor, PriceWaterhouseCoopers, and the Merrill Lynch brokerage firm. The Schemers and Drivers at **HealthSouth** found help from two auditing firms, two investment banks and their analysts, the CEO's wife, various friends, and a political lobbyist.

The External Confederates' support of crookery took various forms. Auditors signed off on procedures that violated generally accepted accounting principles, thereby misleading investors and creditors. Arthur Andersen's auditing and support staff, on the advice of a home-office lawyer, initiated the destruction of potentially incriminating documents at **Enron.** Brokerage and banking analysts, by issuing over-the-top unjustified estimates of company stock valuations (sometimes encouraged by that company's top Schemers), curried favor as a way of promoting their bank's business with the corrupt firm. Some senior banking officers led the cheering for a company's stock while urging their own staffs to "clean up their e-mail files" to avoid possible government prosecution. Government watchdog agencies permitted regulatory rules to be bent. Outside law firms advised in-house counsel regarding legally dubious actions, and one law firm issued a premature and incomplete internal investigative report clearing one of the companies and its executives who had engaged in illegal activities. Close family friends of corrupt corporate executives, along with the spouses of favored officials, served as channels for funneling illicit corporate funds out of the company and into the wrong hands.

The active cooperation of all types of External Confederates makes it abundantly clear that the web of deceit and corruption centered in the host corporation spread well beyond each company's own home-grown Mafia-like mob.

Proposition 7: *Corporate fraud and corruption are opportunistic and episodic, not ubiquitous, are triggered by environmental challenges, and are energized by aggressive, high-velocity, growth-oriented corporate culture.*

The pervasiveness and persistence, not to say the organizational depth and external reach, of fraud and corruption seen in these four companies raises a question of overriding significance for the modern business corporation: Are such acts ubiquitous, representing a continuum of behavior to be expected of all corporations and their top-level executives? Could it be that fraud and corruption are somehow inherent to corporate operations? An affirmative answer would surely shake the very foundations of business life as we know it.

The evidence reported here supports a less dramatic conclusion but one that gives pause nevertheless. All four companies were riding a big wave of expansion and growth in their respective markets. **Enron** had set its sights on becoming, not just the "world's largest energy company" but the "world's greatest company." It also swaggered into the rapidly growing telecommunications market by proposing a vast fiber optics network to compete with cable service. Its energy-trading and market-making skills in a range of commodities became its greatest claim to fame on Wall Street, boosting its stock to ever higher levels. Also during the 1990s **Tyco's** CEO Denis Kozlowski at one point was gobbling up a record 200 companies each year in an expansionist binge started by his predecessor a decade earlier, as Wall Street analysts cheered, investment bankers poured unlimited credit into the company's treasury, and revenues and earnings ballooned. **HealthSouth** prospered for a decade, its revenues fed by an aggressive acquisitions drive to get greater access to Medicare funds which were growing to match an aging population. Its profits soared each year by double digits, and its stock was bid up by nearly one-third from 1987 to 1997. Founded in 1983, **WorldCom's** relentless drive to the top was also fueled by a series of acquisitions and mergers, including two whoppers, $12 billion for MFS Communications (1996) and $42 billion for MCI (1997), and a failed effort to buy Sprint for $129 billion in 1999.

The common denominator and sustaining goal of such expansionist drives is an ever increasing valuation of the company's stock. Stock markets embrace it, creditors extend loans based on it, shareholders covet it, executive stock options soar with it, employee retirement accounts swell along with it. Keeping it spiraling upward becomes key to the fortunes of all involved.

Classic complexity theory says that self-organizing agents interacting with each other and with their environment spontaneously form complex adaptive systems (CAS's) that support the agents' needs (see **Year 1998** chapter above). The better and closer a CAS interacts with its environment, the more successful it is. That means a CAS must be good at meeting and taking advantage of adaptive opportunities that arise from its surroundings. Its strategy by necessity is opportunistic. The same applies to the modern corporation, which is a type of CAS operating in a variety of market environments. As new challenges appear—a new competitor, new products, new technology, political changes—they must be matched by suitable responses. Company strategy necessarily becomes opportunistic and episodic, dependent on both opportunities and threats arising irregularly from the market environment.

For **Enron**, energy markets surged, opening up new marketing vistas, along with fiber optic technology promising new ways of beaming television into millions of homes, plus profit opportunities from market-making commodity trades. Rapid expansion of telecommunications technology paved the way for **WorldCom's** drive for market domination. An aging, health-conscious American public was all **HealthSouth** needed to dream of unending revenues and profits by hooking its economic star to Medicare payments and rehabilitation services. **Tyco**, already an acquisition-built conglomerate, had only to take advantage of a feverish economic expansion cycle during the 1990s to find willing investors and investment bankers to feed its dizzying drive for market domination.

For all four companies, new environments created vast new opportunities for growth, expansion, and profits. They all reacted just as complexity theory predicts: their top-level executives and directors spontaneously self-organized company operations to fit and take advantage of emerging environmental opportunities. The internal excesses of fraud and corruption were spawned by the combined force of external environmental challenges and a corporate culture attuned to power and domination. In that sense, they were episodic and opportunistic, not necessarily a ubiquitous trait of corporate executive decision making.

If not universal, it is possible to conclude that corporate fraud and corruption are ever-present potentialities embedded in the fabric of corporate culture, capable of being activated by hard-wired executive motivational impulses in response to environmental opportunities for personal gain, enrichment, and power enhancement.

Birds of a Feather....

For those who believe that corporate malfeasance and crime are exceptions, or that corporate wrongdoing is normally committed by only a few "rotten apples" or "bad actors," the record and scale of recent corporate scandals will come as a wakeup call. A partial list of only the most well-known cases tells a strikingly different story. All of these companies, their top executives and directors, aided by auditors, law firms, stock analysts, and investment bankers have replicated essentially the same picture of coalitional misdeeds found in **Enron, WorldCom, Tyco,** and **Health-South**.

Here is a very incomplete roster where the webs of intrigue and plundering are virtually identical to those reported in this chapter: **Xerox**, photocopy technology; **Parmalat**, the Italian food giant; **Adelphia Communications**, the Pennsylvania-based cable company; **Lucent Technologies**, well-known telecommunications company; **Qwest Communications**, telecommunications firm; **Gemstar-TV Guide**, publications; **Cendant, Inc.**, travel and real estate; **Rite-Aid** pharmacy chain; **Ahold**, Dutch supermarket chain; **K-Mart** discount chain; **Global Crossing** telecommunications; **Office Max**, office-supply firm; **Bristol-Myers Squibb**, pharmaceuticals; **Symbol Technologies**, bar-code technology; **Beacon Hill Asset Management**, investments; **Bankgesellschaft Berlin AG**, banking; **Dynegy**, telecommunications; **McKesson**, drugs; **Banco Santander Central Hispano Americano SA**, banking; **American International Group (AIG)**, insurers.

Managers and analysts working for **Merrill Lynch, Credit Suisse First Boston, UBS,** and **Citigroup**; other investment banks **J. P. Morgan Chase, Goldman Sachs, Bank of America, Canadian Imperial Bank of Commerce** plus an equal number of others; and audit firms **Arthur Andersen, PriceWaterhouseCoopers, Ernst & Young, KPMG,** and other lesser known ones—all of these firms have supported, condoned, collaborated or colluded with the corrupt, fraudulent actions of companies charged with crimes and civil infractions. Add to this list large parts of the mutual fund industry found cheating investors *en masse* by permitting after-hours trading by a favored few.

Those "few rotten apples" begin to look more and more like an entire orchard.

Whatever Happened to Corporate Social Responsibility?

This paroxysm of corporate dishonesty, thievery, and betrayal of public trust contrasts sharply, even bitterly, with CSR's origins a half century ago. Then, it was believed (as revealed in <u>The 1950s</u> chapter, above) that being socially responsible was the mark of a truly professional corporate leader. Business purpose was *served* by CSR, ennobling the business practitioner and justifying the position of prominence and influence granted to that class by the public.

Are we to conclude that Frank Abrams' 1950s vision of corporate responsibility has been replaced by the turn-of-century corporate piggery of **Enron's** Andrew Fastow, **WorldCom's** Bernie Ebbers, **Tyco's** Denis Kozlowski, and **HealthSouth's** Richard Scrushy?

How far down into the corporate institution, and how widely, do corruption's tentacles reach? Do the genes of greed tug harder at the corporate psyche than the culture of ethical caring? Was Frank Abrams a false prophet? The CSR Grail an illusion?

These hovering questions haunt the hopes of all who seek goodness within corporate enterprise. Is it possible that some of the answers are to be found within the nation's business schools who are charged to prepare tomorrow's leaders? Have they been complicit in corporate crimes? More hopefully, can they restore Frank Abrams' vision? Those challenges are examined next in **Part IV**.

PART IV

TEACHING CORPORATE SOCIAL RESPONSIBILITY

Instilling a sense of social responsibility into the business mind through classroom teaching has long been a controversial matter. Although Joseph Wharton, who founded the nation's first business school over a century ago, boldly proclaimed the importance of developing a broad CSR-like knowledge among business practitioners, most business schools did not follow Wharton's lead. Instead, a sense of practicality came to dominate business instruction, reflecting the ever-more complex technical and financial necessities of the evolving business order. Free-market capitalism being what it is, neoclassical economics became the core discipline around which the business school curriculum was, and is, organized. Social matters—tellingly labeled "externalities"—were, and still are, given lesser standing as topics for classroom instruction. The chapters in Part IV tell some of the story of how the obstacles to CSR teaching have been modified—but by no means removed—through the determined efforts of CSR advocates both within the business schools and the corporate community of practitioners.

YEAR 1961

CLIFFS NOTES FOR THE CSR TEACHER

Setting the Scene. In 1997, The American College honored Clarence Walton with a symposium featuring his many contributions to infusing ethics into the lives, minds, and decisions of business executives. He did so from a variety of impressive positions: classroom teacher, associate dean of Columbia University's business school, dean of Columbia's College of General Studies, and president of Catholic University of America. But it was the 1961 textbook, Conceptual Foundations of Business, written with coauthor Richard Eells, that first gave CSR teachers what they needed to bring CSR awareness to the forefront of business thinking. My review begins with a spoof of the skepticism they were to encounter—and not just in the business schools.

The telephone conversation between aspiring author and potential publisher must have gone something like this:

Walton: *Hello, I've written a book that I'd like you to publish.*
Editor: *Fine, what's it about?*
Walton: *Conceptual foundations of business.*
Editor: *(Pause) Oh?... You mean profits, costs, productivity, and things like that? We already have several books along those lines.*
Walton: *Well, no, not exactly. It's broader than that.*
Editor: *Oh, now I see what you mean. Inflation, the business cycle, unemployment—the bigger economic arena where business is done. That's the kind of practical foundation that business students need, all right. It **is** for business students, right?*
Walton: *Yes, for MBAs. Uh . . but, look, I don't think you...that is, I don't think I've given you a clear picture of what the book is.*
Editor: *Why not tell me how the book begins?*
Walton: *Well, early on we describe how business was done in pre-Columbian Mexico. You know, among the Aztecs.*

Editor: *(A longer pause) Really?... I'll have to contact our sales rep in Monterey and see if he thinks it'll go there. You'll have to write it in Spanish, you know. I'm not sure Aztec is still spoken.*

Walton: *(with a touch of exasperation) Look, maybe I'd better start all over.*

Editor: *Oh, no, that's all right. I'm getting the picture. Tell me some of the authors you cite. That's a good way to get a feel for any book. Especially a book intended for hard-nosed business types.*

Walton: *(perking up at the suggestion) I agree. Richard and I are very proud of the strong case we've made for that kind of business thinking. We have citations to Antigone, Atticus, Engels, Freud, Job, Justinian, Jack London, Baron de Montesquieu, Arthur Miller, Moses Maimonides, Ortega y Gasset, Roscoe Pound, Stalin, and Jimmy Hoffa.... Plus others... Hegel, Hume, Huxley....*

Editor: *(breaking in) Well...that's quite a list, all right. (Pause) Who was Atticus?... Say, did you ever think of using* **The Reader's Digest?** *That has some real meaty stuff sometimes. You know, things like The Most Unforgettable Character I Ever Met. Gives a real human touch to any dull book. Hey, I don't mean that your book would be dull.... It's just that we have to be careful not to talk over the heads of our readers. You know—ha! ha!—the old bottom line is there all the time. Professor, I think I'd better speak to my boss about this proposal of yours and then get back to you. Which business school did you say you're at?*

With this book, called *Conceptual Foundations of Business*, Clarence Walton and his coauthor were trying to convince a doubting world of the need for a textbook that would bring history, philosophy, and literature into the developing consciousness of the nation's future business leaders. Their goal was to point the way to the future by reminding readers of yesterday's ways.

It is worthwhile recalling just what the world was like in the 1950s when this book was in its formative stages. America's war hero, General Dwight Eisenhower, was president. Cold War cynicism had replaced the optimism generated by the defeat of Nazism. The menace of a nuclear Armageddon dominated popular consciousness everywhere. The civil rights sit-ins had begun to stir public awareness of a darker past that lingered on into modern times. John Kenneth Galbraith's *The Affluent Society* raised troubling questions about the excesses of prosperity and the gap between rich and poor.

Other celebrated heralds of cultural trends had not yet been heard from. Rachel Carson's *Silent Spring* would not burst on the scene for another four years (1962), Betty Friedan's *The Feminine Mystique* another year after that (1963), Woodstock, that icon of youth's revolt, was over a decade away (1969). Vietnam was a distant whisper, heard only in the cloistered halls of diplomacy. The youthful John Kennedy and the crafty Richard Nixon waited in the wings for their respective moments of future glory and tragic downfall.

One way to understand this book and its importance is to see it as a reflection of the larger institutional-cultural framework within which the authors pursued their lives and work during the 1950s and 1960s.

The Cultural Setting

In one sense, America during the entire last half of the twentieth century has been convulsed by a titanic struggle between the idea of The Collective and the idea of The Individual. Two main forces have propelled this trend. One is a backlash against the New Deal and its progeny, the Welfare State. The other and more dominant force was the Cold War between a collectivist Communism and an individualistic Capitalism.

In this tense ideological atmosphere, any program, policy, idea, or approach that emphasized or favored The Collective over The Individual could expect to encounter rough going. Labor union leaders saw their union membership rolls steadily shrink, as right-to-work laws began to erode the unions' collective power. Lyndon Johnson's civil rights initiatives, we are now able to see, were the Welfare State's last hurrah, buried under the tumult and debris of the fateful Vietnam encounter. Ronald Reagan embodied the essence of both individualism by defending and reinvigorating free-market principles and practice, and Cold War American intransigence towards communism as he gave the final push that brought "the evil empire" crashing down. We have indeed lived through a gargantuan struggle in which The Individual has been lifted up in glory while The Collective has been buried in shame and dishonor. Little wonder, then, that a theory of corporate social responsibility insinuating the superiority of The Social Good over The Individual Firm's quest for profits would be greeted with skepticism and outright hostility.

On the other hand, even in the midst of this broader cultural contest something might succeed if it could be seen in either of two lights: (1) if The Collective Impulse could be fitted into the larger framework of a capitalist, free-market system without threatening or seeming to threaten its integrity, and (2) if The Individual Impulse could be seen as promoting and strengthening The (minimally necessary) Collective sinews of the larger society.

The Conceptual Foundations

Clarence Walton and Richard Eells, with a touch of genius, seized both possibilities in constructing their theory of business's social responsibilities. They set out to demonstrate that The Collective welfare of business and society is directly traceable to The Individualist philosophy that spawned the entire American experiment in representative government and free-market capitalism. An executive thoroughly seasoned in that tradition, and willing to put it into practice, could not help but make enlightened decisions that were simultaneously supportive of the commonweal and of private enterprise. Far from being foreign to the American love affair with The Individual, their theory of corporate social responsibility was rooted squarely in American individualism. And they were to show in the end that anyone opposed to this view—especially, the practicing manager and business leader—was not just turning away from cherished American traditions but also was rejecting essential ways of getting the world's work done. It was a subtle, daring strategy but one that succeeded beyond all hope and expectation.

Their conceptual foundations of business were none other than the philosophical, ideological stones originally laid down by John Locke, Adam Smith, David Hume, Thomas Jefferson, and James Madison. These included *freedom of association, ownership and private property, constitutionalism, pluralism,* and *liberty*. These core principles anchored the business system, lent it stability, and gave it an enduring quality. Also rationalized were *the free market, the ground rules for competition, the sanctity of contracts, laws to govern and restrain business power, motives for individual economic improvement,* and *political liberties* that segued into and became identical with *market freedoms*. Within such a cocoon of laws, customs, and institutions, the American corporation had prospered and had become the core of a powerful industrial society.

Interwoven into these stabilizing principles were contrasting and sometimes contradictory themes equally a part of the American experience and ethos. They included *technological innovation and social change, the idea of progress, a dedication to work,* and *a devotion to equal opportunity, personal growth, and spiritual enrichment*. Here the corporation faced change, uncertainty, and all of the doubts that social change injects into questions of values, justice, ethics, and social equity.

The authors seemed to say to their student readers, "from these conceptual foundations embodying both stability and change will arise a new business and managerial world that you, the leadership cadre, will confront in all of its overwhelming complexity. You can meet its many formidable challenges with greater professional success and personal satisfaction if you understand clearly that while your decisions may shape the future, they also will reflect a richly textured cultural heritage."

The Quest for Legitimacy

But a single textbook, however well crafted, cannot prevail against firmly entrenched faculty interests. Although Corporate Social Responsibility has now [in 1997] been accepted as a field of management study for roughly three decades, it was not always so. To be admitted into the hallowed and well-guarded curricular precincts of the business school, its supporters had to fight and scratch their way in. The techniques were as varied as they were colorful. Stealth sometimes worked, when newly appointed and innocuous appearing deans quietly seized the reins of power. Forceful takeovers could succeed, as traditional faculty members suddenly found themselves outnumbered by new upstart faculty appointees. Internal rebellions, probably the bloodiest of the various approaches, were not unknown, as the barons of finance and accounting were sent packing. Occasionally, the highly unlikely would occur when a school actually listened—imagine that!—to the voices of business practitioners complaining about the narrowness and lack of creativity of the graduates they hired.

While these internecine struggles were succeeding in schools here and there, they would not have been sufficient to establish a new field of management study on a national scale. That required a body of justifying literature, a central theory of the field, empirical research tools, a group of qualified faculty to do the research and teach the subject, students willing to take the courses (when not coerced to do so by curricular fiat), a way to rationalize the topic as relevant to business practice, and—critically important in the early days—leadership by prestigious schools and universities. Only the last of these vital legitimizing conditions existed when Eells and Walton issued their first edition in 1961. *Conceptual Foundations of Business* proved to be a powerful shield as the authors took their place in the front ranks as the struggle for academic legitimacy began.

During the 1950s, a handful of business schools dared to venture somewhat timidly into these unknown curricular waters. Two of the better known leaders were Harvard and Columbia. The Harvard Business School was first into the fray, aided greatly by a decade of articles about social responsibility, business ethics, and the relation of business and religion in *The Harvard Business Review,* and the teaching of Kenneth Andrews, George Albert Smith, and Raymond Bauer. At Columbia, a new dean from industry ranks, Courtney Brown—none other than executive assistant to

Standard Oil's Frank Abrams (see **The 1950s** chapter in Part I)—appointed Clarence Walton as associate dean, who immediately began teaching a course from which the Eells and Walton text would grow.

At this time, the field's supporting theory was paper thin and the research base was nonexistent. The classic statement of social responsibility had been made in 1953 by Howard Bowen, a former business school dean turned college president, in a book titled *Social Responsibilities of the Businessman.* Richard Eells's *The Meaning of Modern Business: An Introduction to the Philosophy of the Large Corporate Enterprise*, published a year before the Eells and Walton text, contained a remarkably clear version of what is now called the "stakeholder" theory of the firm. In 1963 Joseph McGuire at the University of Washington brought out the only book on business and society relations that ever achieved a semi-popular status, the paperback *Business and Society.* Later still in that decade Keith Davis and Robert Blomstrom, in *Business and Its Environment*, found a formula for describing business and society relations that would hold up through three decades and eight successive editions—and is still going strong. As the decade ended, yet another book destined to become a classic appeared; it was Edwin M. Epstein's *The Corporation in American Politics.*

Achieving Legitimacy

As courageous as these pioneering efforts were, their collective strength could not have prevailed had they not been given a powerful boost by three external events of transcendent importance.

One was the issuance in 1959 of two reports on business school education, both of them a kind of report card or state-of-the-field assessment. The Ford Foundation and the Carnegie Corporation had commissioned the reports independently of one another, but they came to the same stark conclusions. Business schools were not preparing their students for leadership in the postwar world. Their failures were many: a narrow, overly technical curriculum; low admissions standards that encouraged academic mediocrity; a vocational first-job preparation; a short-run professional outlook; an inward-looking domestic, national orientation; an exclusive focus on the mechanisms of a market economy; and an over-reliance on the discipline of economics. In a word, they had evolved into vocational trade schools at a time when national and international conditions called for much larger visions from its business leaders, when the social and behavioral sciences were burgeoning with new insights about organizational dynamics, and when mathematics and statistics were finding new applications in linear programming, inventory controls, and related techniques during the initial years of the Computer Age.

The one felicitous phrase from these famous reports that would forever justify the kind of approach found in *Conceptual Foundations of Business* was the need for schools to provide an education in "the non-market environment of business." Almost overnight, the content of the Corporate Social Responsibility course was anointed as a welcome and needed part of the modern manager's education. This phrase could be hoisted and waved like a battlefield flag in the face of foot-dragging deans and recalcitrant curriculum committees. "See, here," the cry would go up, "our claims to the minds of students are as justified as yours!"

But anyone who has lived in a university for any time at all knows how hard it is to dislodge faculty members from the turf they have occupied for long years. It is probably true, as the old adage goes, that it is easier to move a cemetery than to change a university curriculum. In these struggles, logic and common sense seldom make a difference. What *can* make a difference, though, is the collective judgment of the profession at large, particularly if expressed on a national scale and through academic trade association channels.

And that is precisely what occurred twice. In 1971 The Academy of Management decided to create divisions of its members based on specialization. An alert group of advocates for the Business and Society field, led by Sumner Marcus of the University of Washington, argued successfully for creating a new division in The Academy to be called Social Issues in Management (SIM). This formal recognition of the importance of studying "the non-market environment of business" put a professional seal of approval on what had been favored in principle by the two foundation reports. Social Issues were thus given equal standing with other management subjects.

Three years later, in 1974, the American Association of Collegiate Schools of Business (AACSB)—the business schools' national accrediting agency—included Business and Society in the common body of knowledge required for a school's official accreditation. Full-fledged legitimacy had been won. It was, by no coincidence, the same year that Richard Eells and Clarence Walton brought out the third edition of their celebrated text.

Winning the accreditation battle was a major victory. The principal hero was Walter Klein of Boston College, whose negotiating skills were indispensable to gaining full recognition of Social Issues from AACSB accrediting officials.

Theoretical Foreshadowings

What then can be said of this book's contributions to the Social Issues in Management field? Just how did it make a difference? The answer, in retrospect, seems both astonishing and immensely impressive: *These two authors foreshadowed and gave expression to all of the major components of the field's present theoretical infrastructure.*

They provided a comprehensive statement of **stakeholder theory**, the core concept of current Corporate Social Responsibility thinking. A quarter century before Edward Freeman wrote the "bible" of stakeholder theory, they declared that "everyone has a stake in managerial enterprise" and they saw the business firm as "a constellation of interests."

They fleshed out the classic theory of **corporate social responsibility**, arguing that corporate management has obligations to all of the "direct and indirect contributor-claimants" that made business enterprise possible and prosperous, including workers, stockholders, consumers, suppliers, distributors, local communities, and the general public. A long-run balance-the-best-interests managerial philosophy would have to supplant the short-run profits-only perspective. Long years before plant closings would become the focus of national concern, they pointed out the need to take a socially responsible stance in such cases.

They embraced a primitive version of a **social contract** between business and society—calling it a social charter—and quoted David Rockefeller's support of the idea. They invoked but did not fully develop the rudiments of today's theories of **business ethics**, saying in 1961 that "business, of late, is concerning itself with the question of ethics." They spoke of human rights that entail managerial duties, and of a needed rectitude in corporate affairs, of new values generated both in and around the business firm, of the importance of the "normative sciences" for shedding new light on old problems, and they issued an invitation to "ethicists [to] take the idea of corporate responsibility and join in the intellectual search for answers." They even introduced the idea of a **communitarian ethics**, saying it was "in the ascendance" some twenty-five years before the term and the idea were popularized by sociologist Amitai Etzioni.

As if all this were not enough to establish their place in the Corporate Social Responsibility pantheon, they spoke eloquently and often about issues of **corporate governance** that had been created by the accumulated power of corporate executives. And students were told of the cross-cultural novelties and dilemmas of **multinational corporate operations** that they would face in a rapidly expanding world of commerce and trade. Perhaps most prescient of all was a chapter with the title "Business and Value-Forming Institutions" where they foretold the leadership role that business was bound to take in shaping America's **values** in coming decades.

These are the main ideas and themes that sustained the text's excellence through three editions and nearly twenty years of active classroom use. Its general outlook was moderate, non-radical, mildly managerial and pragmatic, heavily historical, and deeply philosophical. Its level of literacy and sophistication was very high, the breadth and depth of coverage impressively comprehensive. A multi-disciplinary perspective drew on history, politics, economics, anthropology, philosophy, law, the arts, and the humanities. It saddens me to say that no book of this intellectual range and vision could possibly find a place in today's business schools.

The book's life was limited by the inability of its moderate Establishment message of social responsibility to satisfy the intense, turbulent social demands of the late 1960s and 1970s. Those pressures simply overwhelmed the somewhat gentlemanly, paternalistic management attitudes advocated by the authors. Their lessons were not pointed enough for business practitioners suddenly faced with an angry, hostile public and a rising tide of government regulations. Competing texts geared to a simpler level of explanation and to a managerially pragmatic approach, and spelling out specific ways to respond to social and regulatory demands, took over the textbook market.

So, too, was the Eells and Walton emphasis on ethics premature, for neither teachers, students, nor business practitioners were yet ready for *explicit* ethics analysis of workplace dilemmas. That would have to await the ethical transgressions of succeeding decades that shocked the general business conscience and, on the scholarly side, it would depend on the emergence and acceptance of formal philosophic analysis introduced by business ethicists who then became major commentators and contributors.

YEAR 1963

ARE BUSINESS SCHOOLS
REALLY NECESSARY?

Setting the Scene. An air of defensiveness suffuses this early statement, made by a freshman dean trying to justify the existence of business schools to others, as well as to himself. However, it can also be read as part of the managerial educational canon that permeated the thinking of corporate managers and business school educators during the latter half of the 20th century. A later chapter (__Year 2005__ in Part IV.) questions much, but not all, of the rationale found here. Penned before gender sensitivity came to the fore, this statement joins many others of that period in blithely assuming that business is a man's domain. Mea culpa!

A businessman has awesome influence, extensive responsibilities, and profound social obligations. Do business schools adequately prepare him—in fact, can they do so? If not, what is their function? Should they even exist?

There is no person in American society whose education is more important than the businessman. The businessman is the major figure in the American economy. He oversees production, distribution, and financing. He sees that employees are hired and fired and trained to do specific tasks. He is responsible for the conversion to productive uses of human, natural, and technological resources. His influence on consumption is equally great. Through marketing, merchandising, and retailing he brings goods and services to the consuming public, and through advertising he sways them to buy ever larger quantities of this or that product. And since production and distribution are highly specialized, the businessman needs to coordinate the work of specialists and weld them together into an instrument capable of accomplishing the economic mission of American enterprise. This calls for planning; planning calls for budgeting; budgeting leads to forecasting; and all of these call for leadership and economic statesmanship.

So the businessman is producer, marketer, financier, coordinator, planner, budgeter, forecaster, leader, manager, director, administrator, motivator, controller—in short, he is a massive accumulation of highly important skills and techniques necessary to the operation of the American economy.

All of this is impressive enough, but the businessman is more than these things. He is a community leader, charged with many tasks that go far beyond the limits of the business enterprise. By serving as director and adviser to public schools, universities, hospitals, churches, youth movements, and charitable fund-raising campaigns, he vitally affects the ebb and flow of general community life.

A Political Force

He is also a potent political force. He provides many of the funds for local, state, and national political campaigns. He often runs for office and is elected, or he is appointed to serve in some capacity as a public servant. Whether he occupies public office or not what the government does intimately affects his business operations. This means he must be as knowledgeable about politics as about economics. And in these days of global politics and global economics, he must be as well informed about developments in Asia, Europe, or Africa as about the state of the city government in his own back yard.

The businessman is more than economist, manager, politician, and global strategist. Today's businessman must also be a psychologist and even a sociologist. The great emphasis upon human relations in the workplace means that the businessman must be adept in the subtleties of human relationships. He should know what makes people tick and what makes them run down. He needs to know how to motivate workers and how to energize them to seek the goals of the business enterprise. He knows that a coffee break can be as important to increased productivity as a new machine tool.

Science, technology, and the quantification of business operations force him to be a technician, a statistician, a mathematician—or at least, he needs to be able to communicate with these types of personnel. If he lacks this ability, he must either turn the business over to the technicians, the programmers, the computer people, and the data processing specialists, or let the new forms of technology run riot through established business procedures. Both alternatives constitute a vital threat to the businessman.

Adapting to Change

On top of all this, the businessman must be a historian, which means he needs to understand and be able to adapt to change, for if the American enterprise system is any one thing, it is a changing system. Dynamism and transformation have been characteristics of the American scene and the American business system since colonial days, and the pace of change today is swifter than ever. The businessman must be prepared for this change and to adjust himself to new conditions and novel situations. To do so is to prevail and live to see another accounting period; to fail to do so is to court oblivion. Therefore, if he can take deep draughts from the past, learn to identify enduring elements of the economy and the society, learn from past mistakes, and project the past into the future, he will have learned valuable lessons from history that can make him a better and more successful businessman.

Finally, the American businessman is a philosopher. In making business decisions and planning for the future, he needs to be judicious, wise, and of a reflective temperament. He needs to think profoundly about the total consequences of his actions and those of his company. *He needs to be aware of the broad social consequences of his decisions and the deeper ethical implications involved in the relationships between business and the larger society.*

In sum, then, the businessman is economist, manager, producer, marketer, financier, coordinator, planner, forecaster, leader, director, administrator, motivator, controller, politician, community figure, public servant, psychologist, technician, historian, and philosopher. He is all these things rolled into one. His influence is awesome, his responsibilities extensive, his obligations to society profound.

Educating Business Professionals

Creating a businessman with all these characteristics, skills, techniques, and capabilities is the task we have placed at the doorstep of the nation's colleges and universities, and particularly our collegiate schools of business. What can a business school do and what can't it do?

Let us acknowledge at the outset that the job is impossible. No college or university or school of business can create a businessman. The reason is simple: No one can be a businessman without business experience, usually several years of it. Unlike the medical and legal professions, there is no magical moment, symbolized by the conferring of a degree or certificate, when one becomes a businessman. The status of businessman is acquired slowly as one accumulates a great backlog of economic, political, and technical experience.

Although the business school cannot create a businessman out of whole cloth, neither is its function irrelevant to business. Quite the contrary, it can be a powerful ally of the business community. Without the business school, the entire business system would be vastly weakened, impoverished, and perhaps even deprived of one of the key factors that allows it to be so successful.

Training vs. Education

The job of the university business school is to *educate*, not *train*. The business school should not spend its time training students in the specific techniques and skills that are related to specific jobs and tasks. Vocational, highly specialized, technical, how-to-do-it courses have no place in the program of a collegiate school of business. Vocational and technical training can best be done on the job or in specialized institutes by experts who are experienced in the specific requirements of specific jobs and work processes. Each industry, each form of business, each individual firm has its own special way of doing things, its own procedures, its own shop manual. It is the responsibility of business management—not the university—to make these special procedures known to its employees. Although a business school can often provide valuable advisory assistance to business and industry in planning training programs, the school should not attempt, in its regular educational program, to give the equivalent of on-the-job training.

Liberal Education

A business school is designed to teach. But if it can't teach students to be businessmen, what can it teach? Why have a business school at all? The answer to that challenge cuts in two directions.

First, the business school can provide its students with a broad, general, liberal education. "Liberal" here means liberating and unleashing the deeper layers of personality and mentality for coping with the problems of business and for understanding the swift pace of social change. It also means liberating the student from prejudices and ignorance, shaping an alert, well-informed, mentally aggressive person. The business school ought to be interested in the whole person, not just the narrow specialist.

This means that the business student should be introduced to the three broad areas of human knowledge: the humanities, the social sciences, and the natural sciences. The humanities include philosophy, the liberal arts, literature, and languages. The social sciences include history, political science, economics, sociology, psychology, and anthropology. The natural sciences embrace the physical sciences, such as chemistry, geology, and physics, and the biological sciences. A significant educational experience in each of these areas means the student will gain an appreciation of our cultural heritage, of the vastness and complexity of the world of ideas, and of the circumstances that have led to the emergence of mankind's major accomplishments. Mastery will not be achieved in any of these areas of knowledge but it will be another step toward becoming a whole person, capable of reacting significantly in all facets of life that are encountered both on and off the job.

One might argue, though, that these are the things that a liberal arts college does. If the business school is simply to duplicate the work of the liberal arts college, why even have a business school? Can a business school do anything distinctive that the arts college cannot do? Yes, it can. And it would be especially ironic to lose sight of this fact today in view of the exciting and dramatic breakthroughs being made in understanding modern business and management.

The Business Core

The distinctive function of the business school is to introduce the student to the world of business. The business student can learn the meaning of business, the major functions of business, such as production, marketing, finance, and staffing, and the major controls available to management in directing the enterprise, such as statistics and accounting.

Beyond these core functions, the business student should have an education that singles out the stable elements and continuous processes of administration and management, the recurring problems of human relations and adjustment, the hard core of organization and communication, and the arts of leadership and decision making. These elements are particularly important in today's organizational society where leadership, managership, and administration have become more prominent features of the business environment.

Today's business school program is based upon the belief that business management is increasingly a function of the accumulation of a managerial technology and the use of scientific methods for defining and solving business problems. It recognizes that *businessmen and managers need a broad knowledge of society, its institutions, and its values if they are to carry out their functions as leaders of business and general community affairs.* It expresses the belief that business leaders should have a mature understanding of *the place and function of business in society at large and the mutual responsibilities that exist between business and society.* Finally, it urges a careful consideration of *the human element* in business enterprise and proposes an equally careful study of *human values* in their cultural context. These are the things a business school can do—and do better—than a liberal arts college.

Research

A business school must do more than simply teach and prepare young people to enter the world of business. It must also be an active center of research and consultation on problems that confront businessmen. The school should perform its research function so well that the business community should look to the school for leadership in ideas as it looks to the school for future organizational leaders. An active and experienced faculty, brimming over with ideas and understanding, can be a powerful ally of the business community faced with a multitude of problems. Both school and business can enrich themselves by forming a partnership of research, consultation, and mutual support.

It is often not understood, though, that the research function of a business school goes—and should go—beyond the realm of the immediate, day-to-day problems of the business world. Research should carry a faculty into areas where there are no problems—only questions. It is this kind of research, carried on in obscure laboratories years ago, that eventually put astronauts John Glenn, Scott Carpenter, and Walter Schirra into orbit and brought them back safely. Whether an immediate payoff is obvious or not, it is vitally important that this type of research be sponsored by a business school.

A Questioning Faculty

A faculty should constantly question all those things that seem to be most certainly known. For a business school, this involves probing the historical roots of the capitalist system and ferreting out the directions in which that system is now changing. It involves a sober examination of the ideologies that underpin that system and those that challenge it. It requires us to challenge traditions and customs, to question cherished ideas and comfortable habits, to probe deeply and profoundly the moral and philosophical issues of business and the larger society. When these things are done, the school, its students, and its businessmen-supporters emerge with a truer concept of the meaning and function of business in society at large. In this way, we gird ourselves for understanding the complex world of change in which we live and work.

Creating Curiosity

What we should ask of higher education today is that it create in young people a great curiosity about the world around them, a keen awareness of the major developments that have occurred in the past and those that are occurring now, and the courage and ability to face their world and to think their way through the multiform problems that characterize our age.

Robert Hutchins, the former chancellor of the University of Chicago, once said, "Education is not to teach men facts, theories, or laws. It is not to reform them or amuse them or to make them expert technicians. It is to unsettle their minds, widen their horizons, enflame their intellect, teach them to think straight if possible, but to think, nevertheless."

This is what a business school should try to do. This is the greatest contribution it can make to the continued growth and development of business and industry. This is its social function and *raison d'etre.*

YEAR 1977

[Public confidence in big business: 33%]

CSR: Does It Really Belong In The Business School?

Setting the scene. In 1971 the Academy of Management created the Social Issues in Management (SIM) Division of the Academy, which granted official standing to corporate social responsibility as one of the disciplinary fields of management studies. SIM's Governance Committee subsequently put pressure on the American Association of Collegiate Schools of Business (AACSB), the official accrediting agency for the nation's business schools, to strengthen its requirements for CSR education. I was commissioned to draft new accrediting guidelines, with input from other SIM committee members.* It is through such tedious procedures that the real work of educational reform is accomplished. For many years, the guidelines were used by AACSB accrediting teams to encourage the study of CSR and business ethics in the nation's business schools. As the **Year 2005** *chapter in Part IV. reveals, this kind of accrediting safeguard was subsequently watered down by AACSB officials.*

The following guidelines are recommended for use by visitation teams considering schools for new membership in the AACSB Accreditation Council, as well as for periodic review of member schools. The Social Issues in Management (SIM) Division of The Academy of Management is the major professional academic association in the nation whose primary function is to advance the study of business and society issues. The members of SIM'S Governance Committee believe that much can be done to enhance the teaching of these topics through cooperation with the Accreditation Council, and these guidelines are offered in that spirit.

---

* Coauthors: Kathryn M. Bartol, Archie B. Carroll, Gerald F. Cavanagh, John E. Logan, Joseph W. McGuire, James E. Post.

The Business and Society Standard: Standard IV(b)

Presently, the AACSB Accreditation Council provides that programs of its members "shall include in their course of instruction the equivalent of at least one year of work comprising the following areas: ...(b) a background of the economic and legal environment as it pertains to profit and/or nonprofit organizations along with ethical considerations and social and political influences as they affect such organizations;...." The phrase referring to ethical considerations was inserted in April 1976.

There is no clear or commonly agreed on interpretation available addressing precisely what this standard means in practice. As a consequence, schools have sometimes assumed that they have met the standard in a wide variety of ways. We are aware of the problems and dangers of having visitation teams impose rigid curricular requirements upon the diverse membership (present and prospective) of the Accreditation Council. We also sympathize with the Standards Committee which feels pressures from all quarters to legitimize new subject matter and to be more explicit about existing standards. A good case can be made for the existence of broad, flexibly interpreted standards.

We believe, however, that a good case can also be made for focusing interpretation of Standard IV(b) specifically upon a set of practicable curricular practices. Many schools welcome such assistance as they attempt to design courses and prepare teachers. Visitation [i.e., accreditation] teams, too, might be able to conduct their work with more certainty and provide needed suggestions to prospective member schools if they carry with them an approximation of just how this particular standard could be met.

The following suggestions, while stated in the language of curricular design and structure, are intended less as a curricular straitjacket than as a broad set of guidelines. The relative newness and evolving outlines of the business and society field suggest perhaps the greater utility of such broad guidelines for this portion of the curriculum than for other, longer established areas of business and management study.

Suggested Accrediting Guidelines

1. *The curriculum should offer an opportunity to study a broad range of business and society relationships in an integrated fashion.* This threshold course should be *broadly* conceived, should emphasize the *interrelationships* between business as a whole and society as a whole, and should aim for an *integrative* understanding of the business and society interface. The general focus should be on manage-

ment rather than economics or law per se, but all relevant disciplines ought to be brought to bear on the various subjects examined. The management focus would consider how social issues and environmental pressures impact on the management of organizations and how management might respond in order to meet those challenges while maintaining business as a viable institution in a rapidly changing environment.

The content of this threshold course need not be uniform for all schools. Such uniformity would be unrealistic in terms of faculty preparation and interest, diverse student types and needs, and different types and locations of schools.

Core materials for the threshold course can be drawn from the following topics: (1) the historical interrelationships between business and society; (2) a broad analysis of the changing domestic and international environment—social, economic, legal, political, etc.—within which business operates; (3) the power and legitimacy of business institutions; (4) values, ethics, and ideology that are manifested in both business and society; (5) a general appreciation of technology and social change; (6) social responsibility doctrines and theories; (7) analysis of proposals for reforming the business system; (8) major social issues confronting business, such as consumer protection, discrimination, pollution control, employee safety and health, organizational conformity, freedom and autonomy, etc.; (9) business response to social problems and the management of corporate social policy; and (10) a look at possible future business and society relationships.

By far, the preferred course of action for a school—and, in our opinion, the only way to meet the spirit of Standard IV(b)—is to require students to take a threshold course of this general type. An elective course permits students to bypass the subject matter, while inclusion of social issues in standard courses foregoes the desirable integrative course structure and understanding. As SIM has noted in a statement to AACSB, "...courses that only inferentially or peripherally deal with the subject matter are not effective substitutes for the shaping of student thought and effort around the integrative process. ... To permit this subject to be met...as a matter of secondary concern in other courses, no matter how well taught, is to distort the perceived significance of the subject matter in the mind of the student."

The basic recommendation, therefore, is for an integrated course, covering a wide range of subject matter in the business and society interface, utilizing all relevant disciplines in analysis but with a managerial orientation, and emphasizing the whole and the interrelationships among the parts. There are several possible approaches to meeting this objective, provided that the basic components mentioned here are kept in the forefront of course and curricular design.

2. *Traditional functional courses should include social issues relevant to the subject matter.* Marketing courses, for instance, should provide for coverage of controversial social issues surrounding pricing, advertising, product safety and reliability, and similar matters. Production courses should be concerned with employee safety and health issues and with product reliability, as well as with standard materials. While many functional faculty now incorporate socially oriented topics into their courses, it remains true that basic curricular design in some schools tends to seal off and exclude these social matters from the traditional subject matter of the functional fields.

At the same time, we doubt that such broadening alone can provide the student with the necessary integrative understanding of business and society interrelationships. At best, the functional areas can themselves take on a richer meaning for future business practitioners. When taken in conjunction with the broad integrative threshold course recommended above, the functional fields then assume a new significance within the total curriculum.

3. *The capstone policy course should include a significant amount of material dealing with business's social, legal, and political environment, the social issues and problems that arise out of that environment, and the efforts of management to formulate and administer corporate social policies.* Inclusion of socially relevant materials in the policy course should not be considered a substitute for an integrative threshold course. No doubt the policy course can be enriched considerably by giving attention to broad environmental matters, and a student can thereby gain an appreciation for the complexities of business operations and their management. While clear gains can be achieved by including social matters in the policy course, this action by itself is likely to leave the student with an inadequate grasp of how environment and policy mesh with one another.

4. *Where possible, additional opportunities beyond the threshold, functional, and policy courses should be given to students to delve into selected subject matter in the business and society area.* Concentrated, elective studies could be provided in such topics as environmental issues of multinational corporations, business and politics, executive mental health, environment pollution, economic and social costs, social regulation of business, etc.

5. *A variety of faculty members with contrasting disciplinary approaches is desirable for teaching the business and society curriculum.* There are several legitimate ways to conceive and teach business and society courses. Relevant disciplines include law, economics, sociology/anthropology, history, political science, philosophy/ethics, psychology/social psychology, management, and perhaps others as well. Different faculty members will have varying interests and capabilities, and different students will express varying needs. For instance, subject matter may be treated with philosophical orientation in contrast, for instance, to an operational posture. Business may be dealt with as an institution in contrast to specific operational business segments or units. Different subjects may properly elicit different disciplinary emphasis. All of these approaches may be adopted in the same course of study, depending upon the topic and the faculty member's capabilities. Indeed, team teaching may be one practical way to achieve the desired coverage of topics and viewpoints. In general, a broad, multidisciplinary set of concepts—linked to operational knowledge of business and management—is needed in order to teach an integrated business and society curriculum. Those faculty members charged with responsibilities for the business and society courses should collectively possess or be developing such a multidisciplinary and operational capability.

Rationale

The above recommendations are based upon a series of perceived educational needs, certain ideological traditions of business schools, notable trends in course offerings, and the observations and predictions of individuals and study groups concerning the desired content and outlook of management education.

First of all, few persons today would argue with the need for students to be well educated in a broad range of managerial skills and viewpoints, including a knowledge of the turbulent social and political environment within which business is now conducted. One estimate is that some chief executives now spend as much as 40 percent of their time on external affairs, and it is well known that managers in the middle and lower levels of authority can have a powerful effect on a company's social policies and activities. Hence, it now appears to be as important for managers to master the fundamentals of corporate social policy and its management as the more traditional managerial skills.

Secondly, there is no question that including social issues in the curriculum is clearly in the ideological tradition of business schools. The Wharton School, the oldest business school in the United States, was started with a gift to provide for a "liberal education in all matters concerning Finance and Commerce." The reports on business education issued in 1959 by the Ford Foundation and the Carnegie Corporation extended this tradition, urging business schools to offer courses dealing with the changing social, political, legal, and intellectual environment of business. This emphasis is needed "first, to impress on the student the multifarious and changing ways in which business interacts with its institutional environment, and second, to develop in him a sharpened interest in and a sense of responsibility for the kind of society in which he will live and work." George L. Bach echoed the same theme in the Carnegie report by emphasizing "the need for the manager of tomorrow to understand, and be sensitive to, the entire economic, political, and social environment in which he will live and in which his business will operate and be judged."

Matching these traditions and recommended developments are recent trends in increased course offerings in the business and society area. An AACSB survey of 154 business schools in 1968–69 revealed that half of them required work in the social, political, and legal environment of business. The National Affiliation of Concerned Business Students reported in 1974 that 186 graduate business schools were offering more than 650 courses on corporate social policy.

These trends in new course offerings are consistent with projected trends in teaching social responsibility and societal issues to business students. In 1974, over 60 percent of business schools deans expected that the areas of "social responsibility of business" and "business ethics and morals" would be increased.

All of these traditions, trends, and predictions give substance to the case for enriching the curriculum with environmental studies. Turning to the specifics of how this curricular shift is to be accomplished, one quickly encounters the familiar question, "If this goes in, what comes out?" Without wishing simply to duck the tough problems, we believe that this question is one that is clearly to be left in the hands of each individual school to work out according to local circumstances. We remain convinced, however, that all five steps outlined above constitute a reasonable and educationally valid goal for schools to achieve.

An Accreditation Check List

In order to be as helpful and specific as possible concerning the interpretation of the Business and Society Standard (Standard IVb), we offer here a list of questions that can serve as a guide for accreditation teams, deans, and faculty members in assessing business and society curricula.

1. Does the school have an integrated, managerially oriented threshold course dealing with the broad interrelationships between business and society, preferably offered on a required basis?

2. Do the functional courses include coverage of relevant social issues?

3. Does the policy course devote a significant amount of time to social environmental matters and issues?

4. Are advanced business and society electives available on a regular basis?

5. Is there within the faculty a coherent, multidisciplinary view and approach to business and society and especially to the threshold course?

We conclude by emphasizing once again our awareness of the pluralistic character of business and management education institutions. Standards are tools to be used as general guides, not inflexible formulas revealing ultimate truth. If our broad interpretation of Standard IV(b) contributes to the continuing dialogue about how the business and management schools can best serve their respective constituencies, then we would be gratified. At the very least, we hope our thoughts will stimulate further discussion.

YEAR 1977

CSR: Can It Be Taught?

Setting the Scene. A quarter century after CSR had emerged as a business practice, the topic had also found a reasonably secure place within most of the nation's business schools. The Association of American Colleges, representing liberal arts faculty, expressed curiosity about this development and invited me to tell them the story, which gives a bird's eye view of the field's status in those years.

In recent years, a new field of study has emerged in business schools in the United States. It is known variously as "business and society," "business and its environment," "social responsibilities of business," "corporate social policy," and by other titles as well. Its first goal is to understand the social, political, cultural, legal, and ethical environment in which business operates. Its second goal is to bring that understanding to bear upon a resolution of the many human and social dilemmas facing business today and in the foreseeable future. This new field has emerged and come of age since the mid-1950s, largely as a response to the social pressures and moral crises associated with business operations within the last twenty years.

Social Pressures on Business

The moral bill of particulars against business is already a long one and it grows yearly. The major charges now include racially and sexually discriminatory personnel policies.; workplaces that threaten the health and lives of employees; an insufficient concern for environmental pollutants; marketing programs and production methods that often create and sell consumer products that are unreliable, unsafe, ineffective, and/or overpriced; advertising programs that mislead, misrepresent, and appeal to base instincts and psychological fears and uncertainties; sponsorship of television programs, athletic events, films, books, and magazines that teach, demonstrate, and encourage violent aggressiveness as an acceptable form of human behavior; credit and lending policies that bilk the unwary, discriminate against women and minorities, and entrap and burden those already living in poverty; illegal political contributions to presidential, senatorial, congressional, and gubernatorial candidates; secret and questionable payments made to foreign government officials, political parties, and others; conducting business and making handsome profits in foreign nations ruled by repressive, dictatorial governments; exploiting the human, agricultural, and mineral resources of underdeveloped regions with insufficient recompense and little regard for the welfare of the host nation; connivance with the secret intelligence service of the United States to weaken or overthrow constituted governments of other nations; collusion with military forces here and abroad to perpetuate the international arms race; fraudulent reporting of financial data with subsequent losses to shareholders; and a variety of other charges brought by older workers, young workers, the handicapped, blacks, American Indians, ecology-minded conservationists, big city mayors, mental health experts, anti-trust officials, and others.

Add to this dreary indictment the compelling evidence from public opinion polls that reveals a steady decline in the general public's confidence in business and business leadership during the last decade. In 1966, according to *The Harris Survey*, 55 percent of the public expressed confidence in the leadership of major companies. In 1976 only 16 percent felt that degree of trust. Business leaders can take small comfort from the knowledge that all major institutions have suffered a loss of public trust, for business has dropped farther than most and is at an all-time low point in public esteem. Moreover, Harris has also reported that 82 percent of the public believes that "If left alone, big business would be greedy and selfish and would make profits at the expense of the public." It is also reported that 78 percent want Congress to represent the consumer more and big business and big labor less; 73 percent want to reduce the influence of big business in government; and 59 percent want stricter legislation to protect the environment and to curb air and water pollution.

In recent years, also, corporate management has come to expect dissenting shareholders to introduce social-issue resolutions during the companies' annual meetings. In 1976, the total was the highest ever reached—118 resolutions ranging from demands for greater disclosure of political activity and conflict of interest to concerns about environmental impacts, discrimination against women and minorities, doing business in South Africa, complying with the Arab boycott against companies doing business with Israel, nutritional factors associated with baby food, and many others. Although no dissenting shareholder resolution has ever been adopted over the objections of a company's management, the percentage of votes cast for these proposals is now higher than ever before, and in 1976 management actually accepted close to one-third of them.

As if all these social pressures were not enough, the embattled executive looks with growing alarm upon a constantly expanding government regulatory apparatus. From 1962 through 1974, thirty-seven major legislative acts were passed by Congress with the intent of more closely regulating the social and environmental impacts of business. According to one commentator, this new wave of regulations has created "a second managerial revolution," one that is shifting corporate decision making from "the professional management selected by the corporation itself to the vast cadre of government regulators...."

New Focus on Business Schools

With the business world under such a sustained onslaught from so many quarters, one might reasonably ask what the nation's business schools are doing about it all. Do they, for example, teach about—or ignore—these developments? Do those who teach marketing and advertising also emphasize the consumer abuses that often accompany the sale of products and services? Are future production managers encouraged to consider the health and safety of workers? Are racism and sexism in the workplace studied as assiduously as econometrics and probability theory? What about business ethics and social responsibility?

The new field of business and society (CSR) attempts to grapple with just such social and ethical dilemmas of business by incorporating moral and social intelligence into the educational experiences of future business professionals.

The Business School Response

Several developments identify a concern among business schools that social and moral factors should be a part of the curriculum. An AACSB survey of 154 business schools in 1968–69 revealed that half of them *required* work in the social, political, and legal environment of business.

In 1972 Father Thomas F. McMahon sent a survey questionnaire to 847 schools of business and received a response from 54 percent of them. The graduate schools generally reported that they offered a special course on the socio-ethical responses of business to societal needs and pressures. *Almost half of the schools required the course for graduation, and over 60 percent of all the faculty members polled believed it should be required.* The majority of these courses at both the graduate and undergraduate levels had been introduced between 1968 and 1972.

MBA magazine conducted a survey in 1974 among 174 graduate schools of business and found that *60 percent required students to take courses in this general area.* The National Affiliation of Concerned Business Students reported in 1974 that 186 graduate business schools were offering more than 650 courses on corporate social policy and that these courses were being taught by 656 faculty members.

Although precise figures are not available nationally, there are probably between 1,000 and 2,000 business school faculty members who directly teach some aspect of corporate social policy. Additionally, an equal number may indirectly touch upon social factors in the more standard courses such as marketing and personnel administration. Conceivably, these numbers could be much higher.

It is now possible to take a doctorate in business and society (CSR) at Harvard, Columbia, Pittsburgh, California-Berkeley, the University of Washington, UCLA, SUNY-Buffalo, and several others. The business school at the University of Virginia has established a Center for the Study of Applied Ethics. Most of the doctoral graduates of these programs become teachers of business and society courses, although some find positions in business and government.

The documented trends in new course offerings are clearly consistent with projected trends in teaching social responsibility and social issues to business students. Dean Glenn D. Overman conducted a survey in 1974 on behalf of the AACSB and asked 163 business school deans to comment on future trends in the curricula of their schools. Of the 101 deans who responded, over 60 percent expected that the area of "social responsibility of business" and "business ethics and morals" would be increased. The report also noted that emphasis will be placed on "...the ability to solve the social and environmental problems facing the modern executive" and that "...students will spend much more time studying such topics as the social responsibilities of business, business ethics and morals, the role of women in management, consumerism, and problems of racial minorities."

One also finds that AACSB accreditation standards have been adjusted, though insufficiently, to provide for this new and growing emphasis on social matters. Standards now mandate the equivalent of a one-year course involving "a background of the economic and legal environment as it pertains to profit and/or nonprofit organizations along with ethical considerations and social and political influences as they affect such organizations."

A fair conclusion to be drawn from these various surveys and studies is that the nation's business schools have responded to the social upheavals affecting the business system by creating new socially-oriented courses and adding new faculty to teach them.

Major Characteristics of Business and Society Courses

Let us now look more specifically at just how these new courses and their teachers are dealing with the multitude of social problems and discontents contained in the general indictment of business.

Professor George Steiner of UCLA collected course outlines from several hundred schools from 1971 to 1973 and found that they fell into three major groupings.

One group dealt almost exclusively with the idea of business's social responsibilities, attempting to define that concept in an abstract way and to see how it could be made meaningful within the context of specific social issues. A second and the fastest growing group of courses was concerned with the broad range of interrelationships between business and society, placing emphasis upon how corporations interact with political, governmental, legal, social, and cultural institutions. A third type of course was narrower in focus, concentrating on one particular aspect of the business-and-society interface such as minority affairs, advertising and consumerism, business ethics, or selected social problems.

As the field has continued to mature, a fourth type of course has emerged, which stresses corporate social policy and how best a company can manage its relations with its many social constituencies. This managerial approach is likely to become the dominant one because it is consistent with the professional educational mission of the business schools and because it removes the abstract notion of social responsibility from the realm of endless speculation and debate and puts it into a context where meaningful actions can be considered.

A typical business and society (CSR) course today begins with an overview of the social problems, pressures, and dilemmas facing business at home and abroad. It examines the several theories of social responsibility that have been developed in the past twenty years, from Professor Milton Friedman's idea that the only social responsibility of business is to make a profit legally, to the Committee for Economic Development's proposition that government and business should form a partnership for social problem-solving, and on to Professor Neil Chamberlain's theory that most companies are strictly limited in the scope of social problem-solving by both economics and the unwillingness of the public to bear the ultimate cost of social reform in the form of higher prices or fewer jobs. Less moderate views, including the legal, regulatory reforms of Ralph Nader, as well as the radical left's critique of the corporate system, are often treated.

Another major section of a typical course deals with the nature of the modern multinational corporation, with how it is controlled, and with the wealth and power it wields. The social costs of economic programs are considered along with the economic costs of social programs. A study is made of how government and business interact in the social arena, showing the extent to which corporations can influence public policy and how government regulatory bodies intervene in business decision making. In some courses, social class and its relation to the distribution of wealth and income get some attention. Often a series of specific issues, such as sexism and racism, are touched upon to give some reality and specificity to the course. Or the questions of organizational conformity, the preservation of an individual's autonomy and freedom, and the impact of corporate demand upon family and person are studied.

Values, ethics, and ideology are often included, not so much from a prescriptive point of view as from an attempt to point out the genuine ethical and ideological dilemmas that can arise from the normal operations of a business firm in these tumultuous times. Case studies are a useful technique employed to bring these complexities and uncertainties to the fore.

And as noted, increasingly one finds a section on the management of corporate social policy. Here social *responsiveness* is stressed, rather than social *responsibility*. How, specifically, can business corporations actually respond in meaningful ways to tangible social pressures and issues? How, by what means, and facing what kinds of difficulties? This approach assumes that the question of *should* business respond has already been answered affirmatively by public opinion and government regulations.

Finally, a typical course considers the limitations of this managerial approach to social responsibility, pointing out that problems of global dimension and deeply entrenched cultural traditions are not likely to yield to actions taken solely at the everyday operating level of a single company. Large-scale societal strategies are needed to supplement the attempts of individual companies to respond socially.

Overall, perhaps the core principle developed in business and society (CSR) courses is that the modern business corporation is a socio-cultural institution and not merely an economic and technical mechanism. As such, its every act is a social act with moral consequences for people and their environment.

The community of business and society scholars is split regarding the subject of ethics and the use of an ethical approach in thinking about corporate social responsibility. Some eschew ethics on grounds that no generally acceptable ethical principles can be found or, if found, it is felt they will be so general and abstract as to be scarcely applicable to the complex and multifaceted business scene. These critics of the ethical approach favor an analytical attitude toward corporate social responsibility, striving to develop tools and approaches that will have a practical impact on business's social decisions.

The ethicists, on the other hand, insist that the very essence of corporate social responsibility is a commitment to ethical decision making by those who wield significant influence over the lives of many people. They stress the study of values within a historical, cultural, and philosophical context, hoping perhaps to shape the values and attitudes of young business students directly and to persuade mature business executives indirectly by a reasoned exhortation to remember and heed the ethical traditions of Western culture.

Empirical Research in Business and Society

For most of its formative years, the business and society field has based its teaching upon a body of literature that has consisted largely of speculative, impressionistic, abstract, exhortatory, and critical tracts. While a handful of well written and seminal textbooks, as well as a modest number of case studies, were produced in the early years, much of the literature for a long time was marked by a theoretical and conceptual weakness. This state of affairs reflected not just the newness of the subject within the business curriculum but also a failure to match philosophic interest with a program of empirical research.

In these days, no academic field of study is likely to survive very long unless it derives its literature from organized, systematic inquiry. There has been an overabundance of loose speculation, uninformed criticism, and armchair moralizing. What is needed now is more empirical research into the multiform dilemmas of business and society relationships. Presently, that research in insufficient, partly because business is too reluctant to open its doors to professional researchers, partly because business is not generous enough in its financial support of such research, and partly because many business and society scholars prefer to speculate abstractly rather than to study empirically.

But the tide is turning. The Social Issues in Management Division of the Academy of Management surveyed its 285 members in 1976 and discovered a total of 45 empirical research projects under way. Many faculty members active in research are not members of this organization, so the total number of business and society research projects is probably far larger and appears to be increasing yearly. More recently, a series of monographic research studies is being organized by Professor Lee E. Preston which will bring together and publish in serial form the outstanding research of scholars in this field. The principal centers of institutionally supported research are at the business schools at Harvard, California-Berkeley, California-Los Angeles, the University of Washington, Pittsburgh, Columbia, State University of New York-Buffalo, and the University of Southern California. While modest in numbers, these projects and programs represent an encouraging shift toward careful inquiry into complex problems and a move away from interesting but often ill-founded philosophizing.

Also active is the Social Issues in Management Division of the Academy of Management. Created in 1971 as one of thirteen professional divisions of The Academy, it is the only professional association in the nation that focuses all of its efforts on the business and society field.

Outside the academic institutions, some valuable studies are being made by the Council of Economic Priorities, INFORM, and Ralph Nader's Center for the Study of Responsive Law, each of which takes a somewhat jaundiced view of business's social attitudes and activities. On a broader front, useful empirically-derived materials come from the Social Science Research Council's Center for Social Indicators, the Office of Technology Assessment, the Black Economic Research Center, the Brookings Institution, the Committee for Economic Development, and the Conference Board.

Nor would the field be as advanced without the active interest of many socially-concerned individual business executives and such business associations at the Public Affairs Council, the Clearinghouse on Corporate Social Responsibility which represents 189 insurance companies, and the Urban Strategy Center of the U. S. Chamber of Commerce.

Future Directions: A Major Focus on Values

Finally, what can we expect of this new and burgeoning field in the next few years? Four developments will mark its progress.

More attention will be paid to social *responsiveness* and relatively less to social *responsibility*. Corporate managers need all the help they can get in grappling positively with social issues. Managing a large company has always been complicated but those complexities have multiplied greatly in recent years as the environment has closed in on the company. Some chief executives are now said to spend as much as 40 percent of their time on external affairs. If the professional business schools have an educational mission to achieve, it surely embraces an effort to discover and transmit to the management profession fruitful ways to respond to social needs. So the management of corporate social policy will be given increasing time and attention by business and society scholars.

We can also expect to see new forms of social technology invented, refined, and applied to business and society problems. Techniques will be sought to enhance the response process, to ameliorate the corporation's impact upon society, and to bring its activities into greater conformity with humane and widely agreed upon social purposes. New ways of defining social standards of performance for business will be developed, probably by extending the concept of social indicators to the individual business firm and industry. Technology assessment techniques now used by the federal government will probably find their way into general usage in the business world. Social auditing, whether called by that name or not, will find wider adoption as companies try to improve the effectiveness with which they manage resources for social purposes. All of these and probably other new social tools will become a prominent part of the business and society (CSR) curriculum.

A third direction to be taken by both scholars and practitioners is to integrate social factors into long-range corporate strategic planning. To do so requires that the analysis of alternative futures be further refined and brought to a practical level for each business firm. A futures analysis that attempts to anticipate major social trends and to make those trends a part of the company's future planning activities is a definite step toward making social responsiveness a practical reality.

Finally, the study and careful analysis of values will become the centerpiece of all business and society scholarship. Values are what the business and society field is all about. What we witness in confrontations between the corporation and its various social constituencies is a clash of values. Women, blacks and other minorities, youth, the aged, ecologists, consumers, and others are challenging the values that suffuse the corporate enterprise. They want other than the usual values to be instrumental in making the vital decisions that emanate from the corporate boardroom. What is now sorely needed—and what we can expect from business and society scholars—is a more carefully and systematically developed understanding of business values and the values of those who maintain that business serves the community less well than it should. How can these competing value systems be compared? How can the apparent inconsistencies be reconciled? What social mechanisms of compromise, accommodation, and resolution can be brought into play? These are the kinds of questions around which much business and society (CSR) scholarship will revolve in the near future. The effort will bring together the best ideas from those who now favor ethics over analysis and those who urge that conceptual and analytical development should precede ethical formulations.

If these new directions of inquiry into business and society relations are sustained, then it is quite likely that the business schools will move with greater certainty toward creating and providing an "education for practical wisdom" for future business practitioners. What could be more practical—or wiser—than an education which inculcates a responsiveness to one's fellows, in ways guided by new knowledge, fitted within a concept of humanity that shows a concern for tomorrow, and rooted in long-established moral concerns for a just society?

YEAR 1988

[Public confidence in the ethics of big business: 25%]

ETHICS, RELIGION, AND PHILOSOPHY AT HARVARD BUSINESS SCHOOL: A MEMOIR OF TWO VISITS

Setting the Scene. This 1988 memoir records my memories and impressions of two seminars held at the Harvard Business School in 1959 and 1988. Memoirs express personal views, but this one also sheds light on the state-of-the-field of Corporate Social Responsibility at two key points—one near the beginning in 1959, the other well after it had matured. A number of key figures who pioneered the teaching of CSR are identified here.

Harvard Business School, 1959

There we are, arrayed on the steps of Baker Library, aligned in three neat rows with our four HBS instructors seated in front. All of us white and male and with absolutely no consciousness of why it should be any other way, five bow ties, three clerical collars, the *de rigueur* business jackets, most of us with those frozen expressions of pleasantness that we imagine should be assumed on such occasions. The label at the bottom of the class portrait tells that it was the **Danforth Seminar on Religion and Morality in Business Administration**. The date was July 7–17, 1959. We were thirty-six in number.

We had come—chosen equally from religion, academia, and business—to explore the possibilities (considered quite heady at the time) of finding pathways to morality within the normal practice of business. And we struggled mightily—at the time, I might have said "manfully"—with our topic. Laden with articles from the *Harvard Business Review* and charged to prepare case after case heaped upon us by our HBS professors, we were driven to our daily round of case discussions at a relentless pace.

For most of us Danforthians, it was a strange, even bizarre, experience. The business representatives were clearly at sea in this revisited university atmosphere, frequently allowing bluster to substitute for reason and logic. The clerics found themselves somewhat dismayed at what they must have assumed to have been an excessive concern for the pursuit of mammon, as well as to have been lured into the very citadel for instruction in the ways of mammon itself. As the days wore on, though, this discomfiture only hardened their determination to assert ever more strongly their sense of moral authority concerning the doubtful materialistic goals of business.

The academics were a mixed lot, picked from here and there on God knows (pardon me, Mr. Danforth) what grounds. In my own case, my dean brought the seminar's notice to me with great excitement, urging me to apply inasmuch as I had just joined his faculty to teach courses on the relations between business and society (CSR). It may be difficult for those in established, well-known universities to comprehend how remote they appear to be to those who only serve in second- and third-rate, lesser-known (or not known at all) academic institutions. The Harvards, the Yales, the Princetons are as shining temples on some Olympian height where only the greatest of the greatest intellects reside and do their work. Such, at any rate, was my own perception of Harvard at the time.

The catch in the application was having to say something about one's religious convictions. As I was at the exuberant peak of rebellion from a conventional Southern Presbyterian upbringing, the application gave me pause. But not for long. Getting that place at Harvard was worth whatever deviousness might be required in wording my statement on religious association and orientation. I dearly wish that I might be able now to see what I then declared. To my amazement—and no little cynical amusement—I was accepted. But I worried a bit that perhaps the admitting authorities had seen through my somewhat tentative position and would make special efforts to set me on a straighter path once there. It's a price paid by most who are reared in a Calvinist tradition—a stern God is always there, just over one's shoulder, always checking. I never quite figured out just why this Godly presence was necessary since I had absorbed the notion in Sunday School that predestination had pretty well set me up for one fate or another whether I behaved well or poorly.

Today I remember only three of the academic faces in our class photograph. Of those three, only one—Joe McGuire—was to emerge as a leading figure in the field of corporate social responsibility. In another four years, his *Business and Society* book would be widely used by those who were groping for guidance in teaching about business responsibility. The rest returned to their accustomed posts in obscure colleges, to dispense a Harvard-enriched version of what morality demanded of the business practitioner.

The intellectual fare in those days was paper thin. Ohmann's "Sky-hooks" article from the *Harvard Business Review* was the darling of the business school philosophers. The message was pretty simple and straight-forward: business practitioners need to guide their daily decisions by rising above grubby materialism. Rather than bootstraps, they need skyhooks. The religious implications of this metaphor were not lost on any of us, although some of the clerics must have winced at the Dale Carnegie char-acter of it all.

Joseph Fletcher from the Divinity School was called in at one point to instruct us on the felicities of situational ethics, which at the time was all the rage. The clergy did more than wince at this affront. In fact, this episode probably did more than anything else to thrust them into the somewhat mil-itant forefront of the remaining discussions. Before long, the Bible-thump-ing propensities of the Protestant ministers became evident, as the business representatives and academics, not quite sure of their ground, faded into the background.

George Albert Smith (who told us with wry humor that HBS students had dubbed his course, which was officially known as Business Responsi-bility in American Society, as "BRAS, the uplift course"), Ed Bursk, and Ed Learned were among our instructors. They handled us gently and with the skills one associates with classroom instruction at Harvard. With what exasperation they may have returned to their offices and homes after a day with us, one can only guess.

When it was all over, the results were inconclusive, to say the least. After seeing the renowned case study method in the flesh, I remained adamantly opposed to its use in my own classes, and this attitude was to last for many years. I finally came to my senses sometime in the 1970s and dis-covered the virtues of case studies, which I now find indispensable. Neither were the *HBR* articles to my liking—too bland, too diffuse, too goody-goody. As for the Danforth Foundation's fondest hopes that some sense of religious morality would now be insinuated into my classes, it was another disappointment. I did establish a professional friendship with Joe McGuire that has lasted to this day and had a similar but briefer relationship with Cliff Jones. Four years later, I found myself the Associate Dean in Paul Kohberger's business school at the University of Pittsburgh, an outcome that neither of us could possibly have believed possible during that summer seminar in 1959, when I was a faculty member at the University of Kansas City (now the University of Missouri at Kansas City).

In retrospect, I doubt that the Danforth seminars had their intended effect at all. What they may have done, though, was to lend an air of pro-fessional and academic legitimacy to those faculty members who attended and then returned to their campuses. To have participated in such an approved activity at the citadel of business education was thought, rightly or wrongly, to have done something important and significant. For a few of us, it was an early step (and an entirely unsuspected one) on an odyssey that would lead toward the building of a new field of management study. That's not a bad outcome but neither was it what the Danforth sponsors had in mind. As far as furthering the study or comprehension of the moral and ethical components of business decision making, the seminar was a total flop. There was no respectable body of literature, no research capable of creating one, no agreement on the linkages between religious thought and business practice, nothing beyond the diverse and largely primitive theological viewpoints of some of the participants, no particular lessons to be carried home or back to work, no general principles or theory to guide inquiry or teaching. Instruction in business ethics had taken a giant step sideways.

Harvard Business School, 1988

Returning after a 30-year absence carried its own excitement, though clearly not the same kind that one feels at the beginning of a career. True, there was the satisfaction of being included, for I doubt that any of us ever becomes indifferent to the opinions of our professional colleagues. True also that Harvard was to be the host for this gathering, for little had happened in three decades that seriously challenged its preeminence as educational leader in management education. It remained, for me, somewhat Olympian. And, of course, one yearned to know how the B School planned to allocate and direct the largesse of John Shad's $20 million gift that was intended to advance the study and teaching of business ethics.

Beyond these personal interests lay such a vast change in the business world since those dear dead days of the late 1950s! Those gauzy Danforthian ideals had been swept away or trampled underfoot by the social ruffians of the 1960s and the regulatory bureaucrats of the 1970s. The game had turned from principles to power, exercised in the streets (with the media ever present) or in the halls of Congress. The corporate executive had taken a tumble in the public eye, had declined from a near-national hero to a villainous ogre who was best chained up in a network of regulations and public pressures. Granted some relief—actually, a considerable amount— by the Reagan crowd, corporate leaders in the 1980s still found themselves ever on public trial as dozens of stakeholders (itself a newly coined term that had replaced Frank Abrams' "constituencies") put in their claim for attention and action. The newly returned visitor could well wonder how all of these developments, or how many of them, had been incorporated into the Harvard point of view.

It was in this mixed mood of quest and curiosity that we convened as the **Workshop on Ethics and Management Education**. We numbered 40, six of whom were women; all of us were white. It was December 8–9, 1988. One barely noticed that what had taken ten days in 1959 was now to be accomplished in only two. It was safe to assume also that, absent the Danforth sponsorship, we were now to be counted among the beneficiaries of the Shad munificence.

But what of the 1988 participants when compared with their counterparts in 1959? Where were the clergy? Now numbering only two, reinforced by two professors of religion, they seemed to have been invited for reasons other than their standing as "men of the cloth": one was a management professor, the other a doctoral candidate in the Harvard Business School. And of these two, only one injected a note of religiosity into his comments during the workshop conversations, which elicited mild bafflement or awkward silence from those questioned. The Bible-thumpers who had so dominated the earlier Danforth conclave were nowhere to be found. Score one for Harvard, I thought.

And business executives? Again, a striking difference. Only one was present. A giant whose on-the-job actions and corporate philosophy had belied the popular negative image of the business leader, Irwin Miller's workshop remarks hinted at a somewhat antique world view (though one of those cherished antiques, whether furniture or work of art, that one wishes to preserve as a reminder of older and better times). Here was an executive who had instilled into his company some of the very notions that seemed to be the heart of the Danforth approach, and he had made it work in ways that seemed miraculous to outside observers, for he had done it during the tumultuous 1960s and 1970s.

And the rest of the invited guests? This time, professional philosophers outnumbered all others. And the workshop leader, too, was credentialed in philosophy. Where were their counterparts 30 years earlier? Not one of their type had been invited to my Danforth seminar, but now they were the intellectual focus of this workshop. It was their language, their conceptual framework, their way of defining ethics problems, their analytic skills that were now to be built into the consciousness of the Harvard MBA student. True, one of the newly-converted B School ethics professors claimed almost never to have used the term "ethics" in his class discussions, finding it "unnecessary," but all of the teaching cadre had been schooled in the language and approach of the professional philosopher prior to walking into the MBA lions' den where ethics would be made an explicit part of classroom instruction. Small wonder that a number of them found their knees a bit wobbly on the first day of class, or that they needed a boost of morale and helpful hints from the support staff!

The philosophers were the group, of course, that had brought their powerful analytic and normatively-honed tools to bear on the ethical dilemmas of the business order. If anyone had an intellectual claim to speak in 1988, it was they. When the theory of corporate social responsibility that had served reasonably well during the 1950s collapsed under the weight of the social revolutions of the 1960s, the applied philosophers had some answers of their own. While Harvard and other management schools became enamored of the 1970s Bauer-Ackerman theory of corporate social responsiveness that counseled the building of a defensive response mechanism to fend off external pressures, Norman Bowie, Richard DeGeorge, and their philosophic compatriots demonstrated a different and a more critically normative way to pose the needed questions about corporate social performance. It was they, not management scholars, who showed the way.

They too had produced the textbooks and the anthologies, had selected or written many of the case studies, had designed the ethics courses that were found increasingly in business schools, had made the difficult and often frustrating journey across the disciplinary boundary that had long separated philosophy from the business school (as it still does in many universities), had founded the Society for Business Ethics and established the two academic journals devoted to business ethics, and had served as exemplars of an intellectual and normative approach to the core ethical issues of the business order. Without them, no workshop on business ethics in the 1980s would have been conceivable or meaningful.

Most of the rest of the (non-HBS) lot were holders of law degrees or were management professors known for their efforts to incorporate an ethics orientation into their own courses and into the business school curriculum. As translators and integrators of the work of others, their role has become an important part of the business ethics enterprise in schools across the nation. Some of these—one thinks of Ed Freeman and Ed Epstein—go beyond translation to make their own original theoretical contributions. The inclusion of a prominent sociologist, Amitai Etzioni, may be a harbinger of a coming generation of ethics-and-values analysis. Already having integrated philosophic insights into economic theory, an Etzioni could well show the way for other social scientists to join with the philosophers to enrich the normative study of business operations and decision making.

And so we learned that yet another chapter is being written in the history of the Harvard Business School. A required ethics course, albeit a brief one, is in place, a faculty (consisting of "heavy hitters," we were assured) has been schooled in how to teach it, plans are being laid to spread the ethics message throughout the curriculum (Yea, verily, even unto the forbidding precincts of finance!), and a talented support staff continues to work assiduously and enthusiastically to promote this newest cause. Led by the imagination and energy of that scholar with the marvelously apt name of Kenneth Goodpaster, the future of business ethics at this institution would seem to be considerably brighter than the fate that overtook the earlier Danforth efforts. It is a future that will owe not just a little also to the longstanding efforts of John Matthews, Kenneth Andrews, and Ray Bauer, as well as the more recent contributions of Barbara Toffler, Laura Nash, and yet others who now are stepping into the needed faculty responsibilities. It's a comforting thought, given Harvard's leadership role.

And for those who had the opportunity to be 1988's guests, the workshop discharged the usual functions of serving as a badge of belonging, a symbol of participation, and a medal of recognition whose mention on a resume sends a coded signal to one's professional confreres. Beyond these supports for one's self esteem lies a deeper meaning and function of such gatherings. They are a validation of one's commitment to a particular course of intellectual inquiry, a network not just of cherished colleagues but of related ideas and theories, an ongoing dialogue among like-minded scholars searching for a piece of the truth, and a needed and welcome affirmation that questions asked in the dark hours of one's night are shared by others, even though the answers remain elusive.

During the last session of our workshop, as I gazed around the room, my eye rested on Clarence Walton, a longtime friend whose warm and constant support had been important to me personally since first encountering him some 30 years ago. Here, I thought to myself, is the living metaphor of my own odyssey and, in a much larger sense, the odyssey of all those who have sought an understanding of the relationships between business and society. Pioneer of such studies at the Columbia Graduate School of Business in the 1950s, coauthor of the renowned *Conceptual Foundations of Business*, a book that nourished and sustained the field in its very earliest days, an academic administrator who had never left his scholarly activities behind nor forgot his own normative roots that brought him into the study of business institutions, and who had just this year capped his several other books about business values with the eloquence and wisdom to be found now in *The Moral Manager*, he did indeed sum up most of what both the Danforth seminar and this most recent workshop have striven to accomplish and what may be seen, by the perceptive observer, to have been the accomplishments of the entire field in the span of a single generation.

For such understanding, one can be grateful not only to Clarence but to host Kenneth Goodpaster whose workshop encouraged the nourishment of ideas and memories, as well as the deeper reflection that makes those memories worthwhile.

Year 2005

[Public confidence in big business: 22%]

THE BUSINESS SCHOOLS'
MORAL DILEMMA

Setting the Scene. The half-century struggle to find, and then to secure, a respected niche for teaching ethics and corporate social responsibility in the nation's business schools continues to be contentious and with an uncertain outcome. For some, the torrent of corrupt and fraudulent actions symbolized by Enron seemed to justify greater attention to corporate wrongdoing and misbehavior. This chapter grapples with the way business schools have, and have not, risen to this latest challenge.

The moral dilemma is this: Are business schools complicit in the corporate crimes committed by their graduates (1) by inculcating a rationalist mindset in faculty and students that de-centers, or even dismisses, social responsibility and/or (2) by failing to include, or even denigrating, considerations of social responsibility and ethics in their courses of study? Charged with preparing tomorrow's business leaders and professionals, such complicity by the schools would indeed be a serious matter bringing into question the entire role and function of the business schools. A solution to this dilemma is neither readily apparent nor easily discovered, so this chapter will struggle, as have other observers, to find approximate answers. Only by resolving the dilemma would it be feasible and acceptable for business schools to assume a meaningful role in promoting business's pursuit of corporate social responsibility.

Post-Enron Questions

Following the high-profile corporate corruption cases of the late 1990s and early 2000s (see **Year 2005** chapter in Part III), the nation's business schools were criticized for possibly contributing to the widespread fraud and criminal acts by failing to instill a sense of morality and ethical awareness in their students. After all, Enron's Jeff Skilling and Andrew Fastow, two major figures at the center of that company's troubles, held MBA degrees from well-known business schools. But in some circles, the questioning went even deeper, going so far as to cast doubt on the kind and quality of management education itself that was being offered by the business schools. The major target of both criticisms was the MBA degree program, considered to be the schools' premier product and often its major revenue source, not to speak of the continuing reach and influence (and financial advantages) enjoyed by the school from the loyalty of its MBA graduates serving in business, government, and community posts worldwide. Understanding the nature and function of the MBA is therefore key to judging the validity of the attack on the business schools. If the flaw leading to moral compromise or managerial incompetence is located in the MBA program, then the solution to both deficiencies would seem to suggest reform of the MBA curriculum.

Not so fast, some would say, it's not that simple. And they would be correct, of course. First, then, it will be useful to take a hard look at what is claimed for the MBA—what is the competence claimed for it—and what in fact does it accomplish for those who hold it, for the school that grants it, and for the companies that hire MBA graduates. There is a world of difference between what might be called "The Official MBA" and "The Real MBA."

The Official MBA

The general promise and expectation of an MBA educational experience is that it produces leaders who will serve in significant posts in business, government, community, and other influential sectors of the economy and society. The language found at the websites of prominent business schools is invariant. Their aim is "to educate leaders" (Harvard Business School); to create "a principled leader of business and society" (Dartmouth's Tuck School); to produce "general management leadership" (The Wharton School); to provide "leadership" (Stanford Business School). In one way or another, all business schools, whether of elite status or more run-of-the-mill, make the same claims.

For most MBA students, management leadership is to be acquired by taking a two-year course of full-time study on campus, interspersed if possible with an on-the-job training internship between the first and second years of classroom instruction. On this basic theme, many other variations exist: part-time evening courses for working students; executive MBA programs for higher-level managers; weekend courses taken over an extended period of time; distance-learning courses beamed into one or more companies; on-line courses, sometimes paired with occasional campus classes; MBA programs tailored to the needs of a particular company and offered in-house; and other ways of delivering the core elements of an MBA education. The core disciplines and fields are economics, finance, marketing, organizational behavior, operations, controls, information technology, policy, strategy, and the various statistical, mathematical, and analytical techniques that support these functions.

In effect, the business schools are saying, "Take these courses, and you will become a leader. You will be fitted with the skills and knowledge needed to lead and manage an enterprise. Because such leadership competence is in great demand in today's world, you will be financially rewarded in proportion to the importance and contribution you make to your organization's success in the marketplace." As one leading business school states, its MBA students will learn to "refine analytic, decision-making, judgment skills" and gain "lasting knowledge and experience." The Official MBA indeed promises much to students and to the companies who hire them.

The Detractors and Doubters

The official MBA has come under a withering attack for failing to measure up to its rosy promises. Interestingly enough, the harshest criticisms originate from within the business schools themselves.

- Stanford's Jeffrey Pfeffer and Christina Fong cite empirical evidence that the MBA (the "official" one) does not enhance one's professional career, does not exert significant long-term influence on one's salary, and gives too little attention to the kinds of skills important to managers, such as interpersonal relationships, communication abilities, and (ironically) leadership qualities. Taught by faculty members who themselves have no hands-on business or management experience, and whose abstract and highly technical research has little influence on management practice, and who themselves give low priority to classroom teaching, these results are not surprising, though regrettable.

- Another critic, Lex Donaldson of the Australian Graduate School of Management, blames contradictions and inconsistencies between the theories produced in management schools and what is required of managers faced with real world problems. Actions based on the core theories learned by MBAs would be self-defeating in the marketplace. That's not the kind of "leadership" any firm would welcome.

- Two Chinese, one a professor of management, the other a management consultant, analyzed the content of teaching cases widely used in MBA programs in China and the United States. Professor Neng Liang and Jiaqian Wang discovered a strong managerially-oriented rationalistic bias but strikingly less emphasis on human relations, organizational politics, and symbolic factors such as beliefs, ethics, faith, norms, values, and the social meaning of work. They concluded that MBA instruction through extensive use of cases would produce managers who were likely to be strategy-driven but politically naïve, lacking awareness of human and social factors, and having an exaggerated notion of the power of analytic approaches to complex management problems.

- Reinforcing this picture of business school failings, USC business professors James O'Toole and Warren Bennis trace the shortcomings to "a dramatic shift in the culture of business schools" from vocational pragmatics to abstract research. The schools' model of excellence emphasizes "abstract financial and economic analysis, statistical multiple regressions, and laboratory psychology"—at the expense of imparting a practical knowledge of the messy, complex, typically indeterminate world of the practicing manager. Business professors "are at arm's length from actual practice, they often fail to reflect the way business works in real life." MBA instruction fails "to impart useful skills…prepare leaders…instill norms of ethical behavior…[or] lead graduates to good corporate jobs."

- Another trio of business school faculty members—Diane Swanson of Kansas State University, Dwayne Windsor of Rice University, and I—directly accused business schools of being implicated in the corporate corruption scandals by allowing MBA students to bypass entirely any instruction in the ethics and morality of business practice. Only by requiring MBAs to learn about the ethical impacts of business operations on a wide range of corporate stakeholders, their communities, and the global environment would business education become socially acceptable. Backed by hundreds of business faculty who teach ethics plus some management consultants and business practitioners, this call for new ethics accreditation standards to be mandated for all business schools offering an MBA degree was first ignored, then rejected by the Association to Advance Collegiate Schools of Business (AACSB) which accredits business schools nationally. Known informally and derisively as "The Deans' Club," whose member deans accredit each other's schools and who are gatekeepers blocking any nonconforming schools that aspire to membership and accreditation, it was charged by Pfeffer and Fong with acting "to maintain the status quo." That looks suspiciously like a case of the fox guarding the hen house, in this case assuring that the MBA mind is kept free of the clutter of ethics and social responsibility.

- Yet another charge—that business schools have drifted away from instilling a sense of professionalism in their students—was leveled by University of Iowa professors Christine Quinn Trank and Sara L. Rynes. This loss they attribute to a business disdain for theory and research in favor of a narrow focus on first-job skills; an MBA student culture that commodifies learning into packets of technical information fungible in the job market; a media-sponsored ranking scheme that places undue influence in the hands of corporate recruiters and students to the detriment of a broader professional education; an AACSB accrediting process that fails to provide national and professionally-based educational standards for business education; and business school faculties who yield to pressures from students for easier courses, less theory development, and more practical short-run tools. Missing is a sense of professional excellence that nurtures an awareness of social and ethical responsibility.

- Other icons of the management teaching world have weighed in with essentially the same critical views of MBA education: Wharton's Russell Ackoff, McGill's Henry Mintzberg, and USC's Ian Mitroff. Mintzberg particularly has taken the business schools to task for substituting an analytic-technical MBA classroom routine for the richly complex interactive learning that can occur only in and through actual workplace experiences acquired, not in the span of a two-year MBA program, but over a longer arc of time and in varying sociocultural contexts..

The Real MBA

If The Official MBA is essentially a fraud that promises more than it delivers and fails to teach what is most needed by practicing managers, why does it continue to be one of the most popular academic offerings (in spite of a recent decline in MBA enrollments and degrees awarded)? It must be doing *something* to satisfy its supporters. Otherwise, why waste two years and several thousand dollars to attend MBA classes? The answer to this puzzle is found in what might be labeled "The Real MBA."

The Real MBA serves the economic, financial, social, and political interests of the current business order. Students who pass through the MBA system, and the professors who teach them, are part of a wide-ranging, comprehensive business culture that requires the kinds of services that business schools can provide. The MBA program, educationally flawed as it is, may most accurately be seen as carrying out five vital functions that help support and sustain business culture as we know it.

Presumptive business know-how. In spite of known, documented shortcomings summarized above, there is a presumption that MBAs possess a fund of useful knowledge that can be applied to business tasks. The tool kit is thought to be filled with analytic techniques that can support the firm's overall strategy, its marketing aims, its production processes, its financial needs, and the kind of technology and organizational systems capable of achieving these profitable ends. That's what corporate recruiters have been told they will find, so they form long lines to capture the "best and the brightest" of the annual MBA output. They often get just that, particularly management consulting firms, investment banks, auto manufacturers, healthcare organizations, and other highly technologized operations. This kind of technical expertise, though vital to the enterprise, falls well outside the scope of managerial work and does not typically qualify one for membership in the management cadre. John Kenneth Galbraith once referred to the collective skills of this group as a company's "technostructure," and it is indeed one of the few substantive accomplishments of MBA programs. Another is found in the training of what might be called the "corporate soldiery"—those who find useful places within the lower ranks, performing indispensable though unexciting tasks. Neither leaders, hot-shot consultants, nor social climbers, they do not normally enjoy the privileges of The Official MBA and may savor only a few of The Real MBA's benefits. Frequently outsourced, downsized, or out-competed in globalized markets, they lead a more precarious existence than their more well-heeled MBA compatriots.

Pre-screening for the job market. Prospective corporate employers are savvy enough to grasp the advantage of having someone else—in this case, the business school—do the first-level sorting of potential MBA hires. Before being admitted to an MBA program, one must take the Graduate Management Admission Test (GMAT) which is administered and graded by a national testing organization. Scoring high is essential for admission to the top-level business schools. Grade point average (GPA) achieved in prior college or university courses is another marker that can mean success or failure in getting into the program of one's choice. Some schools require applicants to draft essays to demonstrate writing ability and to reveal motives for MBA study. Others interview candidates face-to-face to get a feeling for personality and suitability for MBA study, which can be quite rigorous and time-intensive. Some minimum amount of actual business experience, perhaps from three to five years, is often considered desirable.

Line all of these admissions hurdles up, and you have what corporate recruiters seek—a system that weeds out those who are thought to be not quite suitable for making the MBA run. Pfeffer and Fong reported that when a partner in a leading management consulting firm was asked why companies recruit at business schools, the reply was, "It is a prescreened pool."

Affiliative networking. One of the advertised advantages of the MBA degree is joining an exclusive club whose members speak the same language (of business), share knowledge of analytic techniques, and have experienced all of the disciplinary rigors and monetary rewards common to MBA alumni everywhere. As Dartmouth's Tuck School tells prospective students, "alumni remain involved long after leaving Tuck, creating an unmatched network for graduates at every stage of their careers." Wharton speaks of the "unique bond" formed among its graduates who hold "positions of influence around the world." Here is a professional advantage going far beyond any knowledge found in classroom lectures, case studies, analytic techniques, and between-terms internships. Such affiliative linkages may well pay off as new job opportunities, favored appointments, promotions, board memberships, company-to-company contacts, business deals of one kind or another, and, of course, financial gains for oneself. Quite obviously, these bonds are stronger among the graduates of the elite business schools than the general MBA population. Even in the absence of the affiliative loyalty felt by graduates of a single school, the fact that one has an MBA degree sends a coded signal—almost like the secret signs flashed by urban street gangs—that here is a person of recognized worth, possessing at least the minimum qualifications of membership in the upper echelons of business culture.

Enculturation. Students who first step across the threshold into the business school have already been conditioned to the values, norms, and general viewpoints of business culture—plus a willingness to learn even more about it as a way of finding a job and making a living. They may have been led to the door by family attitudes and parental ambitions, an inspiring teacher, an interesting first-job experience, or simply by living in a society whose political ideology blends easily with the necessities of business and where one hears a constant refrain about the virtues of a free-market economy. In this sense, they are a self-selected group favorably disposed to business. It doesn't take long—only about two years—for this pro-business entering attitude to be strongly reinforced. The Aspen Institute revealed that entering MBA students who believed that a company's top priorities were customer needs and product quality had decided, by graduation time, that top priority should go to "shareholder value." More strikingly, if they found their personal values to be at odds with job demands, they would seek a job in another company rather than challenge the basic values found in corporate culture. This enculturation process—where one learns to accept (or at least not speak out directly against) the values of business culture—is one of the major accomplishments of an MBA education. One learns to be loyal, not just to classmates now and after graduation but to the company, its goals, and the practices needed to achieve marketplace success.

Social symbolism. Society has many ways to signal social class belongingness: ethnic identity, job type, income, place and size of residence, clothing worn, friends and acquaintances, life style, sports preferences, brand of car, vacations taken, jewelry, hair styles, entertainment favored, preferred leisure activities, household possessions, club or association memberships, even religious affiliations, and on and on. One of the lures of the MBA degree is the unspoken signal that it will open pathways eventually leading into the upper reaches of society's class system. The Big Prize is, of course, climbing to the very apex of corporate success— CEOdom itself. After all, the great majority of case studies that the typical MBA analyzes are written and taught from the perspective of top management. It is the guest CEO who is most frequently invited to give tell-it-like-it-is seminars, and to address the graduating class. One visiting CEO who discovered that not all students in his audience wanted to become CEOs became indignant, demanding "Why not!?" Once there, though, CEOs find themselves surrounded by all the trappings that accompany a position of power and influence. The lavish life style signals membership in society's upper classes.

Quite obviously, not all MBAs attain CEOship although many can be expected to hold high-level executive posts such as chief financial officer, chief operating officer, executive vice president, divisional head, plant manager, etc., and to be compensated accordingly. As a group, MBAs are allowed to put their foot on the middle rungs of the social class ladder, a privilege and opportunity to be exploited. Circumstances then determine how far they will climb. Their MBA badge is a subtle reminder to all that the gates to class privilege are now open to the wearer. As the commencement speaker in a *New Yorker* cartoon once emphatically advised members of a graduating class, "Now, go out there and *get yours!*"

The Real MBA and the socio-economic prizes it holds out to those who win it is a powerful attractant, far more than the (doubtful) educational advantages claimed for The Official MBA. Business schools are not permitted—do not permit themselves—to advertise these unofficial benefits openly, with the occasional exception of the affiliative networking enjoyed by graduates of the elite schools. The business schools' most important purpose is to serve the corporate labor market by screening, disciplining, training, and mentally conditioning its graduates so they may be minimally ready for life within the corporate system. Never mind that most of the knowledge acquired by MBA students is irrelevant to the actual conditions and challenges to be encountered in the workplace, as countless critics have demonstrated. Getting in the corporate door is what it's all about.

All else is peripheral and marginal, including ethics, corporate social responsibility, business history, ecology, personal worth, spiritual aspirations, the downside of technological change, the dark underside of market-induced poverty, the emptiness of a work-routinized life. Only where these can be shown to affect a company's goals or managerial strategies are they permitted to become part of classroom instruction.

The upshot is that MBA graduates in effect hold two degrees: An Official MBA that is managerially irrelevant but symbolically meaningful, and a Real MBA testifying that all has been done to discipline the holder to life in the corporate workplace.

The business schools' moral dilemma would therefore appear to be one of their own making, an outcome of the kind of curriculum offered to students—one that educates narrowly (if at all) and without attention to the many social, non-economic consequences of business operations. Those who would change this situation have argued for a greater focus on organizational ethics, corporate social responsibility, stakeholder participation, workplace spirituality, corporate citizenship, the cultivation of virtuous character, regulatory oversight, social contracts, global standards of conduct, and other similar approaches. An unspoken assumption seems to have been that, once in place, these curricular reforms would offset the unethical and socially irresponsible tendencies generated by the rationalist-financial-economic-technical core of MBA instruction. This is tantamount to adding another layer of instruction onto The Official MBA degree, thereby allowing the business school to believe, or at least to claim, that its students are being schooled in ethics and CSR, along with all the rest of the MBA corporate package—and therefore the school is innocent of complicity in corporate wrongdoing.

It is an appealing solution even though unlikely to be accepted by entrenched faculty interests, or supported by AACSB accreditation authorities, or to elicit little more than lip service acknowledgment by corporate recruiters, or to be enthusiastically embraced by students themselves who may wonder how well it suits their immediate ambition and goal of finding a corporate placement. Its salience for coping with the business school's moral dilemma may be questioned on other grounds, as well, this time by stepping away from the pros and cons of business school reform and by stepping into "the natural corporation."

The Natural Corporation

Today's business corporations—their actions, organizational systems, decisions, policies, values, and motivational impulses—are an outcome of evolutionary natural processes (see **Part III. NATURE,** above). So too are their many links to competitors, customers, suppliers, employees, communities, and the ecological environment a manifestation of natural selection pressures operating over long periods of evolutionary time. As Nature's Black Box (see **Year 2000** chapter, above), the corporation conceals these natural forces from public view, hidden behind a screen of sociocultural practices, habits, and customs, so that the cultural factors seem more substantively real than the underlying natural forces.

It follows from this view that nature's laws and nature's limits condition and channel corporate practice generally. Those same limits and laws also contain the firm's normative potentials, i.e., the ability and inclination of the corporation's inhabitants to act in ways judged to be right or wrong, socially responsible or irresponsible, ethical or unethical, morally acceptable or morally corrupt (see **Year 2002, Year 2004,** and **Year 2005** chapters, above).

Given this natural architecture that defines, sustains, organizes, and motivates the modern corporation, the business school's relationship to the corporation—if such ties are to be at all meaningful—is necessarily mediated through the same set of natural processes. That is, if the corporation's normative potentials are a function of nature's limits and laws, then the ability of the business school—or specifically, its MBA program—to affect the values, ethics, and normative inclinations of its students must also be an expression of those self-same natural limits and laws. For this reason, the business school's normative function—the ability to affect the moral consciousness of its students—devolves from natural laws, not simply from culturally imposed rational rules and regulations. The conclusion is unavoidable: only a concept of ethics and corporate social responsibility that is compatible with nature's laws is relevant to the business school's purpose and teaching function.

The two central nature-mediated purposes of the business corporation—**economizing** and **power-aggrandizing**—are at odds with each other and with the interacting **ecologizing** processes of the firm's environment (see **Year 2002** chapter, above). Few, if any, of the major ethics/CSR approaches taught in business schools for dealing with the moral issues generated by corporate operations directly embrace, or even accept the existence of, these three natural values lying at the heart of the modern corporation. As pedagogical techniques, *such ethics/CSR courses appear to be, and perhaps are, managerially and corporately disengaged from morally meaningful analysis for lack of contact with the natural realm.*

Take the much-criticized rationalist mindset found prevalent in MBA programs and said to be at odds with the behavioral realities revealed by the research of social scientists, psychologists, anthropologists, and others. This rationalist notion derives from two sources. One is an economic theory that posits rational self-interest as a basic human trait and then builds analytic models that counsel a rational calculation of benefits and costs as a basis for managerial action. A second source of rationalist thinking is an attitude accompanying and guiding the technology of business operations that calls for pragmatic, instrumental, problem-solving procedures. As presently taught in MBA courses, the resultant rationalist mindset is at odds with the flexible, ever-changing dynamics found in complex adaptive systems like the corporation that operate and try to survive on fitness landscapes (see **Year 1998** chapter, above). Management simply does not lend itself to a purely rationalist approach because it is a non-linear activity, messy, unpredictable, and largely uncontrollable—*made that way by nature.* Contrary to much criticism leveled at the "rationalist" MBA program, the problem with economic analysis taught there is its disconnection from nature-driven behavioral reality, not that it is rationally analytic. So too with the slings and arrows directed at the technology of business; its shortcoming is not in the analytics and pragmatics it necessarily depends on but in its nonlinearity, its open-endedness, the surprising and unpredictable impacts it has on people and society generally—*also made that way by nature.*

The disengagement of the business school from all of the natural sources that make both management *and* normative understanding possible means that much, if not all, that the schools teach their students is sadly deficient. More alarmingly, it suggests that the blame for ethical failure of the corporations and the schools is misplaced. If a nature-disengaged rationalist/analytic management approach is irrelevant, so too would be an ethics/CSR approach similarly detached from a natural base. The recommended remedies—mandatory ethics courses, stronger accreditation standards, corporate citizenship, transcendent spirituality, virtuous character, global citizenship, social contracts, etc.—would most likely not have their intended effect on the MBA/managerial mind. How could they if both managerially and normatively irrelevant?

In the end, one must ask a fearful question: Would these reforms prevent, or even minimize, future Enrons? The equally fearful answer is "not likely," not because the reforms lack all relevance or intellectual and behavioral bite, but because they do not directly address the natural factors that generate the moral quandaries of corporate operations. Just so long as business schools allow this situation to continue, so by equal measure will they continue to be silent partners in corporate crimes, misbehavior, and wrongdoing.

Natural Corporate Morals

A natural system of corporate morals is already firmly in place and need not be imposed by legal or philosophic edict. It exists by virtue of natural selection pressures exerted over tens of thousands of years of human evolution, resulting in behavioral forms and genetically embedded impulses that channel corporate operations into the well known patterns of today's business firm, described elsewhere in this book as The Evolutionary Firm (see **Year 2002** chapter, above).

The evolved moral framework may be understood variously as a set of value clusters (see *Values, Nature, and Culture in the American Corporation*), or as a corporate black box containing and activating those values (see **Year 2000** chapter, above), or as the collective behavioral output of ancestral neural algorithms that shape the modern corporate executive mind (see **Year 2002** chapter, above). The primary natural values, business functions, and algorithmic impulses comprising natural corporate morals are **economizing, power-aggrandizing, ecologizing, symbolizing/technologizing,** and the individualized **X-factors.** Taken together, these naturally evolved values/functions/algorithms create a framework of untold normative significance for the various ways in which business is conducted. As noted in earlier chapters, such moral realizations are themselves a part of human evolutionary experience, centered in and made possible by an evolving brain that interacts adaptively with its environment. Eventually recognized as "values" or "ethical/moral principles" long after their behavioral consequences had been accepted and understood as communal adaptive necessities, their original nature-based provenance is often concealed, ignored, and even denied by those who limit their studies to sociocultural explanations of business (and human) behavior. They are indeed an instance of an evolutionary "is" becoming a sociocultural "ought," a possibility and "naturalistic fallacy" forbidden in formal philosophy. They achieved normative status by their perceived effects on human adaptation, survival, and flourishing.

Here within this evolved moral framework, one finds all that is typical of business behavior: the uncompromising drive for profits and growth (**economizing**); the rationalist, calculative impulse to innovate (**technologizing**); the focused, hierarchically controlled managerial power (**power-aggrandizing**); the strategic goal-seeking in competitive markets (**competitive economizing**); the symbiotic linkages of firm and community (**mutualistic economizing**); and the indeterminacy, diversity, and demographic variations found in individualized **X-factors** of workforce members. *These are the natural normative directions, impulses, and behaviors of corporate business. They will be expressed. They will be acted upon as decisions, policies, strategies, and goals. They are the central values, the normative core of the business order.*

Three central normative issues emerge from this corporate moral system, each taking the form of contradictory behavioral impulses:

- The life-giving, life-sustaining, adaptive benefits flowing from a company's economizing may be offset, canceled, or denied by the self-centered power-aggrandizing behaviors of corporate managers.

- An overzealous, firm-focused economizing drive may disrupt, destroy, and decimate the symbiotic linkages essential to organizational functioning, community life and ecosystem integrity.

- An obsessive quest for managerial power, when linked to a firm's unlimited expansionist tendencies, can greatly diminish and degrade the life prospects of employees, stakeholders, and host communities.

Any business school curriculum that does not acknowledge and address the behavioral urges, attitudes, and impulses implanted by nature in the business mind, as well as the resultant moral contradictions, cannot hope to provide instruction relevant to the moral issues that arise in the workplace. To affect management behavior, one must come to, and be part of, the manager's place of work and decision making. The managerial mind is a pragmatic, problem-oriented mind, *made that way by nature.* It is only doubtfully open to appeals not consistent with nature's traits. Little wonder that such philosophic nostrums as virtuous character, realizing the good society, attaining social justice, or finding transcendent peace of mind—all worthy ends—are so routinely disregarded.

The Natural MBA

What, then, is to be done? Is there a way out for the business schools, a plan of action to restore business education to a place of integrity and managerial relevance? Must the business schools and their prime MBA credential be handcuffed and taken on a perp walk with the other perpetrators of corporate crimes? Can they instead educate, train, and inspire their students to instill a sense of goodness, a moral mission, a goal of socially responsible professional performance into the business corporation?

To this last question, my answer is yes and takes the form of what might be called "The Natural MBA" whose goal, educational rationale, and major curricular components can be summarized briefly.

- Teach business school students—undergraduates and MBAs alike—the core elements of natural process that drive business functions and influence workplace behavior. Topics, viewpoints, and perspectives would embrace evolutionary biology, the genetics of human behavior, the neural basis of decision making and attitude formation as revealed by (f)MRI brain scanning, evolutionary psychology, the dynamics of complex adaptive systems, the natural history of organizational systems, the symbiotic linkages of ecosystems and biotic communities, the parallels and disparities of human and non-human organic life, and the effects—both positive and negative—of all these in forming the business mind and mediating workplace decision making and policy formulation and, ultimately, business practice in general.

- Require of all entering students a basic background in the natural sciences, the social sciences, and the evolutionary history of *Homo sapiens* to be acquired through prior undergraduate study or pre-admission workshops.

- Recruit, and train if necessary, a new generation of scholar-teachers knowledgeable about the impacts of natural forces on the business firm, its managers and executives, organizational systems, motives, and functions. Their disciplinary backgrounds and expertise would likely be in one or more of the natural sciences.

- Design novel computer-assisted delivery systems that can reach directly into the business practitioner's mind *at the virtual point and time of decision making and policy formulation*, presenting an array of natural concepts, analytic techniques, and decision alternatives proven to be relevant to such situations. More than descriptive, these digitized arrays could additionally contain virtual, simulated alternative decision paths derived from different sets of moral assumptions and value commitments held by the involved participants both inside and external to the corporate workplace.

- Discard all claims of leadership learning and immediate professional advantage currently made for The Official MBA, *as well as the belief that the addition of add-on, marginal courses in ethics/CSR will resolve or dissolve the business school's complicity in corporate corruption and criminality.*

- Encourage, by funding, the discovery of innovative models of business practice that incorporate and integrate natural processes and sociocultural concepts across the entire range of the business firm's operations—marketing, production, finance, organization, communication, strategy, policy making, information technology, environmental impact, etc. Only those models having a demonstrated impact on actual workplace operations would be supported.

- Provide reflective insights into the workplace intersections of nature, culture, and personal identity, where the broader societal, metaphysical, and philosophic dimensions of life are realized. These viewpoints might be realized through gifted teachers from the disciplines of history, social science, humanities and arts, philosophy, and the history of science.

- In cooperation with business firms, design an on-going "clinical" activity related directly to the operations of the business firm for the purpose of providing hands-on experience in grappling with actual workplace problems and processes, as well as to test and validate the practical relevance of classroom ideas. Comparable in scope and intention to the legal training of "moot courts" and the clinical experiences of post-medical school "residencies" and "grand rounds," these workplace clinics would provide a needed link between theory and practice.

Realizing such an ambitious, even radical agenda might seem most unlikely at best and impossible at worst. When the nation's business schools were challenged in the late 1950s by the Ford Foundation and Carnegie Corporation to move from narrow vocational training to the broader professional preparation of business leaders, the leading schools adopted and enacted the recommended reforms within a decade, followed by most of the others in relatively short order (see the two **Year 1977** chapters in **Part IV,** above). Helped out by generous funding from both of the foundations and enthusiastic acceptance by the business establishment, the reforms achieved their general aims in a remarkably short period. But to count on that reform model now is probably unwise and unattainable, given the scale, complexities and global dynamics of corporate operations, plus the vested academic interests of the business schools that are ever more conscious of their "national ranking," along with their entrenched and well-paid faculties committed to things as they are. It remains sadly true that it is easier to move a cemetery than to change a university curriculum.

A more likely prospect may be found where least expected: in experimental partnerships between localized but daring business firms and one or more marginalized, out-of-the-way business schools, possibly funded by daredevil high-tech entrepreneurs who seek the sources of innovation underlying their own businesses. Unencumbered by the conventions and shibboleths of both The Official MBA and The Real MBA, these high-tech, nature-inspired, recklessly-naïve educational joint ventures might reach beyond the mere preparation of practitioners and/or leaders to demonstrate the powerfully inspiring creativity and inventiveness hidden within and waiting release from Nature's Black Box—a veritable gusher of ideas and perspectives fungible in intellectual and philosophic fruitfulness for firm, society, and individual—in short, a realization of the natural potentials for life, growth, and opportunity that reside in the practice of business but now securely caged within the stale cultural stereotypes of academia.

The Continuing Dilemma

Not even a shift of this magnitude, with all of its uncertainty, would entirely resolve the business school's moral dilemma, for all of the natural forces that have laid ethical/CSR problems on business's doorstep will continue to operate on the executive mind and to generate self-serving, uncaring, socially disruptive, environmentally disastrous, morally corrupt workplace practices. Nature tells us that much. No single ethics/CSR course, no mandated ethics requirements, no entire MBA program, no philosophic appeal can entirely deflect those darker, antisocial impulses that surface from time to time in corporate life.

On the brighter side, a nature-informed education—The Natural MBA—can reveal to students and practitioners the natural tendencies and long-embedded ancestral proclivities to build systems of social cooperation and exchange, extend reciprocal justice to strangers, form fair and just social contracts, strengthen the symbiotic bonds of family and community—and to explore ways of bringing these socially humane impulses into the workplace. The business schools' dilemma is resolvable, if at all, by redirecting learning efforts away from The Official MBA and The Real MBA and toward The Natural MBA. Therein lies the prospect of avoiding future corporate Enrons by bringing students and practitioners face-to-face with the ethical potentials and opportunities, as well as the dangers, to be discovered within an evolving nature.

In the end, business schools and the corporations they serve share a common moral fate, one set by nature. Thus linked, they must act in concert to avoid nature's normative downside as they seek and find common cause in the more humane potentials that nature holds out to both.

PART V

HORIZON AND HOPE

The active pursuit of corporate social responsibility by U. S. corporations is less than a hundred years old. The modern corporate form itself has existed for no more than two centuries, and even that's a stretch. Neither CSR doctrine nor corporations as we know them have any guarantee of permanency. So, one wonders if what passes for today's wisdom about business's social obligations will be adequate decisional guides into a possibly perilous future. How might executive minds be released from time-bound and culture-bound traditions to seek science-based cosmic and nature-based spiritual perspectives? Is the discipline of business ethics itself trapped in a set of outmoded assumptions about how to confront the moral challenges faced by corporate practitioners? Can science and religion find common moral grounds to instill a sense of global morality in executive minds? Finally, what new generational voices can one hear—voices that speak the language and reflect the needs of a new millennium—voices that can persuade coming generations of business practitioners to heed the call for a higher standard of corporate moral conduct and social responsibility?

YEAR 1998

[Public confidence in big business: 21%]

EXPANDING CSR'S MEANING:
COSMOS, SCIENCE, AND RELIGON
IN THE EXECUTIVE SUITE

Setting the Scene. As the tumultuous 20th century drew to a close, questions of corporate social responsibility seemed to loom even larger than at mid-century. While the corporation's CSR agenda grew longer and more complex, one began to wonder if CSR scholarship could provide the answers so urgently needed by business leaders. Were conventional CSR theories, explanations, and advice up to the task? If not, what should be done to make CSR theory match CSR practice? Here, I urged my CSR colleagues to consider a fourth CSR stage—CSR$_4$—with a far broader reach than the corporation alone.

There are good reasons why scholars who specialize in the study of social issues in management should pay attention to developments in the natural sciences. The principal and most compelling reason is the constant bombardment laid down by natural forces in all areas of human life, including many of the core concerns of business itself (see **Part IV** above). Nature—and especially human awareness of nature's effects—impinges at all hours and often in the most unexpected and sometimes dismaying fashion on what we do, how we do it, and why we are who we are. In confronting this rising tide of existential challenges, it is the natural scientists who can help find a way through present or predicted troubles or, at least, can help us to ask the right questions.

Whether it is Dolly the cloned sheep, or the search for the dinosaurs' demise, or knowing how to deflect errant asteroids headed for earth collision, we are dependent on astrophysicists, geneticists, and fossil hunters for the proximate answers. And this is not to mention such puzzlers as how to keep our heads above ocean waters if the globe truly warms enough to melt the polar ice, or how to head off the further spread of global epidemics such as AIDS, or how to prevent future Chernobyl-like radiation perils. Even people who live in Tornado Alley or near the earthquake-prone edge of the California tectonic plate or in the low coastal areas of Bangladesh where typhoons take their human toll or within sight of any number of not-so-slumbering volcanoes or who crouch in fear of hurricane winds and tides—they too look to scientists for prediction of how and when and with what force nature will unleash its fury.

As cosmologists spin out their theories of how it all began and how it might end, as neuroscientists debate the meaning of human consciousness, as space scientists guide the early Columbus-like explorations of our solar system, as primatologists probe for the moral roots of behavior and language in our near bonobo cousins, as paleontologists uncover yet older fossils of human precursors—as all of these remarkable forays into human meaning and human existence are going on—surely one would be brave and perhaps just a little foolish to believe that this veritable knowledge-gusher from the natural sciences has nothing to say to those who study business and society. It would be as if the entire business system and all business practitioners were sealed within a glass sphere, cut off from nature and all of its myriad effects.

The CSR Trap

CSR thought has been around for about four and a half decades. Within that brief span of time, we who study and teach CSR in the nation's business schools have established a new field of management studies by developing theory and a research literature, have secured its place within the university curriculum, and have moved on to advise business practitioners about their interactions with the social and political world. In spite of these demonstrably important gains, one can still feel a tug of doubt or a sense of incompleteness, as if there is more to do.

CSR's central problem arises from its central strengths. The principal focus of scholarly inquiry has been the corporation-and-society interface, thereby placing emphasis on the various stages through which the corporation has moved as it has become more attuned to its sociopolitical environment: CSR_1 (Corporate Social *Responsibility*), CSR_2 (Corporate Social *Responsiveness*), and CSR_3 (Corporate Social *Rectitude*). However, that is where the problem begins. The three CSRs have ensnared our minds. We are caught within what might be called a "CSR trap." These stages strongly imply that it is *the corporation* that should be the center of our attention. The corporation becomes the sun around which society revolves—the central star of our societal system whose productive rays may now enrich, now impoverish, or at times devastate, the societal satellites that swing around the corporate sun. Lacking *responsibility*, the corporation may breach social expectations and incur penalties. Lacking *responsiveness*, it may fall victim to public wrath and regulatory entanglements. Lacking *rectitude*, it may stand accused of gross moral crimes. Our work has been to head off business's social transgressions, to say to corporate practitioners, "Be socially responsible! Respond to social needs! Act ethically and with moral integrity!"

Important as this work has been, we may have overlooked the pre-Copernican nature of the three CSRs. By turning our analytic telescopes so unrelentingly on the corporation, and by believing that changing its behavior in socially favorable directions is our central task, our analyses may be yielding answers to smaller and smaller questions rather than probing for the grander and more profound questions implicit in business-and-society relations. Could it be that the corporation is not our central star after all? If the corporation does not lie at the center of our whirling and evolving societal system, what does? What should we be looking at, or for? Is there an emerging fourth stage—a CSR_4—enriched by insights from natural science and metaphysics? Getting to CSR_4 is what this chapter explores and advocates.

Moving on Towards CSR_4 Consciousness

New paradigms tend to emerge when conventional ways of thinking no longer provide satisfactory answers or when normal science produces only humdrum answers. But because new paradigms suggest novel approaches, they typically encounter resistance. The new paradigmatic ground symbolized by a new CSR_4 stage rests on several premises about the inadequacies of present CSR theorizing.

- Corporate social performance (CSP) theorizing has reached a crisis point, or very nearly a dead end. Few answers are emerging to the urgent pressures and crises facing today's business and society. These include the unprecedented economic, political, and social upheavals in the former Soviet bloc; the technological revolutions sweeping away many of the familiar traits—as well as millions of jobs—of economic systems here and abroad; the looming and absolutely terrifying global problems associated with ecological transformations; the failure to check ethnic hatreds before they turn into genocide or employee-employer tensions that lead to workplace homicide; the increasing exposure of democratic societies to violent and senseless attacks by terrorists bearing all kinds of instructions from their gods; and on and on. In the midst of this global turmoil, we continue to spin out theories of how corporate good at home can somehow contribute to social good worldwide. We fiddle while the globe burns.

The popularized phrase "corporate social performance" (CSP) itself, often substituted for "corporate social responsibility," provides a clue to the near paralysis of CSR studies. With an emphasis on mere performance, rather than a normatively tinged responsibility, responsiveness, or rectitude, CSP emerges as a morally neutered concept. CSR studies will continue to be morally barren if they focus on performance divorced from the social and moral dimensions of corporate behavior.

- CSR's dominant paradigm—the stakeholder concept—has run its course and now produces few new or theoretically significant insights. Valuable in its time, it has been mined out conceptually, summarized, classified, expanded into ever more complex layers, and examined in minute detail for its connections with social contract theory, virtue ethics, agency theory, strategic management, and so on. These are solid gains to be savored but not lingered over.

- Business ethics theory is hobbled by a failure to acknowledge and integrate contemporary social science and natural science perspectives into the analysis of business operations. A decade of rubbing shoulders with management scholars, through collaborative annual meetings of SIM and the Society for Business Ethics, has not moved business ethics philosophers far beyond their continued devotion to the noncontextualist abstractions found in the lore of conventional philosophy. Theories of rights, justice, and social contract remain firmly anchored in 18th-, 19th-, and early 20th-century perspectives on human nature and human society.

- The role of CSR studies is not to enhance or support the corporation's operations or the work of its managers. We should not see ourselves as intellectual mechanics whose tinkering makes the corporate engine run smoother. Neither is it our job simply to bolster stakeholder claims brought against the corporation. These are important but essentially second-order considerations that have *seemed* central to our scholarly tasks. Our collective concern about the social and moral efficiency of corporations has tended to cloak the main business of CSR scholarship. An emergent CSR_4 consciousness can help clarify the way forward, signaled by a new CSR acronym reflecting a broader and deeper concern.

C = Cosmos

If the "C" phase of CSR_4 consciousness is to touch the most fundamental normative concerns of business and humanity, it must be capable of dealing with the forces and powers that literally define human existence, human consciousness, and human purpose. Those forces are no less than cosmic in their reach, and for that reason it will be helpful *to let the C in CSR_4 stand for* **Cosmos**. The message here is plain: "Corporation, move over. You are being decentered. The cosmos is now to become the basic normative reference for the CSR field."

Even the briefest of glimpses into cosmology demonstrates a compelling, inescapable conclusion: All life, all societies, and all environments—the living biosphere and all non-biotic features, every economy and economic enterprise, all communities and every individual on earth—all are subject to and are a consequence of cosmological processes. Nothing happens anywhere that does not feel the weight of this most comprehensive expression of nature's forces.

All of the important, central normative issues and questions concerning human meaning and human destiny devolve from cosmological processes: the origin of life and the definition of what life is; the origin and evolution of humans; the origin, evolution, and future of the universe; the future fate of the earth; whether there is purposefulness in the universe or within human life on earth; whether there is life and/or intelligent life elsewhere in the universe; if other life is out there, what are we to do about it; if we are alone in the universe, what responsibility if any befalls us to preserve this earthly life.

These are not science fiction questions; they are already upon us. They form some of the central issues of today's public policy. Corporations themselves are frequently caught up in the resultant debates, such as production and use of the medical technologies of abortion, the use of human fetuses and placentas in pharmacological research, genetic engineering and production of genetically altered food products, production and consumption practices that threaten the globe's ecological integrity, the beginnings of extraterrestrial explorations, and many other human issues of cosmic significance spawned at the business-and-society interface.

The basic idea underlying advocacy of this paradigmatic shift is that a corporate orientation is not sufficiently comprehensive to encompass the central normative issues that will challenge business decision makers in the foreseeable future. Business's normative significance cannot be discerned simply by looking into the corporation or by knowing only *its* values. Business must be placed within and understood as part of a cosmological context. Only then will the force and impact of its values and actions become apparent. The cosmos becomes the outer frame within which normative issues arise and answers must be sought. The corporation is a child of the cosmos, subject to its forces and interacting with them. The cosmos does not revolve around the corporation, nor does the corporation deserve a special, centered status. Now is the time to abandon our pre-Copernican-like assumption of corporate centrality and seek instead to describe business's normative function as one part of a larger cosmological whole.

S = Science

If reliable knowledge about business's place in the cosmos is to become an organizing feature of CSR research, it is to scientific inquiry and scientific methods that we must turn. Science becomes the wellspring of cosmological knowledge affecting human and business behavior, and so *the S in CSR$_4$ stands for Science*—all of the sciences, not just the social and behavioral sciences. The needed vision emerges from a broad range of natural *and* social sciences.

An exclusive focus on the social sciences has overlooked a quiet revolution going on in the natural sciences, now in its third decade. This new scientific ferment has been called "The Third Culture" as a play on C. P. Snow's well-known idea of the Two Cultures, one of Science, the other of the Humanities, and their inability to understand one another. Today, all of the truly exciting scientific news comes from Third Culture sciences: artificial intelligence, artificial life, chaos theory, massive parallelism, neural nets, the inflationary universe, fractals, complex adaptive systems, superstrings, biodiversity, nanotechnology, the human genome, expert systems, punctuated equilibrium, cellular automata, fuzzy logic, space biospheres, the Gaia hypothesis, virtual reality, cyberspace, and teraflop machines— among others.

This scientific outpouring signals a needed change in theory and, for business practitioners, changes in the way they conceive their function in society. Rapidly, business is being drawn into the cosmological drama being written in the pages of Third Culture science: agribusinesses are genetically engineering new plant and animal strains; pharmaceutical companies frequently find new biochemical combinations to ward off human ailments ranging from depression (witness the Prozac phenomenon) to

AIDS; insurance companies and private health care agencies probe for the genetic secrets of their clients; aerospace companies are into the fourth decade of space exploration and the quest for extraterrestrial resources for human use; chemical manufacturers and their industrial customers have begun to heed the risks of global warming and overexploitation of earth resources; and business organizations everywhere may soon record productivity gains by drawing on Third Culture theories of chaos, complexity, and self-organization. These are only the most obvious and most directly practical uses of Third Culture discoveries. Others will take us on a wild roller-coaster ride into and through the inner recesses of the mind, the cell, and the psyche—as well as to the outer reaches of space colonization within and perhaps even beyond our solar system. Business will be involved at every stage.

If CSR scholars are to remain theoretically relevant, they have *no choice* but to embrace and explore Third Culture cosmological science. Consider these riveting thoughts: No theory of human behavior is complete without inclusion of genetic components. No concept of organization is complete without acknowledging Third Culture theories of chaos, complexity, and self-organization. No theory of moral action is complete that omits the affiliative biological bonds derived from our evolutionary heritage as a species within the primate order. No theory of human society is feasible that does not place that society firmly within an evolving planetary biosphere. No theory of the corporation is possible that disregards the directive power of the thermodynamic engine buried deep within the bureaucratic layers of people and technology. No theory of business and society is valid that does not take account of these and other Third Culture perspectives.

One more point about the "S" in CSR_4 is worth emphasizing. All Third Culture sciences are *normative sciences*. Their only purpose and significance lies in the light they can shed on the human enterprise, its present character, and its possible future. Their insights greatly enrich all attempts to grapple with the most profound human inquiries. Trying to answer ethical, social, and moral questions without reference to this body of scientific knowledge is futile and ultimately self-defeating.

R = Religion

There is yet another inquiring route by which one can pursue the business-and-society questions and issues posed by the cosmic and scientific dimensions of CSR_4 consciousness: the ways defined by religious viewpoints. Human meaning, destiny, purpose, and morality, along with the practical ways of coping with day-to-day living, have been the province of religionists in all ages and among all cultures. Of whatever stripe of religious affiliation, they have felt free to judge both business and society. It will be useful therefore to let *the R phase of CSR₄ symbolize* **Religion**.

But some will surely protest, "How can this be?" We are not seminarians. Our scholarly work is secular, reflecting the best traditions of science, especially social science. Creedal declarations of faith do not normally preface CSR research or the practical decisions made by business people. Their secular activity seems far removed from the common definition of religion, and indeed we normally pride ourselves for rigorously buttressing the wall that separates scholarly inquiry from faith. How then can it be suggested that scholars should open the door, and their professional minds, to religious phenomena? Or that they should encourage the expression of such views in the workplace?

Nature and Spirituality

The current spate of management treatises about spirituality and soul as a presence in the workplace may signal little more than yet another faddish maneuver invented by consultants eager to peddle their services to corporations. However, as risky as it may be to venture into these waters of unknown depth, even the most devoted empiricist-secularist may be able to find links between the daily work of corporate employees and the broader realms of meaning that are being invoked by today's management soul searchers.

One such possibility is the idea that all people want and need to find meaning within their own lives by relating themselves and their activities to the world around them. This search for meaning and purpose appears to be a constant in human affairs and possibly underlies or at least contributes to the widespread presence of religious activities and philosophic beliefs throughout human societies past and present. That human constant might be referred to as a religious impulse or a spiritual impulse or even a metaphysical impulse.

Though daring, one might hypothesize that such an impulse likely arises from naturalistic processes found within the human genome, particularly from the fertile neural-brain system of the human species. Neuroscientists report that human brains are fully capable of generating a constant stream of symbolic-creative-imaginative-curiosity-play impulses. It seems reasonable that these creative expeditions and explorations by the human mind are at times used by people to seek a clearer picture of their surroundings and, particularly, their personal place in it all. If so, that would signal the active presence of a religious impulse, a trait that impels humans to explore and seek to understand the meaning of their lives within an evolving cosmos.

This nature-based religious impulse, rooted in the human brain, is subject to cultural disciplines of all kinds. Normally, it is passed through diverse sociocultural screens and filters that represent multiple kinds of human experiences, religions, and cultures. It rarely, if ever, finds outlet without cultural shaping of some kind. From time to time, the impulse may be deflected almost entirely away from its original self-fulfilling quest function by legends and ritual beliefs. Students of organizational behavior have noted that the religious impulse within an individual may also be submerged and diminished by suffocating bureaucratic routines of corporations. When that occurs, an employee or manager may then deliberately repress the religious impulse.

But this is an impulse that will not be turned aside. Sooner or later, its influence will be felt, not just as a personal religious experience but also in attenuated form within organizational life, behavior, and decisions. In other words, the impulse and the behavior it drives become one more factor to be understood by those who manage organizations and those who seek to understand and improve workplace life. It may *seem* to be merely personal and, for that reason, not properly within the purview of the student of organizations.

In traversing this terrain, a clear grasp of scholarly purpose is essential if misunderstanding is to be avoided. The argument here is that this human religious impulse is *present* in organizations, including business firms. That is not to say that it *should* be present, although it is difficult to see how it could be excluded, given its neurological base. Nor need it be seen as more important than other natural impulses also present in the workplace. Neither need organizational researchers endorse any particular version of religious dogma or doctrinal creed they may find in the course of their work. As should be evident to any casual observer, some of these doctrinal effusions can be a source of far-reaching mischief, even as others may provide the most subtle satisfactions for their adherents. Brand names here are not as important as the generic product itself.

The basic hypothesis is that people seek to understand their place in the cosmos. The focus is on *the personal quest for cosmic meaning*: Who am I? What am I doing here? Where am I going? And why? In that search, peoples' cultures, their institutions, their religions, and their many other social affiliations provide them with diverse guides, some positive, others negative, some helpful, others a hindrance. But one should not count on finding one's own religious philosophy written on the face of the cosmos.

Rather, what can be counted on is a personal need to make the search. Some people create their own meaning; for them, personal significance is not out there awaiting discovery. Most people fall short of this kind of religious creativity and simply accept (or reject) the metaphysical meanings given to them by their culture.

Religion in the Executive Suite

Corporate managers are caught up in their own personal quest for life's meaning, as are employees and other stakeholders. We are familiar with the perils imposed on society by managers whose personal quest for meaning goes no further than the executive suite and cannot break the bonds of a cramped, self-centered psyche. Or executives whose vision stops at the corporate gates, unable to see beyond the immediate demands of shareholder-owners. Or managers who disregard the planetary damage of their reckless ecological decisions, or who uncaringly cut off at mid-career the productive lives of downsized employees. Their daily worship of corporate power and glory cuts cruelly and deeply into the personal quests of others and countervenes the very cosmic processes from which they—and all of us—draw life and meaning.

Business practitioners may not realize or be willing to admit that their Personal Quest is intertwined with their professional decisions. They too have been taught that business is business whereas religion is personal and private. But it is time to rip the mask of religious furtiveness off the corporate face. Personal religious philosophies of all kinds abound in the workplace.

Timothy L. Fort has made a very strong case for recognizing that the religious beliefs of corporate executives influence their business decisions and that such beliefs should be openly displayed by business practitioners, rather than concealed. Laura Nash's study of evangelical Christian CEOs, on the other hand, reveals some of the problems inherent in mixing one's personal religious commitments with on-the-job responsibilities. Religious proselytizing and/or subtle indoctrination is one of the principal problems found among dedicated evangelicals whose faith may impel them to spread their gospel to others who may or may not wish to hear their pleas. The perceived intrusions, resentments, tensions, and religious rivalries that accompany on-the-job evangelizing can unsettle work routines in even the best-run companies.

In spite of these inherent difficulties, CSR scholars need have no fear of the business practitioner's search for personal meaning when it emerges at work. As teachers, they may open up cosmic vistas and broaden the range of perspectives that carry beyond the individual manager, the company, family, neighborhood, ethnic group, nation, society, planet, and even beyond our galaxy. A *corporate-centered* classroom perspective channels practitioner viewpoints to the narrower, immediate components involved in normative analysis. A *cosmic-centered* perspective beckons the executive to explore a broader, more inclusive range of normative possibilities. By teasing out the practitioner's personal version of a genetically embedded religious impulse, and revealing its broader potentialities, a skilled teacher or researcher might introduce points of view never before glimpsed or imagined by a work-centered business professional.

Here is an instance where the three main components of CSR_4—Cosmos, Science, and Religion—can be brought to bear in broadening and deepening the executive mind. This broader view extends the earlier reach of $CSR_{1,2,3}$, creating a new dimension of normative analysis that supplements—without displacing—responsibility, responsiveness, and rectitude (i.e., moral awareness and action).

Religion and the CSR Scholar

The students of CSR too are caught up in the Quest. Some make no effort to conceal their religious commitments. Most others remain in the religious closet, not out of shame or fear of discovery but because they sense the problems that can easily arise from mixing personal religious beliefs with teaching and research. As children of a positivist age, today's scholars shrink from being pinned with the dreaded label of religious fanatic, crank, or proselytizer.

Given the ethical-moral-societal emphasis of most CSR studies, it would not be surprising to discover that religious conditioning plays a significant, though somewhat muted, role in them. A recent study suggests as much. The religious orientations of 50 organizational leaders of the Social Issues in Management (SIM) division of the Academy of Management, plus 100 others drawn randomly from the SIM membership rolls, were surveyed. Using any definition of religion that they preferred, more than two thirds (69%) said they are committed to a religious philosophy or a set of religious beliefs. Three out of five respondents (63.1%) reported that their religious beliefs/orientation had influenced their choice of academic career. Nearly three quarters (72.6%) said their decision to teach CSR courses was similarly influenced by religious commitment. More than two-thirds agreed that religious orientation was influential in their choice of classroom materials and research topics. Overall, the survey seems to suggest that religious belief is capable of being a major, though mostly silent, partner in the scholarly work of many SIMians.

Those who are committed secularists should not be dismayed by this possibility. Denying the influence of religious belief in teaching and research is to set aside as analytically irrelevant a behavioral and cognitive impulse that appears to be embedded within the human genome. Acknowledging religion's influence need not necessarily lead to an endorsement, or a rejection, of any given doctrinal belief. In their scholarly role, CSR students need not and should not be advocates of any particular religious canon but rather elucidators of the influence that religious impulses exert on organizational decision making and workplace behavior. All beliefs, whether religious or secular, should be judged in their relation to the cosmos and its dominant natural processes, for that remains the core normative framework of a new CSR_4 consciousness. The individual's Quest—whether undertaken as manager, teacher, or student—goes forward within this cosmic realm, no matter what specific religious or metaphysical vehicle guides the seeker.

Getting There

Is the CSR_4 stage "a bridge too far"—a goal stretching beyond the reach and/or interest of the CSR community? Possibly so, but the answer depends on the intellectual and philosophical flexibility of CSR inquiry.

One needs to be reminded of the permeability of the boundaries that have defined earlier stages of business and society thought. As many have pointed out, the distinctions between responsibility, responsiveness, and rectitude have been and remain elusive and ill defined. The same can be said for what is being proposed here as CSR_4. There is a sense in which the use of cosmic/natural-science/religious perspectives in this field began a quarter century ago with the advent of the environmental-ecological movement, particularly if one thinks of the earth as a planet displaying ecological limitations and manifesting a Gaia-like living presence. Another strand of CSR_4 thinking now appears as genetic research into human beginnings, human evolution, human behavior, and human health. To environmental and genetic studies could be added the current attempt to relate chaos and complexity theories to organizational dynamics. Perhaps CSR_4 is already here, needing only to be recognized and deliberately promoted.

Taking a cosmic view of business's social responsibilities is admittedly a very large step, especially for management scholars whose teaching and research is performed mainly within the disciplinary confines, and the pragmatically inclined climate, of the business school. Injecting eschatological issues into the dialogue seems, if not intellectually scandalous, then a waste of valuable time that could be devoted to the more practical concerns of the workplace. Does this mean that seeking the broader meaning of CSR is to be permanently caged within the prevailing culture of business schools, unable to break free for inquiry in a globalized corporate world seething with religious animosities and tensions arising from the widespread use of scientific and technological advances that literally transform and sometimes destroy the lives of people around the world?

One hopes not. CSR is not a trivial game. In the end, it's about life's deepest experiences. We need to say this to our students, the young who aspire and the mature professionals who presently rule the corporate realm.

YEAR 2000

MILLENNIAL CHALLENGES
TO BUSINESS ETHICS

Setting the Scene. Summing up, looking back, and gazing into the future surely occurs at the turn of each century and even more so at the millennial boundaries of human time-keeping. A chance to do so publicly was offered to a group of business ethicists by the journal Business Ethics Quarterly in the year 2000. The questions I posed were aimed at two groups: business ethics scholars and business practitioners.

If business ethics is to remain a viable inquiring enterprise into and beyond the opening years of the third (Christian) millennium, its scholarly advocates will need to cope with a range of questions that have begun to take on new meanings and more complex dimensions not envisioned by established theory or philosophy. The driving force of these intellectual transformations is the heightened pace and range of a human evolutionary process that is opening up new behavioral, cognitive, and societal realms only incompletely understood while simultaneously revealing the inadequacies of present answers and the conventional ways of seeking those answers. Now in its 4,000th millennium (some would say only the 2,500th), human evolution is altering not just the ways in which people behave toward each other but, more importantly, may be removing and replacing the organic limits and constraints previously imposed on thought and action by the traits of a carbon-based organic life. Human attempts to outwit or out-game natural selection, whether successful or not in the far-distant long run, have already gripped the business imagination and spilled a host of ethics dilemmas onto the corporate boardroom table. That business will continue to be drawn into the fierce vortex of managerial *qua* philosophical controversies of the third millennium is of little doubt. That it will be given the guidance it will need, especially by business ethicists, is uncertain. It depends upon the ability and willingness of business ethicists to grasp the nature of the evolutionary transformations taking place and to convey that understanding into the workplace where business managers daily render decisions fraught with personal, societal, and planetary significance.

The questions featured here are by no means a complete register of the normative puzzles newly twisted and transformed by the upsurge of scientific discovery. Some are as old as philosophic inquiry itself, others more recently thrust upon us. But fragmentary as they are, they may serve as symbolic markers of the pathways that business ethicists must tread as they venture into the third millennium.

The Questions

What is the nature of human nature?

An arc traced from Charles Darwin through Sigmund Freud and to Francis Crick pinpoints the journey of modern science toward a greatly modified concept of human nature. Genetics explorations alone have shaken the old Nature versus Nurture conundrum to its foundations. The supreme, dominant posture of culture as the master principle of human behavior suddenly looks less secure. Ethologists and linguists boldly proclaim the presence of innate behavioral impulses that underlie and sustain what has previously been traced to acquired social learning. Culture itself is revealed as a stream of symbols flowing out of complex cognitive networks composed of neuronal circuits activated through electrochemical impulses. In this picture, brain and environment interpenetrate one another, each able to influence the other, with no obvious boundary between the two processes. Nature and Nurture as separate categories literally disappear and dissolve into a common realm of biochemical processes.

The resultant business ethics challenge: Are business practitioners, their actions decisions, policies, and companies, driven and shaped by nature? To what extent, if any, can or should they be deflected from such natural courses? The point here goes far beyond the simplistic notion that the natural business impulse is greed, a comfortable if erroneous assumption of many business ethicists. The issue is broader and more open-ended: Is the business function itself a manifestation of natural forces that are part and parcel of human evolution?

Are values imposed or are they emergent?

The 20th century's social sciences have taught that values are imposed upon the newborn by virtue of learning cultural routines that are socially approved. Parents, peers, teachers, and authority figures, aided and reinforced by institutional and organizational structures, write society's values onto the *tabula rasa* of the young. Laying to one side the still incomplete genetics revolution that in time might cast doubt on the sociocultural origin of values and ethical predispositions, one need turn only to chaos-complexity theory to discover that values appear to emerge spontaneously through natural self-organizing processes as individuals interact in a wide variety of social contexts. In this view, values are *discovered* and are entirely an emergent consequence of one's experienced relationships. Each camp faces further challenges. If values are imposed by society, can they be anything other than culturally relative? If values are emergent, are they in any way constrained toward desirable or sought ethical outcomes?

The resultant business ethics challenge: Whether imposed or emergent, certain identifiable value sets drive business practitioners to do what they do. If one's moral identity has been tattooed indelibly by strong cultural tradition, flexibility in the face of rapid change will be hard to come by; and the business practitioner may project a learned, inflexible set of values into all arenas of business action and policy, regardless of environmental setting and business consequences. If on the other hand business people learn as they go, adapting their value sets to circumstances faced, and giving free rein to their emergent natural impulses, then their firms and the societies they serve may prosper. In either case, the business ethicist will need to identify the moral center of the value sets involved.

Does the global future belong to universalist values or to emergent multi-cultural, multi-ethnic diverse values?

Philosophers have long sought common human values, while culturally inspired clashes of all kinds break out in a rising tide of conflict over right and wrong. With the United States now positioned as the economically and militarily dominant world power, it and its extended family of Western European nations, seem willing (certainly) and able (arguably) to make Euro-American values the core of a world-embracing moral system. Simultaneously and contradictorily, a tidal wave of ethnic identity, diverse and resurgent religious faiths, linguistic separatism, devolution and decentralization of large-scale governmental authority, and a search for new national identities—all of these reflecting value systems of the widest variability—washes across broad regions of the globe. It is at the boundaries where these powerfully driven, diverse moral systems intersect that some of today's most serious and tragic human encounters occur. Finding and agreeing upon common values seems at once less likely and more necessitous.

The resultant business ethics challenge: Global business firms need moral direction if they are to be economically successful and if their presence is to be socially acceptable. These goals would be eminently more reachable if business decision makers could be guided by globally agreed principles and standards. Although first steps have been taken in a number of areas—trade, environment, commercial law, patent protection, exploitation of oceanic resources, and other specific industrial areas—the second millennium has closed on an economic scene of great rivalry, fierce competition, enormous gaps between rich and poor, and a widespread condemnation of the very nations who at times act to promote their own sociocultural values as the world standard. Left to their own naturalistic drives and ethnocentric moral inclinations, business firms everywhere maneuver without either compass or rudder calibrated to the needs of a global economy. Does the corpus of present business ethics theory hold the answers to such puzzles—answers both workable for business practice and morally acceptable to the globe's many diverse peoples?

What methods of inquiry are likely to be the most effective in revealing the core ethical issues of business practice in ways that might lead to improvement in comprehension and resolution of those issues?

The most popular and the oldest methods employed by professional philosophers—abstract, non-contextual, logical analysis—have revealed little of practical import and nothing beyond exhortation that would lead to the direct improvement of ethical practice in business. Social science methods, less frequently applied, have yielded positivist descriptions of business and corporate behavior but only arguable normative propositions and pluralist/relativist interpretations that are of uncertain worth to practitioners. While philosophic method is conceptual but not contextual, social science method is descriptive but not directive. Leading figures on both sides insist that this state of affairs not only should remain as it is but cannot be otherwise. Natural science approaches—such as sociobiological explanations of behavior, evolutionary psychology's emphasis on the persistence of anciently inherited behavioral traits, comparative primate-human studies, genetics theory and analysis, neuroscience and artificial intelligence, game theory, and emergent chaos-complexity theory—are only newly applied, highly controversial, resisted by philosophers *and* social scientists, and largely unknown and inaccessible to practitioners. Could a blend—a consilience, as one observer has called it—of the best from each of these three approaches hold the answer?

The resultant business ethics challenge: The mark of business ethicists on business practice is not large and never has been. Practitioners frequently arrive at an ethical posture on their own and in their own pragmatic way, sometimes from religious precepts absorbed early in life, other times inspired by parental role models or other admired figures. The prescriptions offered by business ethicists may appear, and may be, couched in language and logic not translatable into the routines of the work day, so they are unable to touch the moral sensitivity of the practitioners. Whichever method or approach is to be used, it must come to terms with the kinds of demands the business professional feels on a day-to-day basis.

Why is technology so infrequently discussed by business ethicists?

Technology is a transformative force in human culture, bringing people together and splitting them apart in bewildering ways, thrusting fierce and poignant moral questions forward, generating strikingly new and dazzling dimensions of communicating, sensing, experiencing, and intellectual exploring. Today's technology is literally revolutionizing corporate organization by leveling dominance-and-control hierarchies, de-centering authority, universalizing data possession, creating self-organizing work units, crumbling corporate walls and boundaries, creating cross-cultural alliances and cross-sector coalitions, blurring the lines between buyer and seller, producer and supplier, domestic firm and global enterprise. The Internet alone—that worldwide, never-sleeping, ever conscious intelligent network—promises transformations in human knowledge and conduct never before imagined. Advanced medical technology now reaches into the womb to repair defects at the beginning of life and into the brain of the aging to forestall the end of life. Technology is the fire that heats a roiling stew pot of moral issues and questions that sweep across many facets of human life.

The resultant business ethics challenge: Like it or not, society has made business the arbiter of new technology. Even in those cases where the technology serves governmental purposes, such as military preparedness or space exploration, it is from business laboratories or government-and-business-subsidized university research sites that new technology flows into societal uses. The computerized technology that has cut like a scythe through the ranks of downsized employees has simultaneously opened up a myriad of new professional pathways. The cost-effective technologies that have driven work and jobs from advanced industrial societies into Third World sweatshops has at the same time spawned droves of high technology entrepreneurs who rejuvenate older industrial regions and create new and better jobs. Increasing reliance on electronic technology has somewhat leveled the playing fields on which men and women compete for work and opportunities while still placing much of the environmental burden on minorities and the urban underclass. Justice, fairness, equal opportunity, the preservation of and access to meaningful work, the kinds and quality of public images projected into society, and basic life choices of all kinds are now held hostage to technological decisions made in corporate boardrooms. Count on even more of the same as the third millennium unfolds. One would be hard pressed to find a field more ripe for ethical analysis and workable responses than this one.

What is the moral role of business in geopolitics?

Global free market capitalism is rampant, violating cultural borders as it has long done, repeating many of 19th-century capitalism's worst excesses, at times exploiting Third World workers, raping the globe's environments, stripping away ecological diversity, overworking the earth's fertile soils, amassing and hoarding and wielding mammoth fortunes, recruiting the West's armed might to secure existing markets and open new ones, manipulating world financial institutions to promote market centered economies, resisting full-scale, good-faith United States participation in regional and international environmental compacts, and supporting various saber-rattling and saber-wielding policies of governments here and abroad. Clearly, one cannot treat business actions as if they are separated from today's major geopolitical struggles, because the actions taken by governments often mirror the interests of business.

The resultant business ethics challenge: The need is urgent for business ethicists to step more fully into the geopolitical arena. Some have done so already, proposing global principles of conduct for multinational enterprises, meeting with groups of international business leaders, and participating in international conferences of ethicists and corporate practitioners for several nations. Still others have embraced the sustainability doctrine as one way to move beyond abstract philosophic analysis towards economically workable and environmentally protective possibilities. Ethicists who work out of law school faculties have produced impressive approaches to problems that occur where national jurisdictions overlap. Yet there is a political timidity among too many business ethicists, an apparent hesitation to focus the profession's analytic ethical apparatus on the core nationalistic, ethnic, and religious competitions and conflicts that lie at the heart of today's geopolitical scene. Why should it be left to one of capitalism's most richly rewarded figures [George Soros] to declare that "the system is deeply flawed. As long as capitalism remains triumphant, the pursuit of money overrides all other social considerations"? Or that "Profit-maximizing behavior follows the dictates of expediency and ignores the demands of morality…. We must have a sense of what is right and what is wrong, an inner light that guides our behavior as citizens and politicians…. The profit motive dims that inner light. The principle of expediency takes precedence over moral principles"? There could be no clearer invitation than this to business ethicists to engage business practitioners in moral dialogue about the geopolitics of global capitalism.

What are business's ethical responsibilities when natural disasters occur, or especially before they occur?

Conventional economic theory places nature outside the models of economic behavior, or at best treats nature as an "externality" and therefore not a central part of economic reality. This tendency repeats and reinforces a long-established cultural habit of drawing a sharp line between nature and culture. One result is to insulate human actions from moral culpability when or after natural disasters occur, on grounds that such "noneconomic" events cannot be accurately predicted or controlled or that they are inexplicable "acts of God." This would be true of a long list of natural disasters that have human consequences. Because they seem beyond human ken and control, and because most such events affect large communities of people, any responsibility for preparedness beforehand and recovery afterwards is thought to lie with government and not with major economic actors.

But clearly, the human face-off with nature's rampages is not just a governmental responsibility. Business too incurs a direct moral responsibility well before natural disaster strikes. Business actions or inactions have contributed to or exacerbated the human costs and toll of lives in many of these natural events. Moral responsibility for recognizing and anticipating potential disasters in the making falls heavily, not just on insurance companies but also on builders, developers, bankers, and all others who do business along the margins of nature's most powerful forces. Business is also implicated in a whole range of well-known natural threats such as global warming, habitat and biodiversity destruction, air and water pollution, creation and improper disposal of toxic wastes, depletion of oceanic stocks, etc.

The resultant business ethics challenge: Business ethicists need to recognize that nature is not an "externality." On the contrary, nature not only lies at the very center of human economic endeavors but the powerful and disastrous forces it generates *are integral to the operation of human economy generally.* Simply put, natural disasters are "natural"—an expected, normal, irregular expression of physical, biological, meteorological, atmospheric forces. *Economic behavior is nothing more nor less than nature in action.* Unless and until nature is accepted as integral to human behavior, to economic enterprise, and to moral analysis, it will not be possible to formulate ethics principles adequate for the moral guidance of third millennial business practitioners.

These seven questions are the easy ones. More difficult ones loom in the near future. The combined forces of science and technology are beginning to break down the ancient connection between a carbon-based organic life and an abstract, symbolic realm of human meaning. Humanly created symbolic meanings and actions can now supersede their organic hosts and creators across a broadening range of human endeavor. Myriad electronic pulses, numerous magnetic nodes that define a network of possibilities, computer languages never spoken, the blanket of telephonic signals constantly pervading the air, the ceaseless murmur of the global Internet, the countless computerized data banks, the electronic ears listening for life signals from outer space, the robots that explore other planets—all of these non-organic human creations exist in a techno-symbolic realm that is virtually detached from and no longer dependent upon the organic carbon cycle we call "life." Without exaggeration or excessive imagination, it seems possible to say that human evolution appears to be moving beyond the organic and on into what some have called a virtual dimension, one into which human meanings can be projected *sans* the humans themselves—an ecology of non-organic, largely electronic, silicon-based abstractions. Some notable cosmologists have even suggested that the far distant future belongs to such a virtual ecology, as organic nature subsides and is replaced by hardier human (electronic) forms.

Somewhere and sometime within the third millennium, ethicists who track business practice will need to ponder the moral significance of such science-fiction-sounding scenarios as the following possibilities, all of which are even now in sight if not yet in the range of actual attainment. Each one brings forth a strange virtual world where organic reality fades into an abstract symbolic realm. The third millennium will see:

- Workless societies —-> (leading to) Virtual leisure

- Interplanetary robotic visits —-> Virtual travel

- Genes-by-design —-> Virtual human nature

- Neurochip brain implants —-> Virtual cognition and memory
- Organic programmed nutritional intake —-> Virtual metabolism
- Genetic design of immune systems —-> Virtual immunology
- End of disease —-> Virtual health
- Reproducing all known forms of life and generating new, presently unknown life forms —-> Virtual evolution and retro-evolution
- Human meaning extended to all regions of the cosmos —-> Virtual spirituality
- Infinite stem-cell duplication and end of death —-> Virtual immortality.

Each of these possibilities portends literally unimaginable and presently inconceivable ethical and moral dilemmas, thereby generating virtual ethics and virtual morality. One way or another, and in one form or another, business will be drawn into this vortex of virtualities. Its societal stewardship of technological change puts it in a commanding position to alter, though not to control, the pace of human evolution. Its premier economizing function makes possible the productivity from which the virtual dimensions emerge. Its irrepressible (because nature-based) impulse to grow, to expand, and to dominate makes it a natural ally of a virtual evolution that promises to bifurcate the organic and the symbolic. Indeed, business already sponsors or coauthors some of these movements to break the carbon bond. At every one of these junctures, moral issues will arise.

Toward a New Millennial Manifesto

Business ethicists as a group are not given to political programs or revolutionary upheavals as a way of accomplishing their purposes. Neither are they inclined to post authority-challenging theses on church doors or to issue manifesto calls to arms. But if such a declaration were to be brought forth—a manifesto suitable for the coming moral challenges of the new millennium—its opening paragraphs might go something like this:

"Business ethicists! Awaken from your philosophical slumbers! Social scientists! Cast off your positivist chains! Loosen the grip of encrusted, ancient, outworn philosophies and methodologies! Do not reject but seize the hand of science, the better to guide business into normative channels! Take the outstretched hand of relativism, pluralism, and diversity offered by the world's peoples! Grasp the hand of

nature that rests upon every human endeavor! And yes, grip the hand of the business practitioner who can infuse your moral quest with the experienced dilemmas of the workplace!

"A new millennium beckons, whether the Christian third, the human 2,500th, or the earth's 5,000,000th. Virtual ethicists, arise! The business world awaits your answers and needs your guidance!"

YEAR 2001

[Public confidence in big business: 28%]

GENES, NANOBOTS, AND THE HUMAN FUTURE

Setting the Scene. In March 2000 two seemingly unrelated events occurred. On March 12, Pope John Paul II, in a special Mass at the Vatican, acknowledged certain historical transgressions committed by members of The Church. These were widely interpreted to refer to forced conversions, excesses committed during the Crusades, punitive acts during the Inquisition, negative attitudes toward Jews, and other actions often cited by critics. That same week, Wired, a magazine catering to computer industry aficionados, carried an article by Bill Joy, chief scientist of SunMicrosystems, predicting a future world in which the human species risked being replaced by artificial, computer-generated forms of life. Whereas the Pope seemed to be embracing institutional responsibility for actions taken in the name of The Church, Bill Joy seemed to be searching for some way to have scientists accept a similar moral responsibility for their actions. The following allegorical conversation between two fictional characters is intended to reflect the views and questions that might arise when one considers the intersection of the Pope's homily and Bill Joy's concern. Although fictional, the contemporary patois of the conversation is not intended to demean or diminish the integrity or the dignity of The Holy Father or scientist Joy.

The characters: Bill Jolly, founder of SolarSystems.sci
 John Powell, CEO, RomanoUniversal.vat
The setting: A coffee lounge in California's Silicon Valley
The time: An evening in the summer of 2000
 As the recital auditorium empties out, two figures, one obviously older than the other, move towards a nearby coffee lounge for a post-concert

treat. Newly acquainted, they are eager to share their reactions to the
music. Once settled into a booth, the conversation begins.

Bill Jolly: A marvelous, brilliant performance of Chopin's music,
don't you agree?

John Powell: Oh, yes, absolutely. She captured the essence of the
composer's intention. I always enjoy hearing my compatriot's music.

BJ: I didn't know you are....

JP: ...Polish? Oh, yes.

BJ: John Powell doesn't sound very Polish.

JP: It isn't, of course. It's a name I acquired later in life.

BJ: Did you change it when you became CEO of RomanoUniver-
sal.vat? You know, for PR reasons?

JP: Oh, no, it's a tradition in our firm. But that's a long story. Too
long to tell now. I admire *your* name. It is so pleasant.

BJ: You mean Jolly? Thanks. I try to live up to it. That is, until
recently.

JP: What has happened? Why are you not joyous? Ah, I know. You
took a big hit when the Nasdaq plunged. You're not alone. We lost a bundle
ourselves.

BJ: Too bad. Most startups did. When was your IPO?

JP: Oh, a *long, long* time ago. We've been around a while.

BJ: Oh, Old Economy, huh? Maybe I can help you move over to
where the action is. Firms like yours...well, I hate to say it but...the gas is
going out of them...not much future, I'm afraid.

JP: Hmmmm...I'm sorry to hear you say that. I'll take it up with my
advisors when I get back to headquarters. They're a cardinal bunch. We've
always believed we're on pretty solid ground. We've got good
backing...about the best there is...and a good track record...well, mostly
good...a slippage here and there...the kind of thing you can expect .. . but
generally OK.

BJ: I wish I could say that about my outfit...you know, SolarSys-
tem.sci. I don't mean it hasn't performed well. In fact, it's just like yours in
some ways.

JP: Really?! I wasn't aware you were in our market. Word travels
slowly. Tell me, what's your problem? Why are you worried?

BJ: It's about our product.

JP: A bummer, eh? From time to time, we've had similar problems.
You know, your staff just can't seem to get the message out. We have less
trouble with production, though, than with marketing. Our product is solid.
It's a question of convincing consumers.

BJ: There's nothing wrong with our product either. It's just the opposite. It's *too* good. People are too eager to get hold of it. It's growing like wildfire. Consumers practically pull it off the shelves before we can restock. It's a nightmare.

JP: You puzzle me. You seem to be describing a miracle...if you'll pardon the expression. Isn't that what you're in business for...to push the product out the door as fast as you can? That's what *our* firm tries to do every day. I envy you. Why should that make you sad?

BJ: It's what the product can do...to people, the environment, our entire society, maybe the whole human race. This stuff may wipe us humans off the face of the earth.

JP: You're into munitions?

BJ: No. Life sciences.

JP: Ah! That's *our* line, too. But our goal is to *promote* life...a *very* long life...and to make it rewarding, you might say, and purposeful. Isn't that your goal, too?

BJ: I had always thought so until recently.

JP: What changed your mind?

BJ: Maybe I'd better start at the beginning. Do you know anything about genetics...you know, genetic engineering...the way we can move genes around, turn them on and off, move them from one place to another, even from, say, rats or pigs, to people?

JP: Yes, I've thought a great deal about it. It worries me. What is *your* concern?

BJ: J.P., I know people who may be trying to make a human being in a petri dish! *That's* what I'm concerned about. You have no idea how far this thing has gone. Before long, anyone, say, a young couple, can order up the kind of kids they want...one who can play Chopin the way we just heard it, another who can be a future Einstein, a third who can be a carbon copy of Mother Teresa.

JP: Truly? I wouldn't object to another saintly servant of God. They are rare indeed. She was a blessing to humanity.

BJ: But you wouldn't like it if they decided to make everyone into Hitlers...or if only the wealthy could make these choices...or if, God help us, it becomes possible to make everyone from the same mold. Can you envision the horror of walking down the street and seeing only copies of yourself? Such things are closer than you realize.

JP: Yes, I fear you may be right. All of us are copies, in a way, of Someone greater than ourselves. Of course, each is unique in some ways, too...you know, little imperfections. Over at our place, we specialize in uniqueness. You might say it's the *soul* of our business.

BJ: Well, here's another one for you. If you think copying is bad, think about this. *I have friends who want your job.*

JP: Oh, my. That would be difficult. You see, it takes a while to learn the work. And it involves a lot of travel, too. I've acquired miles and miles of frequent flyer coupons. Besides, not just anyone is qualified. You must be chosen.

BJ: Don't feel bad. They want my job, too. In fact, *all* jobs everywhere are their aim. A mega takeover. An acquisition like none you've ever seen.

JP: But why? I like my job and I'm told I do it well. I'm sure you do, too.

BJ: Well, these guys have figured out a way to have someone else do your work for you.

JP: But I already have a staff for that.

BJ: No, I mean something else. This is a staff that *always* gets things right, is *always* on time, doesn't ask for sick leave, *never* talks back, and *never makes a mistake.*

JP: Another miracle! This is truly a saintly group. What are they called?

BJ: *Robots!* We have them now that can travel to other planets, land there, explore, tell us what they are doing, and then come home. They can deliver medicine to patients in hospitals, direct traffic, run the elevator in your office building, land your airplane, process millions and millions of phone calls clear around the globe, control factories, and in one second can do math tricks that would take you a million years if you did it by pen and paper. J.P., believe me, these robots can do everything you and I can do *better, faster, more reliably, and they can do it over and over and over again forever.*

JP: B.J., I just don't agree. There are parts of my job that only I can do. Those things cannot be roboticized. We humans are not just smart calculating machines. We have another side. We are unique. Our actions are not merely mechanical. They are infused with a different kind of meaning…what some of our people call spirituality. No robot, however clever, can engage in spiritual dialogue.

BJ: Don't be too sure, John Powell. I have a scientist friend who believes it's already in the beginning stages and will be commonplace in another hundred years.

JP: What does he mean by spirituality? I know something about that.

BJ: About what you mean, I guess…he says spirituality is "transcending one's everyday physical and mortal bounds to sense a deeper reality."

JP: That's a little artificial, I'd say…doesn't get to the real core of it…has a kind of New Age ring to it.

BJ: Well, I haven't told you everything yet. There's something else called nanotechnology. It's all about a *very* small world, so tiny you can't even *see* it, smaller even than genes…molecules, atoms, electrons. I mean the most basic parts of life.

JP: I might quibble with you when you say these are life's most basic components. I have a different view on that point. But go on with your story.

BJ: What they're doing with this stuff is to make very tiny computers and chips that can be implanted almost anywhere…in your brain to help you think, or in your heart to make it beat regularly, or they can be installed around your house, or can be strung throughout your car, or used anywhere to do anything you want to do. They're like tiny robots, invisible, never asleep, seeing, hearing, talking to each other, issuing orders, recording everything.

JP: So the goal is to make everything more efficient?

BJ: Oh,, no, it goes much further than that. You see, these little digital robots run without any human help at all. You start them up inside a computer and they take off. J.P., *they reproduce!* New varieties emerge spontaneously. They actually evolve. And you know something else? This will curl your hair. *Someday, they might escape from the computers where they live!* They can already jump from one computer to another, say, from mine here in Silicon Valley to one in Afghanistan and another in Beijing…like fast-breeding viruses. As they grow more powerful and more capable of doing things we want, it is entirely possible they will simply take over everything we do. Once let loose from their computer cage, they can directly compete with us. By then, we'll be so dependent on them, there's nothing we can do. They may even decide to do away with us—the human species—because we are so clumsy and inefficient. The future may belong entirely to genetically engineered nanotechnology robots. That's what scares the hell out of me, John Powell!

JP: I'm truly grateful to hear that *something* can do that for you, Bill. Just kidding, of course. What do you think can be done? Do you have a plan? If your company is partly responsible for these risky projects, can't you just shut them down? You're the chief, aren't you?

BJ: It's gone too far already. For a while, we were the only ones but now it's spread to lots of other outfits.

JP: Why are *they* doing it? Don't they see the dangers?

BJ: Why do they keep on? I'll tell you, John P. They want the power and the privileges and the excitement of making new scientific discoveries. It's like a disease or a drug. They're addicted to it. You know, Nobel Prizes and all that. Don't you have any of that in your company?

JP: Yes, some of our people get rambunctious every once in a while. I have to keep reminding them of what we stand for. I'm sorry to say they don't always listen.

BJ: Well, what do *you* do? Fire them?

JP: Rarely. We have a lifetime retention policy.

BJ: Copied it from the Japanese, eh?

JP: Well, no. We had it first.

BJ: If you can't fire people, how do you handle tough situations? You know, suppose you found out that someone in the past had gone against company policy…and had even caused serious losses…damaged the company's reputation. As CEO, don't you have an obligation to the shareholders to repair the damage?

JP: I'm so glad you brought that up. I've been working on practically nothing else for more than a year. It's been an enormous crisis for us, truly threatening our very base…or at least, some of my advisors believe it's that bad.

BJ: Why not tell me about it? Maybe it will help me with my own problem.

JP: Some of the incidents go back a long way, into the early history of our organization.

BJ: What kinds of problems were they?

JP: Well, in one case, we were just trying to defend what was ours. One of our foreign installations—actually, it was where our business had its beginnings—was taken over by a competing group. When they wouldn't give us access, we sent out groups of people to pressure them into giving it back to us. You know, like a crusade. It led to a tragic loss of life on both sides. I'm afraid in their zeal, our people acted rashly and unwisely, although their hearts were pure. I very much regret that such a thing happened.

BJ: Yes, I can understand how you feel, but since it was a long time ago maybe the laws they acted under at that time could explain…or even excuse…their behavior.

JP: There is something to be said for that, I agree. Laws and attitudes change. But as we look back on it, I feel they overlooked our basic charter…what we stand for. They were, I guess you could say, like children who had not learned all their lessons. We wouldn't tolerate something like that now.

BJ: Have you had other kinds of problems?

JP: Oh, yes, several. One of the most regretful was one that a scientist like you might be especially interested in. Once long ago, our predecessors had a bitter dispute with a famous expert, an Italian astronomer. He caused us grave problems when his discoveries appeared to be at odds with our fundamental policy and goals. He was a stubborn fellow and wouldn't back down. So he was disciplined in the only humane way we knew how.

BJ: How was that?

JP: We told him he would be, in a manner of speaking, "fired"if he persisted. He was also asked to agree that our policy was the correct one, and we reassigned him so he could no longer do the kind of work that had gotten him into trouble.

BJ: Did he come around?

JP: Yes, he accepted the punishment.

BJ: So, what's the problem?

JP: To our discomfort, we found out much later that he had been correct all along.

BJ: So your policy had been wrong.

JP: Not at all.

BJ: I don't get it, John Powell. If *he* was right, how could you *not* be wrong?

JP: It wasn't our *policy* that was wrong, Bill. It was the way our predecessors had been interpreting it.

BJ: Ah, I see. Another case of changing attitudes over time. In other words, your people in those days couldn't be blamed if they weren't up to snuff on what we know now. They thought this guy's new ideas were out of whack with policy, and they cracked down on him, even though they were wrong. Is that what you're saying, J.P.?

JP: You would have to agree, wouldn't you, Bill? After all, how many people today know as much as you do about genetics and nanotech robots? Maybe you and your friends who are doing this kind of work today are like the scientist who was condemned by our people. With your superior scientific knowledge, you may turn out to be doing the right things in the long run...and you may find that your present fears are unjustified.

BP: But I've got a precedent to back me up. The scientists and engineers who made the two atomic bombs that were dropped on Japan...and who went on to build hydrogen bombs...they didn't give a hoot about the long-term consequences.

JP: But B.J., those scientists must have believed there were good reasons at the time for making the bombs.

BJ: That's the irony of it all. Long afterwards, one of them was said to feel a "pride of achievement" but also a lingering "shame of being associated with it." Another one said, "I feel I have blood on my hands." At the time, they thought they were saving civilization from a worse fate. They said if they didn't do it, someone else would.

JP: Theirs was a noble cause, wasn't it? At the time and under those circumstances, what else could they have done? That's what I was trying to tell you earlier about *our* company's past problems. I don't see any real difference. In both cases, people acted in good conscience to promote what they thought was right. What's wrong with that?

BJ: I'll tell you what's wrong with it, J.P. Noble cause or not, most of those bombs—around 25000 of them—are still out there, just waiting to be primed and launched. They can still destroy civilization as we know it. I'm just saying we don't want to repeat their mistakes. It could happen again, believe me.

JP: In other words, in both cases, it was and is a failure of both policy *and* implementation...purpose *and* people.

BJ: Yes. The whole idea...the basic aim...is wrong. It's taking us where we shouldn't go. And the ones who are doing it...making those robots, jiggering those genes...they're guilty as hell, if you'll pardon the expression, J.P.

JP: Your problem brings to mind a somewhat similar one I've had to grapple with.

BJ: Oh, what is it?

JP: You're speaking of a failure to act *now* when one believes there is a *future* danger. What our outfit once had to face was a little different. Some say it was a hesitation...perhaps one could say, a genuine doubt...to speak out about a *present* danger.

BJ: What kind of danger was it?

JP: The worst kind. The possible death of many, many people...as many as six million.

BJ: Could the people in your firm have prevented it?

JP: No. No one could...or did. Not even the mightiest armies...nor the governments who sent those armies. Our leaders did try. Some protections were offered, but our critics say not enough was done.

BJ: What else could they have done?

JP: Some say we might have brought more pressure to bear...taken a more forthright stand. It's hard to say in hindsight.

BJ: Ah, there's that attitude thing again. In other words, looking back on it now it's easy to say what might have been done...but, as before, you're saying we can't judge yesterday with today's standards. In your opinion, was it a failure of policy or of the people involved?

JP: Bill, we believe our organization's policy...its aims and goals...its central purpose is *never* wrong. What happens sometimes is the people who carry out that purpose...well...none of us is perfect...we all have imperfections, as I said earlier. At times, they fall short of achieving our policy goals.

BJ: Would that be true of your CEO, too...the one who was in charge then?

JP: It's a deeply troubling question, Bill. The answer needs much thought....

BJ: How do you explain that to your critics, J.P.? I can't imagine it would be much comfort to them to be told that your top managers may have goofed up big time.

JP: I know, I know. What else can we do now but acknowledge our errors...say we now recognize our tragic failure to act more vigorously when it might have made a difference? I've gone personally and directly to their leaders...met with them on their own ground...meditated with them on the horror of it all...told them we have purged ourselves and have vowed never again to permit such things to occur.

BJ: And did that help? Did it allow you to put it all behind you and go on?

JP: We have no choice but to go on, Bill...but with a contrite heart. For others, perhaps even many, it remains an open wound.

BJ: Oh, look, John, the piano recitalist just came in. She's having a coffee with the sponsors.

JP: Yes, I see. I wonder if we could get her to play an encore on the café's piano...just informally, of course. I may ask her in a few moments...using my Polish heritage might persuade her.

BJ: Worth a try, J.P. While she's finishing her coffee, let's see if I can pin down some of what you've told me. Your views are very impressive. There may be a lesson here for me and my fellow scientists. As I see it, the secret of your outfit's success over the years...in spite of being Old Economy...is your basic purpose and policy. You anchor everything in it and then judge your managers by how well they carry out that policy and achieve that purpose. And you seem to be saying that the policy is always solid, so that gives the organization a strong anchor...a way to give directions to your people. Learn the policy, follow it, and be rewarded. That's simple and straightforward. I just wish my situation was as simple as yours.

JP: Bill, don't all scientific firms have a policy and a purpose? I don't see how they could get along without one.

BJ: *Discovery* is what drives all science, J.P. One very famous scientist said it's about "the pleasure of finding things out." If science has a purpose, that's it.

JP: With no regard for *what* is found? Or what to look for? Unrestrained discovery as a purpose and policy seems unsound. Doesn't discovery need to be bound by some Larger Purpose...by humane values...by considering the whole human community...by what I might even call a communion of souls? Don't you need an absolute standard to guide discovery?

BJ: I'd say our absolute standard is the search for truth.

JP: We're ahead of you on that one. We've found Truth.

BJ: But not how to make it work, at least not all the time. We scientists *do* know what we are looking for.

JP: But as you've said, Bill, you don't know how to put it to humane uses, at least not all the time. Besides, you may be looking in the wrong place.

BJ: There's a lot of argument over that. Most would say that what is sought is intended to improve the human condition. And I would say that's what has happened most of the time. We're a lot better off now than during the Middle Ages.

JP: Humph! That depends *entirely* on your point of view.

BJ: But you see, J.P., when *you* find someone in your firm out of line with policy, all you have to do is to issue a reminder...like, get with it, or else. At our place, though, we actually *encourage* people to break away from policy...create something new...take chances...the crazier, the better...do it differently...improve...discover...no matter it hasn't been done before...novelty is what we want...old is out...new is in...find it before our competitors do. Science is entirely different from your business. We *seek* change and improvement. Success is measured by how far our people *depart* from established policy. We don't *want* them to stay put. They might get fired if they don't produce novelty...and they know it.

JP: Well, then, you've created your own dilemma, haven't you? If discovery is the name of the game, and if you've lit a fire under all employees to find new things, how can you possibly blame them if they invent these nanobots or clone—of all things—*a Lamb*?

BJ: J.P., for me personally, it's even worse. I've done lots of that kind of thing myself.

JP: So the scientists like you who *make* policy and the ones who carry it out...both are...umm, should I say...guilty?

BJ: Yes! That's the problem. And it's leading us directly to our own doom. We're not talking about just thousands or millions of people, the way you were. *The whole human race—all 6 billion of us—are endangered.* We've become the most endangered species on earth.

JP: Thanks to science?

BJ: No, not science alone. Science and technology are always channeled and given direction by society's institutions...by religion, government, and business.

JP: What do you mean?

BJ: The atomic and hydrogen bombs were built by government money. The military wanted them.

JP: But only when urged to do so by scientists. Didn't they appeal directly to your President...plead with him to begin work on the bombs?

BJ: Yes, you're right about that. Scientists did take the initiative. And the link to business isn't much different, I guess. Much scientific work is done directly because companies...like mine, I have to admit...pay scientists to make discoveries, which the company patents, and then turns those discoveries into profits...regardless of the human consequences.

JP: Give me an example.

BJ: Take genetically modified foodstuffs...you know...soybeans, corn, stuff that winds up on your breakfast table or that parents feed to their infants. Scientists have figured out a way to modify the genes so the soybean plants and corn stalks have built-in herbicides and insecticides. That not only protects the plant but means less chemical pollution of the fields and the farm workers. And it also means bigger crop yields and more food for everyone in the world.

JP: Isn't that good?

BJ: Yeah, but there's a down side, too.

JP: Like?

BJ: Like...well...no one knows what might happen if some of those gene-jiggered seeds get scattered around just anywhere. You know, if they escape from the fields where they're planted. Their modified genes might mix with the genes of other kinds of plants and...well...you just don't know what might happen in the long run.

JP: So you're saying business firms have a responsibility to keep that from happening?

BJ: Yes, they'll be as much to blame for what happens as the scientists...the bad along with the good.

JP: In other words, business *and* science can give us many material blessings but each of them bears a moral responsibility for any negative outcomes.

BJ: Precisely. That's the way it looks to me.

JP: Well, what is to be done? Anything?

BJ: I think there's a way out...maybe...if it isn't too late. People like me can speak out...tell others about the threat...warn them what can happen to their families, their children if we keep on this way...*let them know that their very essence as a human being is at stake.*

JP: We've had a lot of experience in getting *that* message out, Bill.

We've sent people around the globe. I myself go when I can. We have out-posts...even in the midst of some leading scientific centers...right here in Silicon Valley. We try to get The Word out.

BJ: There's one other thing, J.P., that's worth a try.

JP: I'm all ears, Bill.

BJ: I'm going to ask all scientists who are working in these new fields—genetic engineering, nanotechnology, and robotics—to stop their research, close their labs, burn their papers. I want them to relinquish their grip on the discovery process. That would break the momentum that has built up.

JP: But you've been saying all evening that creativity is what causes scientists to tick. How can you expect them to stop their life's work...turn off that which excites and animates them? As much as I admire your goal, I just don't see how it would be possible. I don't like to discourage you, Bill, but I think you and I must accept that your business and mine have some fundamental differences that are extremely difficult to bridge. Your products and ours are too different, our respective policies set us off in different directions and in pursuit of different kinds of goals; we have different ways of dealing with disputes over the purposes we seek. *Our* organization, after all, has been in business much longer than yours and others like yours. We've learned, often the hard way, how to keep on the path we have chosen...or the one chosen for us. I personally, as today's CEO, have acknowledged our firm's past mistakes. *You could say I have assumed, in the name of the company and as its top representative, the moral responsibility for our errors of the past.* Can't you and your fellow scientists do the same? We've taken a step that you need to take...and we've shown you how it can be done.

BJ: I see that, but there's still a problem. Your purposes and goals and moral leadership are OK but they're not always followed. On the other hand, my people are good at doing what we hire them for but our policy and purpose sometimes encourage mischief, recklessness, and potential destruction. For you, the problem is *people*. For us, it's *purpose*.

JP: Yes, Bill, but your *solution* focuses on changing *people*, not your policy of constant innovation. Without new policy guidelines—some standards about what is desirable and what is to be avoided—how can you expect the highly motivated scientists, yourself included, to change their present behavior?

BJ: That may be true, but *your* solution focuses on reaffirming your *policy*, and just hoping or praying that people will do better. That leaves your firm vulnerable to repeating the mistakes of the past. A fine-sounding policy won't necessarily get good results. I'm not sure you're any better off than we are. We seem to be at an impasse, J.P.

JP: Bill, the evening has been so pleasant and rewarding, let's not end our discussion in dissension. In spite of our differences, I feel we may be closer than is apparent, and with the help of our recitalist I think I can show you why I am optimistic. When I asked her a few moments ago, she agreed to play an informal encore for us...a Chopin *Etude*, the one in E minor from Opus 25. Listen to it carefully. It mirrors our conversation this evening. As it begins, you'll hear harsh-sounding discords that grate against one another, but then slowly they are blended into two separate melodies. They are like our two differing points of view...not always harmonious...each one independent of the other but interwoven so that each gains strength and beauty from their mutual association. Each stands within its own magisterium...touching one another but independent...neither one entirely whole without the other. Perhaps that is what we have sought tonight. The voice of human endeavor mingled with a Larger Meaning, each separate but respectful of the other, each discovering something the other offers. There is something here, I suspect for both of us. She's about to play now. See if you hear what I hear....

The Polish expatriate's music floods the coffee lounge, silencing all other conversations as it tells its own story.

For the many readers who will not have a recording of Chopin's *Etude* handy, a good nonmusical substitute that makes the same point is Stephen Jay Gould's *Rocks of Ages: Science and Religion in the Fullness of Life*. Biologist, geologist, paleontologist, science writer *extraordinaire,* Gould argues that science and religion are separate but equal human accomplishments, each deserving the respect of the other but each also authoritative in its own magisterium—factuality for science, morality for religion. That is the message that John Powell hears in fellow compatriot Chopin's music.

YEAR 2005

[Public confidence in big business: 22%]

LAST LIGHT: NEW VOICES, NEW HOPE

Setting the Scene. A summing up of CSR's status after a half-century of evolution, what has been accomplished and what remains to be done, as new voices emerge to point the way.

One wonders what CSR pioneer Frank Abrams would think if he could be teleported through time to the world of 2004. You will remember Abrams from **The 1950s** chapter where he was described as the first herald of a new management philosophy that assigned top priority to a company's social responsibilities. Abrams' prescience was all the more remarkable for coming from one of the nation's best known corporate executives. He might well have rolled his eyes in dismay as the tidal wave of corporate corruption broke over America some 50 years after he had charted a nobler course for business.

So, too, do I, at the end of my own journey to understand the possibilities and limitations of corporate social responsibility, need to pause and reflect on its larger dimensions. Two questions are foremost in my mind, and I imagine Frank Abrams would ask them, too, were he here.

- What has been achieved in a half century of pursuing and promoting corporate social responsibility?

- Was the pilgrimage, the search for this earthly Grail, worth undertaking?

This final chapter seeks the answers. In general, they run along the following lines. Corporations and their executives have learned not only to embrace CSR principles but to make them a part of policy and practice. Academics who study and teach CSR have made giant strides in developing analytic tools and useful techniques to aid executive decision making that promotes CSR. Yet, shortcomings persist in both practice and scholarship, and the business system remains vulnerable to outbreaks of unethical, immoral, and socially irresponsible behavior. But help may be on the way, as new voices emerge to point the way to a better future for both business and society. First, then, what can be claimed for progress in the business sector?

Practitioner Outcomes

For CSR advocates, there is much to celebrate when looking at the actual practices and policies of business corporations. Generally speaking, they've come a long way since the 1950s.

Greater Awareness. There is a greater awareness by business of what CSR means and what it demands of business firms. Hardly a week goes by without a potent reminder of the missteps that can lead a company into the tangled thickets of criminality or civil infractions, whether it is consumer fraud, environmental destruction, or investor cheating. While distressing, and distressingly frequent, these cautionary tales create an atmosphere of public concern which promotes a counter desire by business to protect its image and restore the public's trust. That may be achieving reform the hard way but it's the usual way.

Higher Public Expectations. Beyond imagery, though, is the knowledge that the general public simply expects more from business than a good bottom-line report. The public opinion data found at the beginning of most chapters in this book shows quite clearly that big business has never scored very high in public esteem. If only one in four or five people express high confidence in large scale enterprise, that means four or five others have negative or less than full confidence that business is doing the job it should. Savvy companies read these polls and draw the obvious conclusion: "We need to raise our standards of operation; it isn't as simple as just making a profit and satisfying our shareholders. The public wants, and expects, more of us."

Clearer Transparency. To move in those directions, both advocates and critics of business now possess a far wider range of information about business practices and their social impact than was true five decades ago. "Transparency" has emerged as a new requirement for businesses: the doors of low-wage foreign sweatshops must now be open to NGO inspections; the nutritional content of foods is now exposed to buyer view; ratios of male to female jobs, along with their relative pay scales, may no longer be hidden behind a corporate veil; sky-high executive salaries, bonuses, and perks are public knowledge; tests of the crash-worthiness of cars and SUVs are regularly televised; pollutants that contribute to global warming are traced to specific industries and companies; and when companies are slow to keep an alert public informed about its deeds and misdeeds, they may find their secrets leaked by e-mail, photocopies, or cell phone cameras and presented in living color and streaming video on the World Wide Web. It may be as true for errant corporations as for terrorists that President Bush's warning applies: "You can run but you can't hide."

More Oversight. The public fishbowl that has become today's corporate reality is open to the gaze of an ever increasing number of organized watchdogs. Over 2,000 United Nations-registered non-governmental organizations (NGOs) keep watch on U. S. corporations. Transparency International, which keeps an eye on bribery and corruption, is symbolic of NGOs worldwide, which may number in the millions. The always-open media eye focuses laser-like on corporate wrongdoing, through docu-dramas, prime-time investigative reports, whistleblower interviews, talk radio (pro and con), hidden-camera plant visits, films and videos exposing corruption and bribery. New laws and government regulations have mushroomed to match questionable business practices, often as a response to such spectacular misdeeds as those committed at Enron and WorldCom. Stock exchanges rushed to toughen trading rules as mutual fund managers were found to be favoring some clients with after-hours trading opportunities. The circle of watchers and rule-makers has drawn tighter around the business sector, causing some of its leaders to wonder if the noose is too tight, so we will return to this possibility later in this chapter.

More Credit for Good Deeds. Having taken its lumps over the years for not living up to public expectations, the corporate sector now finds that its good behavior can be rewarded and publicized by the very groups who make it their business to be critical. Best-company lists and rankings are in vogue, singling out firms whose social performance stands out. The Council on Economic Priorities issues such a list annually and has done so for more than a decade. *Business Ethics* magazine's annual awards to companies leading the way ethically and environmentally get much attention, along with its yearly naming of the best socially screened mutual funds. One of the first to recognize best-company CSR practice was the Business Enterprise Trust, and new ones join in yearly, one of the most recent being the Leeds Summit Awards issued by the University of Colorado's business school for "profitable activities that leverage social initiatives or environmental leadership." Business takes notice, with some firms making special efforts to clean up in-house practices to boost their CSR rankings.

More and Better CSR Tools. In Frank Abrams' day, companies who wished to put CSR into practice were pretty much on their own. Much depended on the CEO's personal commitment to honesty and integrity; some took their cues from personal religious belief; others supported their favorite philanthropic organizations; no reliable, tested tools existed for helping a company to be socially responsible or for knowing whether its best efforts were going anywhere or even to be sure just what CSR actually meant in practical terms.

What a contrast with today! Entire tool kits are available—through training programs, ethics consultants, web-based learning systems—for any company that is prepared to make ethics an integral part of its operations. Social audits, ethics audits, codes of conduct, analysis of a firm's ethical climate, demonstration of corporate culture's impact on social performance, designing social contracts, stakeholder mapping, enhancing social capital, charting strategic philanthropy, building social alliances, undertaking environmental impact studies, social mission statements—all of these and more are now part of the corporate scene. A new CSR technology is there. All it takes is a willingness and determination to use it. Many, many corporations have done just that.

A Broader Global Vision. Like it or not, corporations have been forced to take a larger view of their responsibilities in a world increasingly given over to international business alliances and cooperative agreements among governments. CSR principles are now found embedded in cross-border compacts, such as the Montreal Compact and the Kyoto Protocol, both aimed at reducing industrial pollutants that contribute to global warming. Several prominent U. S. corporations did not wait for official government ratification of the Kyoto principles and moved ahead with their own plans for cutting harmful emissions. Earlier, the Sullivan Principles laid down CSR guidelines for corporations conducting business in a South Africa riven by apartheid and racism, an effort now expanded to embrace human rights on a global scale. CSR ideas have been codified and promulgated by business leaders in Europe, Asia, and the U. S., including the Coalition for Environmentally Responsible Economies (CERES), the Caux Roundtable emphasizing good human rights practices for business firms, the United Nations Global Compact that features labor, human, and environmental rights, now endorsed by hundreds of leading companies around the world, and such other efforts as the Amnesty International Human Rights Principles for Companies.

More Inclusive Stakeholder Orientation. The confrontational and occasionally violent social upheavals of the 1960s and 1970s—when consumers, women, blacks, environmentalists, peace activists, and safety conscious workers insisted that business adopt more ethical practices (described in the **YEAR 1973** chapter, above)—signaled the end of the corporation's exclusive concern for the shareholder. These newly active and outspoken groups were what Frank Abrams had called the corporation's "constituencies," known to a later generation as "stakeholders." Effectively mobilized, they could be potent rivals to business power. Ignoring them was no longer a choice. Serving their interests, negotiating a series of informal social contracts with them, shaping and softening new laws aimed at promoting their anti-corporate views became a new kind of corporate strategy. Given legs (and a new name) by R. Edward Freeman's 1984 *Strategic Management: A Stakeholder Approach*, a corporation's stakeholder orientation became key to its social acceptance. Not just the shareholder but the entire gamut of stakeholders now had to be served. CSR had morphed into a much bigger enterprise than imagined by Abrams and his gentlemanly comrades in the executive towers whose views of CSR were to toss a little philanthropic money over the ghetto wall, or to believe that blacks and women could be mollified by a few token appointments to powerless jobs, or that Ralph Nader and his consumerist legions could be "stuffed" legally. In the end, though, the lesson was learned. To run today's corporation, you have to be mindful of stakeholder interests. Another bridge on the way to CSR had been crossed.

A Practitioner CSR Infrastructure. Helping to build that bridge into CSR Land is a burgeoning network of business-supported organizations who sponsor annual conferences for business practitioners on how to manage the ethical dilemmas that arise on the job (The Conference Board); conduct research, training, and consultancy services for companies experiencing ethics problems (Ethics Resource Center); organize conferences, professional development activities, and research for ethics officers of major corporations (Ethics Officer Association); offer assistance to companies wanting to improve their social and ethical accountability (Business for Social Responsibility); and the newly established Business Roundtable Institute on Business Ethics to provide ethics training for corporate leaders, following the outbreak of major corporate corruption scandals. These and other such business initiatives, many at the local level, have created a supportive infrastructure that gives well-intentioned companies a leg up in attaining an improved level of CSR performance.

Symbolic Endorsement of CSR. One way companies signal their commitment to higher ethical and social performance is to develop a code of good conduct. These ethics codes typically cover a wide range of do's-and-don'ts for employees, managers, directors, suppliers, and other stakeholders. Agreeing to abide by these codes is often a job requirement signaled by an employee's signature, which can then be the basis of dismissal when laws or company rules are broken. Research (some of it reported in the **YEAR 1987** chapter of Part II) has revealed that ethics codes, now adopted by most major corporations, are more symbolic than behaviorally practical; that is, they declare a company's good intentions and provide behavior guidelines but do not in themselves guarantee ethical outcomes. The emphasis tends to be on legal compliance as a way of protecting the company from its own managers and employees, rather than avoiding actions that may be legal but unethical. Cynics like to point out that Enron Corporation, the poster child of corporate corruption, boasted of having an elaborate code of conduct for its managers and employees. Enron's board of directors actually suspended the code on two occasions to allow its chief financial officer to engage in ethically questionable activities. On a more positive note, Johnson & Johnson's ethics code has been widely credited with saving the company from financial disaster and possible ruin when its leading product, Tylenol, was criminally contaminated with poison and totally withdrawn from store shelves. J&J executives could point to the company's ethics code as justifying this massive, expensive recall. By thus protecting its customers, the company's own financial interests were given a boost by restoring customer confidence in J&J's products, which is a prime example of harmonizing the needs of both business and society. One can say that in spite of their behavioral flabbiness, codes (along with a company's mission statement) may be counted among the positive signs that today's corporations have taken a public stand on the importance of ethical and socially responsible operations.

The Overall Conclusion. All of these positive steps by corporate practitioners are gains worth preserving, celebrating, and expanding. Progress has indeed been made in refocusing corporate goals towards wider and more inclusive social and ethical perspectives. CSR advocates can count among their allies large and growing numbers of business practitioners who accept and enthusiastically pursue CSR agendas in their daily operations.

Scholarly Outcomes

From practically nowhere at mid-century, CSR theory and research—the stuff that constitutes a legitimate field of academic inquiry—has much to show and be proud of at the dawn of the 21st century: From rudimentary, even primitive beginnings, to an intellectually sophisticated, practice-oriented present; from windy theory to useful analytic tools; from top-down paternalism to bottom-up communalism. Unknown to the early CSR pioneers, a new field of management studies was in the making.

Theory and Concept Development. Largely unaware of the theoretical edifice they were constructing, or the potential effect their efforts might have on workplace ethical dilemmas, CSR academics who labored mostly in business schools and philosophy departments produced the major building blocks of today's CSR understandings. Looking back on those years of

accumulating knowledge, much of it forged as a response to repeated
instances of a shocking disregard for the public interest and social welfare
by major corporations, the essential CSR theoretical structure is now apparent.

- **Stakeholder Theory.** This idea grew legs beginning in the mid-
  1980s when a Wharton Business School professor, R. Edward
  Freeman, wrote the "bible" of stakeholder thinking. Its lesson was
  simple: companies who wish to be successful economically must
  consider all who have a "stake" in its operations. The key stakeholders are shareholders, customers, employees, suppliers, host
  communities, creditors, governments, the media, and others with
  significant influence. CSR is achieved when a company's managers
  recognize and balance the interests of all its multiple stakeholders,
  including but not limited to the shareholder-owners. Expanded and
  enriched later by the empirical work of Max Clarkson and the conceptual models of Lee Preston and Thomas Donaldson, stakeholder
  thinking has become the keystone holding the entire CSR theoretical edifice together.

- **Business Ethics.** In the late 1970s, philosophers specializing in
  ethics began applying their concepts and theories to the thorny
  moral dilemmas of the business firm. Their main role models
  turned out to be Aristotle, Immanuel Kant, and John Rawls, whose
  name recognition was not exactly high in the corporate workplace.
  The sustaining rationale for this turn to philosophy was a belief,
  indeed, an absolute certainty by its adherents, that workplace ethical dilemmas differed little if at all from the large, universal moral
  issues of humanity at large (at least, as seen through Western eyes).
  Put those same analytic tools—the wisdom of the ancients—in the
  hands of tomorrow's business leaders, and the practice of business
  would surely improve, or so went the thinking. Three approaches
  vied for attention.

Virtue ethics. Aristotelian scholars, University of Texas Professor
Robert Solomon our exemplar, say personal character counts for
everything if business firms are to be ethical and socially responsible.
The virtues of honesty, integrity, fairness, trust, and moral courage not
only build individual character but also contribute to the realization of
general happiness and community goodwill within the business firm.
CSR is not so much a set of rules imposed on a company as it is a
result of the virtuous actions of the people who work there. Business

itself is a worthy undertaking because it contributes to the building of a good life for all. The virtuous character of all who participate in business can therefore be reinforced through a company's social policies and programs that contribute to general community welfare. David Hart and Edwin Hartman made notable additions to this Aristotelian dialogue.

Human rights ethics. The idea that human beings possess fundamental rights, should be treated with dignity, and are owed respect as persons is traceable to 18th century German philosopher Immanuel Kant. Kant's principal champion among today's business ethicists is Norman Bowie of the University of Minnesota who applies these principles to life in the modern corporation. A corporation is moral if employees are treated with the respect due to all human beings and are not used simply for the company's benefit or its profit goals. Wages should provide a decent living standard, and work should be meaningful and fulfilling. All stakeholders, not just one or a privileged few, should benefit from their ties to the corporation, and management should work to see that just relations prevail among all. All of these prescriptions are obligatory for the firm's managers and directors; they are duty bound to uphold and pursue them. In doing so, the corporation becomes a moral community serving the public interest through service to humankind. In this tradition, Patricia Werhane has shown how the rights of employees are central to the moral obligations of today's corporations.

Social contract ethics. The idea that business and society should draw up a contract that defines the rights, obligations, and duties of each to the other is an appealing way to think about a company's social responsibilities. In the early 1970s, the Committee for Economic Development (CED), a business association of corporate leaders, proposed it as a way of coping with the intense anti-business pressures of that era. About the same time, David Rockefeller, a corporate titan and head of Chase Manhattan Bank, floated the idea to fellow members of the business establishment. This general openness and willingness by business leaders to think about a collaboration between business and society set the stage for the notion that social contracts for business firms are not only feasible but morally necessary. Corporations are ethically obligated to protect the rights of employees (fair wages and safe working conditions), customers (fair prices, reliable quality and service, marketplace honesty), suppliers (fair pricing and delivery schedules), local communities (fair share of taxes, pollution control), and other affected stakeholders. The core idea of a social contract is to establish fairness and justice for all stakeholders while protecting their rights. Social contract thinking that has attracted the most attention among both practitioners and scholars is the work of philosopher Thomas Donaldson and legal scholar Thomas Dunfee of the Wharton School. Grounded philosophically in John Rawls's concept of justice, their Integrative Social Contracts Theory (ISCT) puts some practical legs on the social contracts envisioned earlier by the CED and David Rockefeller. Conceptual groundwork for ISCT had been developed previously by Michael Keeley.

- **Corporate/Global/Business Citizenship.** A new jewel in the CSR crown emerged as part of the globalization movement. An outgrowth and extension of the earlier way of thinking about a company's social responsibilities, "corporate citizenship" takes the voluntary, single-society orientation of CSR a further step outward to embrace a multi-societal, global viewpoint, with a strong focus on protecting human rights of all participants. Though still urged to be responsive to a wide range of stakeholders, the corporation-as-citizen is now seen as only one-among-equals in a large worldwide community. Its work, its economic output, takes on a public dimension that is to serve the general public citizenry. Its citizenship status compels it to favor the commonweal, to respect the rights of all other citizens, and to promote societal and environmental sustainability. Whether companies are labeled "corporate" citizens (as by Sandra Waddock), "global" citizens (preferred by James Post), or "business" citizens (touted by Donna Wood and Jeanne Logsdon), the CSR charge to all alike is to accept and act upon one's ethical responsibilities as citizens of civil society. That global corporations have duties to respect human rights everywhere and in all of their operations has long been emphasized by a corps of scholars, led by Richard DeGeorge, Thomas Donaldson, and S. Prakash Sethi.

- **Public/Social Policy.** These newer citizenship concepts of business rest on a firm theoretical foundation of political science laid down in earlier years by Edwin Epstein who analyzed the corporation as political actor. That allowed Lee Preston and James Post to propose that the surest path to CSR leads through an active public policy process where government regulations set guidelines for corporate behavior. Rogene Buchholz reinforced their views by insisting that *public* responsibility, as defined by laws and regulations, therefore becomes more tangible and achievable than an ill-defined though sincere *social* responsibility. Corporations can then take their place as citizens of civil society.

- **Other Theoretical Perspectives.** Today's CSR theorizing is based
principally on the Big Five approaches above—stakeholders, business ethics, social contract, corporate citizenship, and public policy—but finds outlet in other directions as well. Most notable of
these are the pragmatic management of specific social issues confronting companies, as in the work of Steve Wartick, Philip
Cochran, and others; public affairs and public relations management from the research of John Mahon and associates; social crisis
management pioneered by Ian Mitroff; Archie Carroll's four-phase
model of ethical decision making; global puzzlers such as doing
business in South Africa or selling infant formula in poor nations,
addressed by Karen Paul, Prakash Sethi, and James Post; finding a
place for workplace spirituality as developed by Robert Giacolone;
corporate citizenship models from Sandra Waddock and colleagues; and searching for the evolutionary/biological/genetic
underpinnings of corporate behavior, values, and culture (see the
chapters in **Part III**, above). These and other theoretical initiatives
constantly renew and refresh the established base of CSR understandings, providing new vistas, behavioral openings, and operational potentialities for receptive corporate minds.

Empirical Research. Among academics, the CSR enterprise has
from its beginning been mainly a talking exercise. It tries to persuade,
cajole, urge, and implore business practitioners to adopt socially responsible and morally desirable policies and practices for their companies. Without doubt, theory has overweighed both practice and empirical research.
Many CSR theorists continue to this day to argue that normative theory and
empirical research live in different domains, never the twain to meet, thus
echoing the ancient and now questionable separation of (scientific) "facts"
and (unreachable or untouchable) "values." Never mind. Empiricists,
though in the minority, continue to reveal some of the subtle under layers
of business behavior that affect CSR's prospects, and this research gives
managers tangible guides as they move to integrate CSR into their companies' operations. Researchers Linda Trevino and Gary Weaver empirically
chart the critical role played by managerial values, ethical commitments,
and ethical climates. They demonstrate how prevailing concepts of fairness
and ethics training programs can make the difference between socially
responsible activities and those behaviors less morally desirable. Social scientist David Messick and colleagues produced a treasure trove of scientif-
ically discovered truths about organizational wrong doing, patterns of
organizational authority, and internal social structures that affect CSR outcomes. A multivolume series of research studies dealing with corporate

social performance was initiated in the late 1970s. The research of James Weber, Elizabeth Scott, and Thomas Jones elucidates the nature and behavioral impact of managers' values. Comparative field research conducted in eight nations on three continents by Richard Wokutch has helped clarify global ethical issues regarding worker safety and health, sweatshop abuses, and child labor. Hundreds, perhaps thousands, of case studies describe episodes of corporate misbehavior as morality lessons for learning to achieve CSR standing. Still sparse when compared with the CSR theory gusher, the totality of these and other empirical research studies adds a significant component to scholarly work about CSR.

Teaching Resources and Professional Infrastructure. The first CSR textbook for classroom teaching, written by Richard Eells and Clarence Walton, was published in 1961, in the very early years of what was to become a full-fledged field of management analysis (see the **YEAR 1961** chapter in Part IV). Other texts followed, giving teachers a systematic way to convey the key ideas of socially responsible corporate performance to their young students. In general, they reflect and summarize the five major theory orientations identified above. Today, case studies exist in ample numbers to illustrate the right way and the wrong way to implant CSR values into company operations. Internet exchanges, web sites, and search engines have become a fruitful source of information never imagined in the early days of CSR thinking.

The profession itself—that is, the several hundred scholars whose main interest is to teach and conduct research on CSR—operates through an extensive and collaborative professional infrastructure not unlike those that sustain scientists, artists, lawyers, engineers, and numerous other professions.

- Five major professional associations: The Social Issues in Management (SIM) division of The Academy of Management; The Society for Business Ethics (SBE); The International Society for Business and Society (IABS); the Organization and Natural Environment (ONE) division of The Academy of Management; and the European Business Ethics Network (EBEN).

- Major publication outlets: *Business & Society; Business Ethics Quarterly; Journal of Business Ethics; Business and Professional Ethics; Business and Society Review;* and the magazine *Business Ethics*. Additionally, major management journals, such as *Academy of Management Review, California Management Review, Academy of Management Executive, Harvard Business Review*, and others frequently publish CSR articles.

- Outreach business ethics centers exist at several universities, including Bentley College, Santa Clara University, the Darden School, the Wharton School, and Duquesne University. All offer ethics training programs for companies and help companies develop codes of conduct, ethics hot-lines, etc.

The Overall Conclusion. It is clear that scholars, as well as business practitioners, have made immense progress in thinking through the controversial issues associated with corporate social responsibility. Their work has created tools of analysis, practical ways of responding to social pressures, safeguards for stakeholders, wider visions for corporate leaders, two-way communication channels between business and society, and a rich research base of information enabling managers to direct their companies towards both social and economic goals acceptable to the general public.

Vulnerabilities and Evolving CSR Challenges

Though secure in both practice and scholarship, the CSR show is far from over. The forces that brought it to the fore as a national issue are still very much alive, some impelling business towards more socially responsible behavior while other influences are more negative. Major pitfalls and challenges remain.

- Periodic breaches of CSR trust can be expected to occur. Deeply embedded, biologically driven impulses to achieve economic goals at the expense of stakeholder rights, community welfare, and environmental sustainability cannot simply be wished aside, nor can regulatory controls anticipate and prevent all irresponsible corporate actions. More Enrons, Bhopals, and Exxon Valdezes are in our future.

- Contrariwise, an excessive enthusiasm for promoting stakeholder rights, in defiance of valid business needs and goals for cost-effective, technologically efficient, economical production can override and diminish business's major contributions to an adaptive life process for human society at large. Over-burdening the corporation with social functions—employee healthcare programs being one example—carries a price harmful to all.

- A failure to curb the inherent power-aggrandizing behavior of hierarchically organized corporate executives—behavior manifested in the wave of recent corporate corruption scandals—can destroy public trust in business, roil the stock markets, greatly increase costly regulatory controls on business, and defeat the pursuit of community goals that mutually benefit business and society.

- A persistent ideological rigidity by many business leaders, think tanks, and the business press that diminishes and dismisses the importance of ecological problems such as global warming, the declining quality of water resources, eroded agricultural lands, etc., and that simultaneously whines about new social regulations such as the Sarbanes-Oxley Act, can undermine collective, global efforts to achieve a larger measure of corporate social responsibility worldwide. In today's complex, multicultural world, the free market is not the answer for everything, as some ideologues would have us believe.

- Not helpful at all is a disdainful, dismissive, anti-business attitude registered by many CSR scholars. Little wonder that corporate leaders often have trouble taking advice from an academic community that frequently brands them as preferring "profits before people," "greed over good," and "short-run company gain over long-run community benefit."

- A reluctance by CSR academics to rub shoulders with business practitioners, or to invite them into their classes to talk directly to students, or to spend time in the business workplace actually observing the ethical quandaries faced daily by managers diminishes the quality of business education and conveys an abstract, non-contextual, non-practical understanding of what it is to "run a business." Business ethics theories that rely on morally spontaneous expressions of goodwill arising from personal character traits and a "well-managed" corporate culture are no substitute for encountering the actual day-to-day, month-to-month, quarter-to-quarter ethical dilemmas and the imperfect solutions fashioned on the spot by workplace managers. Experience is, if not everything, about 95% of what it takes.

- The general reluctance of the nation's business schools to embrace the teaching of ethics and corporate social responsibility is a blot on their honor and, worse, an invitation to graduate future business leaders who lack a strong moral compass to navigate the workplace. With less than one-half of the schools mandating ethics/CSR courses, plus lax, permissive, flexible accreditation standards of the Association to Advance Collegiate Schools of Business, many business schools run the high risk of overlooking, underemphasizing, and diminishing the importance of ethics as a core component of business decision making.

New Voices, New Visions

All of the practitioner and scholarly advances described above—including even all the remaining warts—convey an affirmative and positive answer to the first question posed at the beginning of this chapter: **What has been achieved in a half century of pursuing and promoting corporate social responsibility?** Much has been accomplished that would satisfy the early yearnings of CSR pioneer Frank Abrams who believed there was "no higher responsibility, no higher duty of professional management" than to help society solve its many complex problems.

And the other question, **Was the pilgrimage, the search for this earthly Grail, worth undertaking?** Does it, too, have a welcome answer? This entire account, after all, has recorded my own personal intellectual and philosophic journey, taken against the background of large-scale societal movements. My answer can be mercifully brief.

I wrote this book to give a new generation a sense of how Corporate Social Responsibility began and why it continues to be important today and will be tomorrow. It is a story of human values, good ones and bad, that impel business people and their companies to do what they do. Unlike most books, this one took an entire lifetime to write. Finishing it is even more difficult because it has no real ending, no final conclusion, no moment of closure, and leaves no feeling of comforting resolution. It records only a moment of the world's infinite time that I witnessed during my own brief visit. But rather than being disappointed by the absence of resolution, one should rejoice for it means that the CSR spirit remains vibrant and meaningful for the coming generation of practitioners and scholars.

New voices are blowin' in the wind. They speak less of theoretical purity, more of practical solutions (Kay Plantes). They replace condemnation of wrongdoing with a more mature search for workable solutions (Tammy MacLean and Barrie Litzky). They seek new forms of corporate governance that mediate between personal morality and organizational needs (Timothy Fort). They call for value attunement, not value clash (Diane Swanson). They carry a pragmatic, organization-specific, get-real edge (Joshua Margolis), yet offer new philosophic framing for old and well-known problems (Robert Phillips). They find kindred spirits in poets and entrepreneurs (Susan Harmeling). They call attention to the political dynamics that shape the public mind of business (Richard Marens). They speak the new languages of chaos-complexity (Mollie Painter-Morland), global multiculturalism (Sandra Waddock), evolutionary psychology (David Wasieleski), neuroscience (Paul Lawrence), and biology (Ronald Hill and Debbie Cassill). Facing Robert Frost's "two roads [that] diverged in a wood," they take "the one less traveled by, And that has made all the difference." They explore imaginative possibilities and persistently ask of business, "Can't we do better?"

I invite you now to listen to these and other new voices of how a nobler vision of business practice might emerge. It is they and their counterparts across the cultural landscape who now run the race to secure CSR in business and society. What a joy to pass the baton to such fleet minds! Hear their voices, share their visions.

One of the most famous passages in all of science, penned by Charles Darwin on the final page of *The Origin of Species*, goes like this: "It is interesting to contemplate a tangled bank, clothed with many plants of many kinds, with birds singing on the bushes, with various insects flitting about, and with worms crawling through the damp earth, and to reflect that these elaborately constructed forms, so different from each other, and dependent upon each other in so complex a manner, have all been produced by [natural] laws acting around us. ... There is grandeur in this view of life [that] from so simple a beginning endless forms most beautiful and most wonderful have been, and are being evolved."

And so, in parallel fashion, does my story, my journey, my pilgrimage to discover the meaning of Corporate Social Responsibility end. There is indeed a grandeur in the CSR view of business and a wondrous personal awe that from so simple a beginning endless forms most beautiful and wonderful have been, and are being, evolved.

CSR ANALYTIC CONCEPTS

Business ethics
Corporate culture
Corporate enlightened self-interest
Corporate governance
Corporate mission
Corporate moral agency
Corporate political strategy
Corporate public affairs
Corporate social audit
Corporate social performance
Corporate social policy
Corporate social responsibility
Corporate social responsiveness
Corporate stakeholder
Corporate voluntary stewardship
Corporate/business/global citizenship
Crisis management
CSR public policy
$CSR_{1, 2, 3, 4}$ phases
Environmental audit
Ethical climate
Ethics codes
Global human rights
Government-business social partnership
Iron law of responsibility
Managers' moral development
Managers' values
Marketplace morality
Natural law
Naturalist ethics
Organizational justice
Organizational values
Shareholder activism and resolutions
Social contract
Social issues management
Social justice

Social regulations
Strategic corporate philanthropy
Sustainable development
Value attunement
Virtue ethics
Vision-values
Workplace spirituality

LANDMARK CSR EPISODES AND CRISES

1950s

Civil Rights Sit-Ins
Tobacco Industry and Human Health (1950s-2000s)

1960s

Cummins Engine and Civil/Social Projects
General Motors, Ralph Nader, and the Corvair
Love Canal & Hooker Chemical
Manville Corporation & Asbestos Claims (1960s-1980s)

1970s

A. H. Robins and the Dalkon Shield
Discrimination: Coca-Cola, Eastman Kodak, AT&T
Dow Chemical and Napalm
Dow Corning and Silicone Breast Implants (1970s-1990s)
Firestone Radial-500 Tire
Ford Pinto's Exploding Gas Tanks
Foreign Bribery: Lockheed, Gulf Oil
General Public Utilities and 3-Mile Island Nuclear Accident
Nestle Infant Formula (1970s-1980s)
U. S. Corporations in South Africa (1970s-1990s)

1980s

Bhopal and Union Carbide
Exxon Valdez Oil Spill (1980s-1990s)
Johnson & Johnson's Tylenol recall
Lincoln Savings & Loan collapse
Merck Free Drugs for River Blindness
Procter & Gamble's Rely Tampon
Wall Street Financial Scandals: Ivan Boesky, Dennis Levine, Michael
Milken

1990s-2000s

Abbott Labs and Habitat for Humanity Homes for the Homeless
AIG insurance scandal
Clothing Manufacturers and 3rd World Sweatshop Labor
Corporate corruption: Enron, WorldCom, Tyco, HealthSouth, et al.
Drug Companies and 3rd World HIV/AIDS
Ford SUV Explorer and Bridgestone Tire Recall
Malden Mills and Aaron Feuerstein
McDonald's and Obesity
Mutual fund after-hours trading scandal
Public accounting firms and corruption: Arthur Andersen, KPMG, Deloitte & Touche, PriceWaterhouseCoopers, Ernst & Young
Shell Oil in Nigeria

ACKNOWLEDGMENTS

Pitt's Social Environment group—the faculty who taught Business and Society courses—was an exciting place to be from the mid-1960s into the early 1990s. Sustained by the strong administrative support and encouragement of Dean Marshall A. Robinson and Dean H. Jerome Zoffer, Pitt became one of the nation's main centers for the study of Corporate Social Responsibility. Our success, I believe, was due largely to a conscious effort to seek out faculty with diverse disciplinary backgrounds: law (Francis Eugene Holahan and John Murray), sociology (Donna Wood), socio-psychology (James Wilson), economic history (Robert Krueger), philosophy and philosophy of science (Ian Mitroff), political science (David Blake and Barry Mitnick), and economics and anthropology (William Frederick). Collectively, this group taught, conducted research, and developed two or three generations of students who became key players in the Corporate Social Responsibility field of management studies. So, thank you, Marshal, Jerry, Gene, John, Donna, Jim, Bob, Ian, David, and Barry.

Sad to report, the vigor of the Social Environment group faded in time. Dean Zoffer held his finger in the dike as long as possible against those who were skeptical that CSR and ethics could be taught to adult students. But at the very peak of the corporate corruption scandals in 2002, a new dean joined these ethics Luddites to abolish the school's required MBA courses in CSR and ethics. One is tempted, though not too strongly, to recall the spirit of that familiar Biblical quotation, "Forgive them, Father, for they know not what they do."

The names of several doctoral graduates are reported in the text as contributors to the field's literature, while others have served primarily in the nitty-gritty work of making CSR and ethics come alive in the community. Three who deserve mention are William Tiga Tita who founded Pitt's Student Consulting Project that aided minority business firms in the Southwestern Pennsylvania region , was a high-tech entrepreneur in his African homeland,and who then served as United Nations consultant linking Third World entrepreneurs to the Internet; Robert Hogner, inspiring teacher at Florida International University, initiator of environmental reporting of hazardous chemical pollutants from industrial operations, and sparkplug organizer of on-the-ground and distance-learning centers for business students in Thailand and Nicaragua; and Robert Toy who worked side-by-side with laid-off steelworkers like himself to rescue their jobs and their dignity from the ravages of Pittsburgh's industrial decline. Thank you, Bill, Bob, and Rob.

In my formative years as a scholar when the ideas in this book were emerging, Violeta Rodriguez served ably and loyally as field companion, professional aide, language translator, and cultural synthesizer on four continents. Thank you, Violeta.

When the credits are given out, there remains a phantom group of people whose names do not appear here, a casualty of my own faulty memory. Though nameless here, they ran the race with the rest. As the Dodo in Lewis Carroll's *Alice in Wonderland* said when asked who had won the Caucus-Race, "*Everybody* has won, and *all* should receive prizes." Thank you, phantoms.

I am grateful to three seasoned corporate executives for offering advice and making suggestions to me about the ideas in this book: Benno A. Bernt, Thomas Petzinger, Jr., and Richard P. Simmons. Their experienced viewpoints brought the book's message closer to the realities of corporate life and practice as they have known it than I would have been able to accomplish alone. Thank you, Benno, Tom, and Dick.

The source of greatest encouragement and support, as well as allowing me to draw upon her bountiful knowledge of rhetoric and executive communication, was Dr. Mildred S. Myers, Teaching Professor of Management Communication in the Tepper School of Business at Carnegie Mellon University. Thank you, Millie.

PUBLICATION CREDITS

Some of the chapters in this book contain materials previously published as articles in journals or as chapters in other books. For ease of reading, all such items have been shortened and stripped of all references and footnotes, and new titles have been adopted in some cases. Anyone who wishes to consult the original sources will find a complete list below.

INTRODUCTION Written for this book. Not previously published.

Part I. EMERGENCE AND STRUGGLE

The 1950s Written for this book. Not previously published.

Year 1960 Adapted from William C. Frederick, "The Growing Concern Over Business Responsibility," *California Management Review*, 2 (4), summer 1960, 54-61. Copyright 1960, by The Regents of the University of California. Reprinted from the *California Management Review*, Vol. 2, No. 4. By permission of The Regents.

Year 1973 Adapted from William C. Frederick, James A. Wilson, and Mildred S. Myers, "Business in a New Social Role," Working Paper WP37, Graduate School of Business, University of Pittsburgh, January 1973. Not previously published. Used with permission of James A. Wilson and Mildred S. Myers.

Year 1978 Originally a Working Paper, Graduate School of Business, University of Pittsburgh, dated 1978. Published as William C. Frederick, "From CSR_1 to CSR_2: The Maturing of Business-and-Society Thought," *Business & Society*, 33 (2), August 1994, 150-164, copyright 1994 by Sage Publications, Inc. Reprinted by permission of Sage Publications, Inc.

Year 1981 Adapted from William C. Frederick, "Free Market vs. Social Responsibility: Decision Time at the CED," *California Management Review*, XXIII (3), 1981, 20-28. Copyright 1981, by The Regents of the University of California. Reprinted from the *California Management Review*, Vol. 23, No. 3. By permission of The Regents.

Year 1983 Adapted from William C. Frederick, "Corporate Social Responsibility in the Reagan Era and Beyond," *California Management Review*, XXV (3), Spring 1983, 145-157. Copyright 1983, by The Regents of the University of California. Reprinted from the *California Management Review*, Vol. 25, No. 3. By permission of The Regents.

Part II. VALUES AND CORPORATE CULTURE

Year 1985 Adapted from William C. Frederick, "Embedded Values:

Prelude to Ethical Analysis." In Patricia H. Werhane and Kendall D'Andrade (eds.), *Profit and Responsibility: Issues in Business and Professional Ethics*, New York: Edwin Mellen Press, 1985, 46-64. Reprinted by permission of the Edwin Mellen Press.

Year 1986 Adapted from William C. Frederick, "Toward CSR_3: Why Ethical Analysis is Indispensable and Unavoidable in Corporate Affairs," *California Management Review*, XXVIII (2), Winter 1986, 126-155. Copyright 1986, by The Regents of the University of California. Reprinted from the *California Management Review*, Vol. 28, No. 2. By permission of The Regents.

Year 1987 Adapted from William C. Frederick, "From Bhopal to Boesky: New Research Perspectives on Corporate Ethics and Managerial Values." Associates Lecture, Katz Graduate School of Business, University of Pittsburgh, October 6, 1987, 1-32. Not previously published, but details of the reported research are in William C. Frederick and Lee E. Preston (eds.) *Research in Corporate Social Performance and Policy: Empirical Studies of Business Ethics and Values*, vol. 9, Greenwich, CN: JAI Press, 1987.

Year 1991 Adapted from William C. Frederick, "The Moral Authority of Transnational Corporate Codes," *Journal of Business Ethics*, 10, 1991, 165-177, copyright 1991 Kluwer Academic Publishers. With kind permission of Springer Science and Business Media.

Part III. NATURE AND CORPORATE MORALITY

Year 2000 Written for this book. Not previously published.

Year 1998 Adapted from William C. Frederick, "Creatures, Corporations, Communities, Chaos, Complexity: A Naturological View of the Corporate Social Role," *Business & Society*, 37 (4), December 1998, 358-389, copyright 1998 by Sage Publications, Inc. Reprinted by permission of Sage Publications, Inc.

Year 2002 Adapted from William C. Frederick, "The Evolutionary Firm and Its Moral (Dis)contents." In R. Edward Freeman and Patricia H. Werhane (eds.), *Business, Science, and Ethics: The Ruffin Series No. 4*, Society for Business Ethics and University of Virginia Darden School Foundation, 2004, 145-176. Copyright 2004 by Society for Business Ethics and the University of Virginia Darden School Foundation. Reprinted by permission of the Philosophy Documentation Center.

Year 2004 Adapted from William C. Frederick, "$T^2 + D^2 + E^3 = $ ISCT-II: A Biocultural Guide to Social Contract." A paper presented to a conference on Contractarian Approaches to Business Ethics: The Evolution of Integrative Social Contracts Theory, The Wharton School, University of

Pennsylvania, November 12-13, 2004, 1-44. Not previously published.

Year 2005 Written for this book. Not previously published. Primary sources: News reports in *The Wall Street Journal, New York Times, Business Week,* and other press reports during the years 2001-2005.

Part IV. TEACHING CORPORATE SOCIAL RESPONSIBILITY

Year 1961 Adapted from William C. Frederick, *"Conceptual Foundations of Business:* A Book That Made a Difference." A chapter in Ronald F. Duska (ed.) *Education, Leadership and Business Ethics: Essays on the Work of Clarence Walton.* Dordrecht: Kluwer Academic Publishers, 61-73, copyright 1998, Kluwer Academic Publishers. With kind permission of Springer Science and Business Media.

Year 1963 Adapted from William C. Frederick, "Are Business Schools Really Necessary?" *California Management Review*, V (4), Summer 1963, 85-89. Copyright 1963, by The Regents of the University of California. Reprinted from the *California Management Review*, Vol. 5, No. 4. By permission of The Regents.

Year 1977 Originally published as William C. Frederick, "Business and Society Curriculum: Suggested Guidelines for Accreditation," *AACSB Bulletin*, 13 (3), Spring 1977, 1-5. Republished by permission of the Association for Advancement of Collegiate Schools of Business.

Year 1977 Adapted from William C. Frederick, "Education for Social Responsibility: What the Business Schools Are Doing About It," *Liberal Education*, LXIII (2), May 1977, 190-203. Reprinted with permission from *Liberal Education*, May 1977. Copyright held by the Association of American Colleges and Universities.

Year 1988 William C. Frederick, "Ethics, Religion, and Philosophy at the Harvard Business School: A Personal Memoir of Two Visits." Not previously published.

Year 2005 Written for this book. Not previously published.

Part V. HORIZON AND HOPE

Year 1998 Adapted from William C. Frederick, "Moving to CSR_4: What to Pack for the Trip," *Business & Society* 37 (1), March 1998, 40-59, copyright 1998 by Sage Publications, Inc. Reprinted by permission of Sage Publications, Inc.

Year 2000 Originally published as William C. Frederick, "Notes for a Third Millennial Manifesto: Renewal and Redefinition in Business Ethics," *Business Ethics Quarterly*, 10 (1), January 2000, 159-167. Copyright 2000 by Society for Business Ethics. Reprinted by permission of the Philosophy Documentation Center.

NAME INDEX

SUBJECT INDEX

AACSB. *See* American Association of Collegiate Schools of Business
   and Association to Advance Collegiate Schools of Business
A. H. Robins, 95, 310
Abbott Labs, 310
Accrediting standard, for business and society courses, 216-217
Adelphia Communications, 196
Ahold, 196
AIG (American International Group), 196, 310
Algorithms
   economizing, 156, 157
   emotive, 156, 158-159
   neural, contradictions in, 156
   power-dominance, 156
   social contract, 157
   symbiotic-moralizing, 156, 157-158
Altruism, definitions of, 170
American Association of Collegiate Schools of Business, 206, 216, 221,
   225. *See also* Association to Advance Collegiate Schools of Business *and* AACSB
American Enterprise Institute, 47
American International Group (AIG), 196, 310
Amnesty International Human Rights Principles for Companies, 297
Anti-War, Anti-Militarist Movement, 28
Arthur Andersen, 155, 182, 189, 193, 194, 197, 311
Association to Advance Collegiate Schools of Business, 243, 249, 306.
   See also American Association of Collegiate Schools of Business *and* AACSB
AT&T, 310
Banco Santander Central Hispano Americano, 196
Bank of America, 197
Bank of Boston, 95
Bankgesellschaft Berlin AG, 196
Beacon Hill Asset Management, 196
Bhopal, 95, 110, 305
Black Economic Research Center, 230

Religion
>   and corporate decision making, 267-268
>   and CSR scholarship, 268-269

Rio Conference, 147

Rite-Aid, 196

Sarbanes-Oxley Act, 306

Schemers/Drivers, definition of, 184, 190

Shareholder resolutions, 224

Shell Oil, 311

Social contract, 37, 48, 166, 207, 301-302. *See also* Integrative Social
Contracts Theory
>   adaptive advantage of, 174-175
>   definition of, 173
>   and pragmatism, 177-178
>   cultural forms of, 173-174

Social equity, as normative source, 114

Social exchange, 169-170

Social Issues in Management (SIM), 92, 206, 216, 229, 268, 304

Social partnerships, 66-67

Social reciprocity, 173

Social responsibility, 228, 230. *See also* Corporate social responsibility

Social responsiveness, 230. *See also* Corporate social responsiveness
>   management of, 228

Social revolutions, 25-28
>   and corporate power, 35

Social role of business, 23
>   and nature, 146-147

Social voluntarism, 48, 51-52

Socially negative business actions, 223-225

Society for Business Ethics, 92, 238, 261, 304

Spirituality and nature, 265-267

Staff Cooperators, definition of, 184, 190

Stakeholder, 9
>   concept, 261, 297
>   theory, 205, 207, 300

Standard Oil of New Jersey (Exxon), 7

Strange attractor, as corporate values, 144, 149. *See also* Complexity
theory